TIMOTHY D. KANOLD
Series Editor

COMMON CORE
Mathematics
in a PLC at Work™

HIGH SCHOOL

Gwendolyn Zimmermann
John A. Carter
Timothy D. Kanold
Mona Toncheff

FOREWORD BY Richard DuFour

A Joint Publication With

NATIONAL COUNCIL OF
TEACHERS OF MATHEMATICS

555 North Morton Street
Bloomington, IN 47404

800.733.6786 (toll free) / 812.336.7700
FAX: 812.336.7790

email: info@solution-tree.com
solution-tree.com

Visit **go.solution-tree.com/commoncore** to download the reproducibles in this book.

Printed in the United States of America

16 15 14 13 12   1 2 3 4 5

Library of Congress Cataloging-in-Publication Data

Common core mathematics in a PLC at work. High school / Gwendolyn Zimmermann ... [et al.] ; foreword by Richard DuFour ; Timothy D. Kanold, series editor.
    p. cm.
  Includes bibliographical references and index.
  ISBN 978-1-936765-50-8 (perfect bound : alk. paper) -- ISBN 978-1-936765-51-5 (library ed. : alk. paper)
  1. Mathematics--Study and teaching (Secondary)--Standards--United States. 2. Professional learning communities. I. Zimmermann, Gwen. II. Kanold, Timothy D.
  QA13.C5657 2012
  510.71'273--dc23
                        2012008000

Solution Tree
Jeffrey C. Jones, CEO
Edmund M. Ackerman, President

Solution Tree Press
President: Douglas M. Rife
Publisher: Robert D. Clouse
Vice President of Production: Gretchen Knapp
Managing Production Editor: Caroline Wise
Senior Production Editor: Joan Irwin
Copy Editor: Sarah Payne-Mills
Text Designer: Amy Shock
Cover Designer: Jenn Taylor

Acknowledgments

Thank you, Tim, for having the faith in me for my contributions to this book. As always, my love and gratitude to J. Z. and G. G. for all their support and patience.

—Gwendolyn Zimmermann

Thanks to all of our mentors who have provided guidance, feedback, and leadership over the years. We have been blessed to experience the guidance of caring individuals who recognized the importance of helping others reach their goals. It is my hope this book will provide that same type of assistance to others.

—John A. Carter

Since no one writes alone, I have a team of family and friends, including the coauthors, who support me in my passion for mathematics education. I also fully recognize the sacrifice and devotion of my husband. I am blessed that he constantly encourages me from the sideline. And I work with amazing students, teachers, and leaders who have confidence in me. They diligently work to support the vision of *equity and excellence* in our high school mathematics departments. Thank you!

—Mona Toncheff

My heartfelt thanks to Gwen, John, and Mona for their dedicated, creative, and tireless effort to turn the idea of this book into a collaborative reality. They are each champions for the cause of improving 9–12 mathematics education as a major aspect of their life's work. Personal thanks also to the men and women of Adlai E. Stevenson High School, who embrace great mathematics teaching and pioneered the transparency and hard work of collaborative team learning in a PLC.

Special thanks to Solution Tree—Jeff, Douglas, Gretchen, Joan, and Sarah—for their time, tireless effort, commitment, and belief in the importance of this work for the mathematics community.

Sincere thanks to the National Council of Teachers of Mathematics and the Educational Materials Committee for their support of this series and their leadership in the mathematics education of teachers and students.

Finally, thanks to all of the authors and reviewers for this series. Many of their great ideas surface across the books and serve to bring coherence to the Common Core mathematics message.

—Timothy D. Kanold

Solution Tree Press would like to thank the following reviewers:

Roger Day, NBCT
Department of Mathematics
Illinois State University
Normal, Illinois

Richard DuFour
Author and Consultant
Moneta, Virginia

Vanessa Cleaver
Director of Mathematics
Little Rock School District
Little Rock, Arkansas

Linda Fulmore
Mathematics and Educational Equity
    Senior Associate
Cave Creek, Arizona

Darshan Jain
High School Mathematics Teacher
    and Teacher Leader
Adlai E. Stevenson HSD 125
Lincolnshire, Illinois

Henry S. Kepner Jr.
Professor, Department of Curriculum
    and Instruction
University of Wisconsin–Milwaukee
Past President, National Council of
    Teachers of Mathematics
Milwaukee, Wisconsin

Edward C. Nolan
PreK–12 Mathematics Supervisor,
    Department of Curriculum and
    Instruction
Montgomery County Public Schools
Rockville, Maryland

Kit Norris
Senior Associate, Common Core PLC
    Learning Group
Boston, Massachusetts

Sue Pippen
Past President, Illinois Council Teachers
    of Mathematics
Plainfield, Illinois

Connie Schrock
Professor, Department of Mathematics,
    Computer Science, and Economics
Emporia State University
Emporia, Kansas

John W. Staley
Secondary Coordinator,
    Office of Mathematics
Baltimore County Public Schools
Baltimore, Maryland

Visit **go.solution-tree.com/commoncore** to download the
reproducibles in this book.

Table of Contents

About the Series Editor

Timothy D. Kanold, PhD, is an award-winning educator, author, and consultant. He is former director of mathematics and science and superintendent of Adlai E. Stevenson High School District 125, a model professional learning community district in Lincolnshire, Illinois.

Dr. Kanold is committed to equity and excellence for students, faculty, and school administrators. He conducts highly motivational professional development leadership seminars worldwide with a focus on turning school vision into realized action that creates greater equity for students through the effective delivery of professional learning communities for faculty and administrators.

He is a past president of the National Council of Supervisors of Mathematics and coauthor of several best-selling mathematics textbooks over several decades. He has served on writing commissions for the National Council of Teachers of Mathematics. He has authored numerous articles and chapters on school leadership and development for education publications over the past decade.

In 2010, Dr. Kanold received the prestigious international Damen Award for outstanding contributions to the leadership field of education from Loyola University Chicago. He also received the Outstanding Administrator Award from the Illinois State Board of Education in 1994 and the Presidential Award for Excellence in Mathematics and Science Teaching in 1986. He serves as an adjunct faculty member for the graduate school at Loyola University Chicago.

Dr. Kanold earned a bachelor's degree in education and a master's degree in mathematics from Illinois State University. He completed a master's in educational administration at the University of Illinois and received a doctorate in educational leadership and counseling psychology from Loyola University Chicago.

To learn more about Dr. Kanold's work, visit his blog Turning Vision Into Action at http://tkanold.blogspot.com, or follow @tkanold on Twitter.

To book Dr. Kanold for professional development, contact pd@solution-tree.com.

About the Authors

 **Gwendolyn Zimmermann**, PhD, is the director of mathematics of Adlai E. Stevenson High School District 125, a model professional learning community district in Lincolnshire, Illinois.

She has served as journal editor for the National Council of Supervisors of Mathematics. She served on the committee that revised the adolescence and young adulthood mathematics standards for the National Board of Professional Teaching Standards and has served as chairperson for the National Council of Teachers of Mathematics Educational Materials Committee. In 2001, Dr. Zimmermann received the Presidential Award for Excellence in Mathematics and Science Teaching.

She earned a bachelor's degree in mathematics from Northeastern Illinois University and a master's of science in teaching mathematics from the University of Illinois at Chicago. She received educational administrative certification at North Central College and a doctorate in mathematics education from Illinois State University. Dr. Zimmermann is currently working on her dissertation toward the completion of a doctorate in educational leadership from Loyola University Chicago.

 **John A. Carter**, PhD, is the principal of Adlai E. Stevenson High School in Lincolnshire, Illinois. He previously served as the director of mathematics and the assistant principal for teaching and learning at Adlai E. Stevenson. He taught mathematics for nineteen years at Community High School in West Chicago and at Stevenson High School.

As a teacher and professional developer, Dr. Carter has focused his work on teaching mathematics for understanding, student-engaged learning, and developing student reasoning. As a presenter and lesson-study facilitator, he regularly works with teachers to examine their instructional practices, further their content knowledge, and improve student achievement.

Dr. Carter has served on the Board of Directors for the National Council of Teachers of Mathematics as well as been a member of National Council of Teachers of Mathematics committees, task forces, and writing groups. He received the Presidential Award for Excellence in Mathematics Teaching in 1993 and was awarded the T. E.

Rine Secondary Mathematics Teaching Award from the Illinois Council of Teachers of Mathematics in 2000.

Dr. Carter earned a bachelor's degree in mathematics, a master's degree in education, and a master's degree in educational administration from the University of Illinois at Urbana-Champaign. He earned his doctorate in mathematics education from Illinois State University and completed postdoctoral work in educational administration at Loyola University Chicago.

Mona Toncheff, MEd, is the math content specialist in the Phoenix Union High School District, an urban school district in Phoenix, Arizona. She has served in public education for twenty years, twelve of them as a high school mathematics teacher. She received her masters of education in educational leadership from Northern Arizona University and has been the district's mathematics leader for eight years.

As the math content specialist, she oversees mathematics curriculum, instruction, and assessment at the twelve comprehensive and four special high schools in the district. Her experience includes supervising the culture change from teacher isolation to professional learning communities, creating articulated standards and relevant district common assessments, and providing the ongoing professional development for over two hundred high school mathematics teachers regarding best practices, equity and access, technology, and assessment for learning.

Mona served as the National Council of Supervisors of Mathematics secretary (2007–2008) and currently serves the National Council of Supervisors of Mathematics board as the Western Region 1 director. In 2009, Mona was selected as the Phoenix Union High School District Teacher of the Year.

To book Gwendolyn Zimmermann, John A. Carter, or Mona Toncheff for professional development, contact pd@solution-tree.com.

In addition to being the series editor, **Timothy D. Kanold**, PhD, is a coauthor on this book.

Foreword

The initiative to establish Common Core standards in language arts and mathematics is the most comprehensive and coordinated effort to utilize curriculum to impact student achievement that has ever been undertaken in the United States. Forty-six states and the District of Columbia have endorsed the Common Core standards as a key strategy for helping students learn at higher levels.

The impetus for the Common Core came from the growing recognition that the current system of allowing each state to establish its own standards, assessments, and benchmarks for proficiency resulted in enormous disparity in the educational experiences of students across the United States. The rigor of curriculum those students pursue, the quality and degree of difficulty of the assessments they take, and the standards for defining their success have varied dramatically from state to state.

The Common Core seems to offer the perfect remedy to the huge discrepancies that exist in the current system. It will replace the myriad state standards with one well-defined set of rigorous standards designed to provide all students with access to a high-quality curriculum. The assessments that will ultimately accompany the Common Core will be more challenging and will establish higher expectations for student achievement than existing state assessments. The economy of scale that results from this coordinated national initiative will eliminate the inevitable redundancies, duplication of effort, and waste that occur when each state is creating its own standards and assessment. The resulting savings can be used to support student learning rather than merely measure it.

I am among those who believe that creating the Common Core is an important step in the right direction for U.S. education. I am concerned, however, that not enough attention is being paid to an important fact—merely adopting a new curriculum, even a challenging curriculum, will not improve student learning.

There is a long history of failed attempts to raise student achievement in mathematics through curriculum reform—from the National Defense Act of 1958 passed in response to the Russian launching of *Sputnik*, to the reforms spurred by the *Nation at Risk* report of 1983 (U.S. Department of Education), to the *Curriculum and Evaluation Standards for School Mathematics* the National Council of Teachers of Mathematics (NCTM) adopted in 1989, to the mandate for each state to establish mathematics standards with the passage of the No Child Left Behind Act in 2002, to NCTM's K–8 *Curriculum Focal Points* and *Focus in High School Mathematics Reasoning and Sense Making* articulated in 2006 and 2009, respectively. What has become increasingly apparent is that even a well-articulated rigorous curriculum will have little impact on student achievement unless attention is paid to the implementation of the curriculum and the quality of instruction with which it is taught. As Dylan Wiliam (2011) puts it succinctly, "Pedagogy trumps curriculum" (p. 13).

A 2012 study of the Brooking Institute found that there was no correlation between the quality of the mathematics standards adopted by the various states and actual student achievement in mathematics. The benchmark established for proficiency in mathematics by the various states was also unrelated to student achievement. Students in states with a well-articulated, rigorous curriculum and high benchmarks for proficiency fared no better than students from states with inferior curriculum standards and easier assessments on the National Assessment of Educational Progress. In fact, the study found that the differences in student achievement in mathematics were four to five times higher between schools *within* the same state than it was *between* the states. As the study concluded, "The empirical evidence suggests that the Common Core will have little effect on American students' achievement. The nation will have to look elsewhere for ways to improve its schools" (Loveless, 2012, p. 14).

The reason that *Common Core Mathematics in a PLC at Work™, High School* is so powerful is precisely because it looks beyond the adoption of curriculum to improve student learning. To their great credit, the authors recognize several critical elements that have historically been overlooked in curriculum reform efforts.

1. There is a difference between the *intended* curriculum an external authority establishes (whether it is a national commission, a state department of education, or the central office) and the *implemented* curriculum that individual teachers teach in the classroom each day.

2. Students cannot learn what they are not taught. Therefore, to ensure all students have the opportunity to acquire the knowledge, skills, and understanding essential to their success in mathematics, a school must take steps to ensure all students have access to a guaranteed *implemented* mathematics curriculum. Teachers must acquire a shared, deep understanding of the curriculum and its intended goals. Even more importantly, they must be committed to teaching that curriculum.

3. The quality of the instruction students receive each day is the most important factor in their learning of mathematics. No curriculum will compensate for weak and ineffective teaching. Therefore, the school must address the challenge of providing more good teaching in more classrooms more of the time.

4. Providing more good teaching in more classrooms more of the time requires high-quality professional development for those who deliver mathematics instruction. This professional development must be ongoing rather than sporadic. It must be embedded in the routine practices of the school, occurring in the workplace rather than relying on workshops. It must be collective and team based rather than individualistic. It must focus directly and relentlessly on student achievement rather than adult activities.

Very importantly, the authors recognize that helping all students learn at high levels in mathematics requires educators to build their collective capacity to transform their schools into high-performing professional learning communities. This book offers so much more than a review of the Common Core standards in mathematics. It articulates the specific steps a school must take to move from a culture focused on covering mathematics curriculum to a culture fixated on each student's learning, from a culture of teacher isolation to a culture of purposeful collaboration and collective responsibility, from a culture where assessment is used as a tool to prove what students have learned to a culture where assessment is used to *improve* student learning, and from a culture where evidence of student learning is used primarily to assign grades to a culture where evidence of student learning is used to inform and improve professional practice.

One of the great strengths of this book is its specificity. The authors do more than present the questions that drive the work of teams in a PLC; they go into considerable detail about how the teams should address those questions. They provide practical strategies to help teams work their way through questions such as:

1. How will we determine the knowledge, skills, and understanding each student must acquire as a result of this unit?

2. How will we know if our students are learning?

3. How will we respond when at the end of the unit some students have not yet demonstrated proficiency?

4. How can we enrich and extend the learning for those students who are proficient?

5. How can we use the evidence of student learning to inform and improve our own professional practice?

Each chapter's Extending My Understanding section is another valuable aspect of this book. The questions for reflection and the recommended activities will help educators begin to think like members of a true professional learning community.

In short, this book is exactly what mathematics educators need as they face the challenge of implementing the Common Core curriculum. It merges the potential of the Common Core to be a positive force for student learning with the power of the Professional Learning Community at Work process to provide an invaluable framework for school improvement. It offers much more than a book about curriculum. The authors draw on their expertise in mathematics content, good instruction, and the complexity of school change to present the comprehensive support educators will need as they face the challenge of bringing the Common Core to life in their schools and classrooms.

There will undoubtedly be many books written about implementing the Common Core, but I am certain that none of them will offer more constructive, practical, and insightful recommendations for creating the conditions that lead to higher levels of learning for both students and educators. It warrants the careful consideration and collective dialogue of all mathematics educators in the United States.

—Richard DuFour, Educational Author and Consultant

Introduction

These Standards are not intended to be new names for old ways of doing business. They are a call to take the next step. It is time for states to work together to build on lessons learned from two decades of standards based reforms. It is time to recognize that standards are not just promises to our children, but promises we intend to keep.

—National Governors Association Center for Best Practices &
Council of Chief State School Officers

One of the greatest concerns for mathematics instruction, and instruction in general in most school districts, is that it is too inconsistent from classroom to classroom, school to school, and district to district (Morris & Hiebert, 2011). How much mathematics a high school student in the United States learns, and how deeply he or she learns it, is largely determined by the school the student attends and, even more significantly, the teacher to whom the student is randomly (usually) assigned within that school. The inconsistencies high school teachers develop in their professional development practice—often random and in isolation from other teachers—create great inequities in students' mathematics instructional and assessment learning experiences that ultimately and significantly contribute to the year-by-year achievement gap evident in many schools (Ferrini-Mundy, Graham, Johnson, & Mills, 1998). This issue is especially true in a vertically connected curriculum like mathematics.

The hope and the promise of *Common Core Mathematics in a PLC at Work, High School* is to provide the guidance and teacher focus needed to work outside of existing paradigms regarding mathematics teaching and learning. The resources in this book will enable you to focus your time and energy on issues and actions that will lead to addressing the Common Core State Standards (CCSS) for mathematics challenge: *All students successfully learning rigorous standards for college or career-preparatory mathematics.*

Most of what you will read and use in this book, as well as this series, has been part of the national discussion on mathematics reform and improvement since the National Council of Teachers of Mathematics' (NCTM) release of the *Curriculum and Evaluation Standards* in 1989. In 2000, NCTM refocused the U.S. vision for K–12 mathematics teaching, learning, and assessing in *Principles and Standards for School Mathematics* (PSSM), and the National Research Council (NRC) followed by providing supportive research in the groundbreaking book *Adding It Up* (NRC, 2001). NCTM (2009) followed with *Focus in High School Mathematics: Reasoning and Sense Making* for high school teachers and leaders. (For a full description of the changes in mathematics standards from 1989–2012, see appendix A, page 155.) The significance of these developments for your professional development is discussed in chapters 2 and 3.

So, what would cause you, as a classroom teacher, to believe the national, state, and local responses to the CCSS for mathematics will be any different this time than previous reform efforts and recommendations? Will your professional learning opportunities and activities be any different this time than those that accompanied previous changes in mathematics standards and curriculum programs?

The full implementation of the previous mathematics teaching and learning frameworks and standards was limited by a lack of a coherent and focused vision *implementation* process at the local level. In many cases, the very system of the previous states' standards mathematics *assessments* caused local district resistance to teaching the deeper, richer mathematics curriculum described in the CCSS. This resistance was primarily due to state testing that reflected only the lower cognitive, procedural knowledge aspects of the states' standards. In many school districts, it often felt like a race to get through the grade-level or course curriculum before April of each school year as the *wytiwyg*—what you test is what you get—phenomenon kicked in. For the most part, therefore, significant improvement in student learning of high school mathematics has been happenstance. If a student happened to attend the right school with the right conditions, with the right teacher, with the right program, and with the right processes for learning mathematics in place, then he or she might have a chance for a great mathematics learning experience.

Since 1989, high school mathematics teaching and learning in the United States has been mostly characterized by *pockets of excellence* that reflect the national recommendations of improved student learning, disposition, and confidence for doing mathematics well. The lack of coherent and sustained change toward effective practice has been partially caused by a general attempt to make only modest changes to existing practices. In this context, professional learning opportunities in mathematics were often limited or, in some cases, nonexistent. This situation is defined as *first-order change*—change that produces marginal disturbance to existing knowledge, skills, and practices favored by faculty and school leaders who are closest to the action.

The CCSS expectations for teaching and learning and the new state assessments of that learning usher in an opportunity for unprecedented *second-order change*. In contrast to first-order change, where there is marginal disturbance to the existing knowledge and practices the faculty and school leaders favor, second-order change requires working outside the existing system by embracing new paradigms for how you think and practice (Waters, Marzano, & McNulty, 2003). Furthermore, the Education Trust (Ushomirsky & Hall, 2010), in *Stuck Schools: A Framework for Identifying Schools Where Students Need Change—Now*, indicates that in an environment where funds and capacity are limited at best, educators and policymakers need to establish clear priorities. The CCSS will be your catalyst for providing the support you need as a high school teacher or teacher leader to effect real change.

In this book for high school teachers and teacher leaders, the five chapters focus on five fundamental areas required to prepare every teacher for successful implementation of the CCSS for mathematics leading to the general improvement of teaching and learning for all students. These areas provide the framework within which second-order change can be successfully achieved. The five critical areas are the following.

1. **Collaboration:** The CCSS require a shift in the *grain size of change* beyond the individual isolated teacher or leader. It is the grade-level or course-based collaborative learning team (collaborative team) within a Professional Learning Community (PLC) at Work culture that will develop the expanded teacher knowledge capacity necessary to bring coherence to the implementation of the CCSS for mathematics. The grain size of change now lies within the power and the voice of your collaborative team in a PLC.

2. **Instruction:** The CCSS require a shift to daily lesson designs that include plans for student Mathematical Practices that focus on the process of learning and developing deep student understanding of the standards. This change requires teaching for procedural fluency *and* student understanding of the CCSS. One should not exist without the other. This will require your collaborative team commitment to the use of student-engaged learning around common high-cognitive-demand mathematical tasks used in every classroom.

3. **Content:** The CCSS require a shift to *less* (fewer standards) is *more* (deeper rigor with understanding) in each course. This emphasis will require new levels of knowledge and skill development for every teacher of mathematics to understand *what* the CCSS expect students to learn at each grade level within each course blended with *how* they expect students to learn it. What are the mathematical knowledge, skills, understandings, and dispositions that should be the result of each unit of mathematics instruction? A high school mathematics program committed to helping all students learn ensures great clarity and low teacher-to-teacher variance on the questions, What should students learn? How should they learn it?

4. **Assessment:** The CCSS require a shift to assessments that are a *means* within the teaching-assessing-learning cycle and not used as an *end* to the cycle. These assessments must reflect the rigor of the standards and model the expectations for and benefits of formative assessment practices around all forms of assessment, including traditional instruments such as tests and quizzes. *How will you know* if each student is learning the essential mathematics skills, concepts, understandings, and dispositions the CCSS deem most essential? *How will you know* if your students are prepared for the more rigorous state assessment consortia expectations from the Partnership for Assessment of Readiness for College and Careers (PARCC) and the SMARTER Balanced Assessment Consortium (SBAC)?

5. **Intervention:** The CCSS require a shift in your team and school response to intervention (RTI). Much like the CCSS vision for mathematics teaching and learning, RTI can no longer be invitational. That is, the response to intervention becomes R^2TI—a required response to intervention. Stakeholder implementation of RTI programs includes a process that *requires* students to participate and attend. How will you *respond* and act on evidence (or lack of evidence) of student learning?

Second-order change is never easy. It will require your willingness to break away (or to help a fellow teacher break away) from the past practice of teaching one-standard-a-day mathematics lessons with low-cognitive demand. This change will require all teachers to break away from a past practice that provided few student opportunities for exploring, understanding, and actively engaging and one that used assessment instruments that may or may not have honored a fidelity to accurate and timely formative feedback. Now every teacher will be required to embrace these new paradigms to meet the expectations of the CCSS Mathematics Standards for High School.

Based on a solid foundation in mathematics education research, *Common Core Mathematics in a PLC at Work, High School* is designed to support teachers and all those involved in delivering meaningful mathematics instruction and assessment within these five second-order change areas. It is our hope that the suggestions in these chapters will focus your work on actions that really matter for you and for your students.

Each chapter's Extending My Understanding section has resources and tools you can use in collaborative teams to make sense of and reflect on the chapter recommendations. As a collaborative team, you can make *great decisions* about teaching, learning, assessing, and how your response to learning will impact student mathematics achievement. As Jim Collins and Morten T. Hansen (2011) indicate in *Great by Choice*, you may not be able to predict the future, but you and your team can create it. Our professional development goal is to help every teacher and teacher leader make great decisions toward a great mathematics future for students—every day.

CHAPTER 1

Using High-Performing Collaborative Teams for Mathematics

*The Common Core State Standards provide a consistent, clear under-
standing of what students are expected to learn, so that teachers and parents know what they need to do to help them learn. The standards are
designed to be robust and relevant to the real world, reflecting the knowledge and skills that our young people need for success in college and
careers. With American students fully prepared for the future, our communities will be best positioned to compete successfully in the global economy.*

—National Governors Association Center for Best Practices &
Council of Chief State School Officers

The mission of the K–12 CCSS for mathematics is ambitious yet obtainable. To successfully implement the CCSS Mathematics Standards for High School, you need to be
engaged in a meaningful process of implementation. Such a process allows you a rich
opportunity to be engaged in effective and significant professional development and
learning with your colleagues. The primary purpose of your collective and collaborative teamwork is to develop a coherent, ongoing unit-by-unit cycle of *teaching-assessing-
learning* around the robust mathematics curriculum of the Common Core mathematics.
This cycle (detailed in chapter 4) uses a collaborative approach of planning before a unit
of instruction begins; collecting evidence of student learning needs before, during, and
after the unit; interpreting that evidence in terms of mathematics practices and content; and shaping instruction to support student learning. Working together on activities within this cycle, you and your team have the opportunity to fulfill the expectations
of the CCSS and, at the same time, build a supportive environment for the professional
development of one another.

Research affirms the value of your collaboration with others and its positive impact
on student achievement (Learning Forward, 2011). Many professional organizations
include teacher collaboration as an essential part of professional growth and responsibility (Learning Forward, 2011; National Board of Professional Teaching Standards, 2010;
National Council of Supervisors of Mathematics, 2007; National Council of Teachers
of Mathematics, 1991, 2000). Whether you are a veteran or novice mathematics teacher,
your participation in collaborative teams benefits student learning.

Just as students in groups need direction and support to work together well, high school teachers in collaborative teams need direction and support to effectively collaborate as well. This chapter defines and details how to create *collaborative teams* within a PLC. You will discover how to operate successfully as part of your team and learn the high-leverage collaborative actions that support the authentic implementation of the CCSS. Whether you are part of a new team or a veteran team with deep experience in the PLC process, this chapter helps you identify the current stage of your collaboration and the types of work and discussions in those stages, and it provides several critical collaborative protocols through which you can measure your team's continued progress.

The Professional Development Paradigm Shift

One of the reasons the CCSS have attracted so much attention and gained traction is the potential to address the prevalent concern that U.S. students have historically learned mathematics content in a superficial manner in which concepts and skills are approached as discrete and unrelated topics without application. As a high school mathematics teacher, how often have you heard from others or personally felt that you are obligated to reteach much of what students were supposed to have been taught the previous year?

Although great teaching does not look the same in every classroom, the Common Core standards expect you and your colleagues to commit to high-quality instruction as an essential element of successful student learning. Implementing the CCSS with fidelity requires you to not just teach mathematics content but to teach students processes and proficiencies for ways of thinking and doing mathematics—a habit of mind, so to speak. In the CCSS, these learning processes are referenced within the eight Mathematical Practices (see chapter 2) and the Standards for Mathematical Content (see chapter 3). Your participation in collaborative team discussions allows for the creation and implementation of a rigorous and coherent mathematics curriculum and prevents ineffective instructional practices. Implementing the CCSS for mathematics means you and your colleagues, working together in collaborative teams, must "balance personal goals with collective goals, acquire resources for [your] work, and share those resources to support the work of others" (Garmston & Wellman, 1999, p. 33). Kanold (2011a) explains it this way:

> This is the wonderful paradox of the loose-tight or "defined autonomy" leadership culture. . . . Adults can work within a defined set of behaviors [the CCSS expectations] *and* have an opportunity for freedom and choice. Autonomy is different from independence. Autonomy in the loose-tight PLC world does not mean the individualistic going it alone, relying on nobody. Yet as Daniel Pink (2009) points out, autonomy "means acting with choice—which means we can be both autonomous and happily interdependent with others." (p. 48)

The issue is not about protecting individual teacher autonomy. Rather, the issue is teaching and supporting your collaborative team autonomy with the tools necessary to collaboratively reflect and experiment in ways that are connected to the vision and mission of your school district and the CCSS, supported by research, and that have direct impact on improved student learning.

At your high school, teachers and administrators might equate PLCs with teacher collaboration. As such, *PLC* is a fairly ubiquitous term in education. At the same time, various definitions and understandings regarding a PLC culture abound. In this book, we use the work of DuFour, DuFour, and Eaker's (2008) *Revisiting Professional Learning Communities at Work* and DuFour, DuFour, Eaker, and Many's (2010) *Learning by Doing* to define the conditions for collaborative mathematics learning teams in an authentic PLC school culture. For our purposes, we will refer to grade-level or course-level groups of faculty and resource staff working together in a PLC as *collaborative teams*.

Figure 1.1 lists the primary characteristics that define collaborative team expectations. These actions of shared visioning, collective inquiry, collaborative action, and continuous improvement are foundational to you and your team's ability to answer these four critical questions of a PLC as you implement the CCSS Mathematics Standards for High School.

1. What are the knowledge, skills, and dispositions we want all students to acquire as a result of their experience in our course? (See chapters 2 and 3.)

2. How will we know each student has acquired the intended knowledge, skills, and dispositions? What is our process for gathering information on each student's proficiency? (See chapter 4.)

3. How will our team and school respond to students who experience difficulty in acquiring the intended knowledge and skills? How will we provide them with additional time and support for learning in a way that is timely, directive, precise, and systematic? (See chapter 5.)

4. How will our team and school provide additional enrichment for students who are already proficient? (See chapters 2 and 5.)

Collaborative high school mathematics teams do the following:

1. Work toward a shared vision of mathematics curriculum, instruction, and assessment tied to the school and district vision as aligned with the Common Core standards' expectations

2. Engage in collective inquiry around rigorous mathematical practices and content, high-quality instruction, and formative assessment practices that provide meaningful feedback on student progress

3. Remain focused on a collaborative action orientation, experimentation, and reflection by all team members

4. Use assessment data to guide continuous and formative improvement of student learning and teacher instruction

---

Figure 1.1: High school collaborative team expectations and activities.

Visit **go.solution-tree.com/commoncore** for a reproducible version of this figure.

You often work toward success for every student by yourself, without an articulated or shared image of what that might look like in a high school mathematics classroom. For example, if you asked each teacher on your team to list his or her top three non-discretionary teaching behaviors critical to student success, would the response reveal a coherent and focused vision for instruction from your team?

Similar to providing students with a learning target to aim toward, a first step for your collaborative teams is to create a shared vision of curriculum, instruction, and assessment specific to learning high school mathematics. As Danielson (2009) argues, "It's not sufficient for a school to be comprised of individual expertise; that expertise must be mobilized in the service of a common vision" (p. 17).

A shared vision is a necessary cornerstone to the work of your collaborative team. You might already have that vision for instruction and assessment in place, which is a good start. However, vision alone is not sufficient. Collaborative teacher inquiry, action orientation, experimentation, and reflection will enable you to make progress toward implementation of the vision. This brings an intentional purpose to your daily work. In many high schools, teachers are working in teams and using data to set goals and monitor student progress. Does this describe your work at your school? If so, this is important and necessary, but not sufficient if it is carried out in isolation from your colleagues.

Although given less attention, the difficult team*work* of collective inquiry together with action orientation and experimentation has a more direct impact on student learning (Hattie, 2009). It is in the process of inquiry and experimentation that you find meaning in your collaborative work with colleagues. It is through respectfully challenging your peers about what does and does not work in the classroom that you take ownership of your own beliefs, learning, and professional development.

Through the collective creation, modification, and ongoing reflection of what is taught and how instruction and assessment impact student learning, you begin to pursue your personal growth as a professional. When you and your collaborative team focus discussions on the mathematical content and processes students engage in and how instruction and formative assessment sustain meaningful student learning, your professional growth becomes continuous and embedded in your daily work, and your students' performance will soar. This book is designed to support your professional growth work as teachers and collaborators at your school.

Your collaboration with colleagues is about "purposeful peer interaction" (Fullan, 2008, p. 41). Purposeful peer interaction begins as you use a common vocabulary for your team discussions. It is an important factor contributing to your focused interactions with colleagues. The vocabulary and format of the CCSS Mathematics Standards for High School may be somewhat different from what you are accustomed to using. Figure 1.2 presents some key terms for the Common Core Mathematics Standards for High School, and the complete text for Common Core Mathematics Standards for High School is presented in appendix C (page 165).

The **conceptual categories** of the CCSS Mathematics Standards for High School are: Number and Quantity; Algebra; Functions; Modeling; Geometry; and Statistics and Probability. Each conceptual category consists of several domains, with the exception of Modeling.

Domains are larger groups of related standards. Standards from different domains may sometimes be closely related. For example, Number and Quantity has four domains (see appendix C, pages 165–169): the Real Number System (N–RN); Quantities (N–Q); the Complex Number System (N–CN); and Vector and Matrix Quantities (N–VM). An acronym accompanies each domain title.

Content standard clusters are groups of related standards. Note that standards from different clusters may sometimes be closely related because mathematics is a connected subject. The domain the Real Number System (N–RN) has two content standard clusters: (1) Extend the properties of exponents to rational exponents, and (2) Use properties of rational and irrational numbers.

Standards define what students should understand and be able to do. The two content standard clusters in the Real Number System domain include three standards: N–RN.1, N–RN.2, and N–RN.3.

1. Extend the properties of exponents to rational exponents

   › **N-RN.1:** Explain how the definition of the meaning of rational exponents follows from extending the properties of integer exponents to those values, allowing for a notation for radicals in terms of rational exponents. For example, we define $5^{1/3}$ to be the cube root of 5 because we want $(5^{1/3})^3 = 5^{(1/3)3}$ to hold, so $(5^{1/3})^3$ must equal 5.

   › **N-RN.2:** Rewrite expressions involving radicals and rational exponents using the properties of exponents.

2. Use properties of rational and irrational numbers.

   › **N-RN.3:** Explain why the sum or product of two rational numbers is rational; that the sum of a rational number and an irrational number is irrational; and that the product of a nonzero rational number and an irrational number is irrational.

Source: Adapted from National Governors Association Center for Best Practices & Council of Chief State School Officers, 2010, pp. 5, 60.

Figure 1.2: How to read the CCSS mathematics standards for high school.

Visit **go.solution-tree.com/commoncore** for a reproducible version of this figure.

According to Reeves (2010), high-impact professional development and learning in collaborative teams is:

1. Focused on student learning

2. Focused on assessment of the decisions teacher team members make

3. Focused on people and practices rather than programs

Based on these features of collaborative teams, your professional learning takes place as your team discusses questions such as, How might we teach the Complex Number

System (N-CN) so students understand the concept of complex numbers? (see N-CN, appendix C, page 167). During the unit, your team collects and analyzes data to determine if your instructional decisions had an impact on student learning of complex numbers. In this process, your team attends to the needs of teachers by creating and supporting their collaborative work in the critical examination of student learning. Together, team members analyze student work and classroom practices and exchange ideas about mathematics content and the assessment of that content. This unit-by-unit cycle of dialogue with your peers results in a greater impact on student achievement and brings a focus and coherence to your work as a team.

Collaboration is not necessarily efficient or easy. However, when you and your peers have the skills and knowledge to collaborate through professional conversations focused on student learning, the dialogue, reflection, and actions that characterize your collaborative team emerge as a significant part of your ongoing professional learning. As Fullan (2008) indicates, your collaborative learning is the work.

Teacher Collaboration Versus Cooperation or Coordination

Without teacher collaboration, the Common Core Mathematics Standards for High School are merely another set of standards: "These standards are not intended to be new names for old ways of doing business. They are a call to take the next step" (NGA & CCSSO, 2010, p. 5). When you and your colleagues collaborate through discussion and dialogue about the impact of the CCSS on curriculum, instruction, and assessment, your content knowledge capacity will increase and you will develop effective ways to approach mathematics instruction—with pedagogical content knowledge.

The only sustainable form of mathematics professional development in high school occurs when you work in highly effective collaborative teams around issues of curriculum, instruction, and assessment (NCSM, 2008a; Learning Forward, 2011). Given the high stakes of increased academic achievement for students, your collaboration with peers becomes a nondiscretionary reality of your work, and the mathematics teachers in your high school should not be allowed to opt out of working with you and your peers when it comes to issues related to student learning.

The act of becoming an effective teacher can no longer be about *my students* or *your students*. It is about *our students* and what each teacher can do in the courses he or she teaches to benefit all students—including those students in need of the various and multiple RTI options discussed in chapter 5. Teachers accustomed to going into their classrooms, closing the door, and making decisions in isolation, separate from colleagues, are missing the opportunity to share their knowledge and experience with colleagues. If such individuals are in your school, they miss the chance to learn from others and lose out on the benefits of participation in a collaborative team. Taking advantage of opportunities to interact with your colleagues on matters of mutual interest and concern enables you to grow professionally.

Although teacher collaboration is an essential aspect of a PLC, what is often considered *collaboration* is actually cooperation or coordination. *Cooperation* is an informal process for sharing information with no goal or outcome in mind (Grover, 1996). Cooperation is about being a team player. One potential danger of cooperation is the exclusion of a diversity of team member ideas. Consider a scenario in which your team members share ideas and lesson plans about how they each teach a learning target about triangle congruence to geometry students. In this case, teachers cooperate by sharing resources, although each teacher retains his or her own authority to teach and assess the learning target as he or she best understands it.

Coordination, on the other hand, requires more planning and increased communication by the teacher team than does cooperation. Efficiency regarding the management aspects of the course tends to drive teachers to coordinate. For example, your Algebra 1 Team may coordinate a schedule so all teachers have access to graphing calculators for the unit on graphing linear equations, or it might divide up different content standards from a particular CCSS content standard cluster in order to design lessons for the team. Note that coordination can serve purposes of efficiency but do little to push peer inquiry and student discussion as part of the daily instruction and assessment in the classroom—the true purpose and high-leverage work of the high school collaborative teams in a PLC.

Whereas *cooperating* and *coordinating* are about individuals on the teacher team making decisions, *collaborating* is about creating interdependence with your colleagues as you work beyond consensus building. When your team is collaborating effectively, members are creating new structures and ways of working that are focused on academic success for all students, not just the students in their own classes. Graham and Ferriter (2008) offer a useful framework that details seven stages of collaborative team development. The level at which teams fall within Graham and Ferriter's framework is directly correlated to each team's level of effective collaboration. Table 1.1 highlights these seven stages.

Table 1.1: The Seven Stages of Teacher Collaboration Diagnostic Tool

Stage	Questions That Define This Stage
Stage one: Filling the time	What exactly are we supposed to do? Why are we meeting? Is this going to be worth my time?
Stage two: Sharing personal practice	What is everyone doing in his or her classroom? What are some of your favorite problems you use for this unit?
Stage three: Planning, planning, planning	What content should we be teaching, and how should we pace this unit? How do we lighten the load for each other?
Stage four: Developing common assessments	How do you know students learned? What does mastery look like? What does student proficiency look like?

continued ▸

Stage	Questions That Define This Stage
Stage five: Analyzing student learning	Are students learning what they are supposed to be learning? What does it mean for students to demonstrate understanding of the learning targets?
Stage six: Adapting instruction to student needs	How can we adjust instruction to help those students struggling and those exceeding expectations?
Stage seven: Reflecting on instruction	Which of our instructional and assessment practices are most effective with our students?

Visit **go.solution-tree.com/commoncore** for a reproducible version of this table.

Teams at the first three stages of collaborative team development are trying to understand what they are supposed to do and accomplish. Consider the following scenario. The Precalculus Team began meeting weekly at the beginning of the year with little direction as to the purpose of meeting (stage one). Shortly, the team began to share how each teacher approached conditional probability (S-CP, see appendix C, page 190) in his or her respective classrooms (stage two). By the end of the semester, the Precalculus Team began to discuss the homework problems that best represented what students should know and be able to demonstrate related to radian angle measure (F-TF.1, see appendix C, page 179) and had decided who would compile the assignment sheet to be distributed to students (stage three). At this stage, the precalculus teachers are *cooperating* as they begin to share their own classroom practices and delegate team responsibilities.

Teams in stages four and five are *coordinating* around common planning of instruction, developing common assessment instruments and tasks, and analyzing student learning results. An Algebra 2 Team (or a Mathematics 3 Team, if integrated course sequencing) comes together (stage four) to develop a common quiz to assess students' ability to solve rational and radical equations (A-REI.2, see appendix C, page 173). The following year, the Algebra 2 Team creates common assessment instruments for all course units or chapters and uses collaborative team time to analyze and compare results in order to determine how all algebra 2 students are performing on the learning standards for the course.

It is in the final two stages that teams are actually *collaborating* as members take collective responsibility for ensuring all students learn, differentiating instruction, and designing assessments based on student needs by reflecting on the question, Which practices are most effective with our students? (Graham & Ferriter 2008, p. 42). After analyzing the data from the unit's common assessment, a Geometry Team (or a Mathematics 3 Team, if integrated) has identified a small group of students struggling to apply some of the chord relationships in circles (G-C.2, see appendix C, page 186). The teams develop a differentiated re-engagement lesson to extend the knowledge and reasoning of students who have mastered the learning target and provide targeted support for struggling learners (stage six). The Geometry Team will reach stage seven when team members regularly make adjustments to instruction using the teaching-assessing-learning cycle (described in chapter 4) based on learner needs and discuss instructional strategies that have the greatest impact on student learning.

You can use table 1.1 to determine your collaborative team's current stage of development and to consider what might be done to move to the next stage. In a mathematics department with several teams, you and your colleagues may be interested in comparing notes about issues other teams address and how they conduct their meetings. When your collaborative team works together, are discussions focused on sharing each teacher's lessons or activities without inquiry into assessing student learning? Are meetings centered on when the unit or chapter assessment instruments will be given in class, rather than whether or not the instrument is a high-quality exam? Is your focus mostly on scheduling or on how you and your colleagues are connecting the learning standards with context throughout the unit? Discussions with your team colleagues can help you determine whether the team is cooperating, coordinating, or collaborating.

Collaborative Practices

The goal of collaboration is deep, widespread knowledge of subject-area content and consistent implementation of best-practice instruction for that content. McKinsey and Company (Barber & Mourshed, 2007; Mourshed, Chijioke, & Barber, 2010) conducted two studies of the world's highest-performing school systems. According to these studies, the world's highest-performing school systems are able to "decrease the pedagogical variability between teachers and increase the quality of instruction. . . . They do this by establishing clear instructional priorities and investing in teacher preparation and professional development" (Barber & Mourshed, 2007, p. 12). The structure designed for collaborative efforts to support teachers in their professional learning is critical. Five aspects of collaborative practice can be considered:

1. Collaborative team participants
2. Collaborative team commitments
3. Collaborative team leaders
4. Collaborative team agendas and meeting minutes
5. Collaborative team time

In order to do the work of the team described in figure 1.1 (page 7) and to move effectively and efficiently to the more advanced stages of team collaboration, it is important that your team responds to each of these five collaboration factors.

Collaborative Team Participants

The needs, interests, and expertise of individual team members will often affect the flow and the work of your team. The members of your collaborative team may also vary according to the needs of your school or district. For larger schools, collaborative teams may be comprised of all teachers of a particular course, subject, or grade level. For example, a collaborative team may be all teachers of advanced honors algebra, teachers of all levels of geometry, teachers of your mathematics 1 ninth-grade course, or all honors mathematics teachers. Your collaborative teams might also benefit from other faculty and staff members participating on your team, including faculty members from other departments and school support personnel, such as counselors, special needs or English learner (EL) teachers, or paraprofessional tutors.

Team members need only have a common curricular, instructional, and assessment focus about which to collaborate. While there is no ideal or magic number of teachers on a collaborative team, experience seems to suggest that teams much larger than seven or eight can be challenging (Horn, 2010). When your teams are too large, discussions become unwieldy and a few extroverted teachers can hijack participation, limiting other team members' voices. It is possible for larger teams to engage in productive dialogue; however, a higher level of facilitation will be required. Your mathematics department chairs or instructional leaders should also consider individual compatibility when determining assignments to collaborative teams. The ability to work with colleagues who understand how to share information and how to work with a positive attitude on various team projects is important. One way to nurture this expectation for becoming an effective contributor to the team is through the development of clear team commitments and behaviors.

Collaborative Team Commitments

Expectations for how collaboration looks and sounds need to be clearly and explicitly communicated. In *What Works in Schools*, Marzano (2003) identifies the necessity for collegiality. *Collegiality* is defined as the way teachers interact with each other in a manner that is professional. Roland Barth (2006) provides a description of collegiality.

> When I visit a school and look for evidence of collegiality among teachers and administrators—signs that educators are "playing together"—the indicators I seek are:
>
> 1. Educators talking with one another about practice
> 2. Educators sharing their craft knowledge
> 3. Educators observing one another while they are engaged in practice
> 4. Educators rooting for one another's success (p. 10)

Fullan and Hargreaves (1996) explain that professional behaviors include respect for one another, a willingness to share mistakes, and an openness to critique practices and procedures (as cited in Marzano, 2003). Sharing mistakes and being open to criticism can be daunting. Thus, teams need to establish norms or collective commitments of conduct and behavior if members are to work collaboratively in ways that promote a level of openness and vulnerability and the ability to play together.

The purpose of team collective commitments is to create a respectful, open environment that encourages diversity of ideas and invites criticism combined with close inspection of practices and procedures. Various protocols are available to assist you and your team in establishing actions that team members agree to follow. The process need not be arduous, complicated, or time consuming. The protocol in figure 1.3 is one model your team can use to establish and review collective commitments throughout the year.

Setting Team Collective Commitments

Because we need our best from one another in working as a team, it is essential that we set collective commitments for our work cultures. Collective commitments are values and beliefs that will describe how we choose to treat each other and how we can expect to be treated.

As we set three to four collective commitments for ourselves, please note that establishing these does not mean that we are not already good people who work together productively. Having collective commitments simply reminds us to be highly conscious about our actions and what we can expect from each other as we engage in conversations about our challenging work.

Step one: Write three or four "We will" statements that you think will have the most positive influence on our group as we collaborate on significant issues about teaching and learning. Perhaps reflect on past actions or behaviors that have made teams less than productive. These are only a jumpstart for your thinking.

Step two: Partner with another colleague to talk about your choices and the reasons for your selection. Together decide on three or four commitments from your combined lists.

Step three: Move as a pair to partner with two to four other colleagues to talk about your choices and the reasons for your selection. Together decide on three or four commitments from your combined lists.

Step four: Make a group decision. Prepare to share your choices with the whole group.

Step five: Adopt collective commitments by consensus. Invite clarification and advocacy for particular commitments. Give all participants four votes for norm selection. It is wise not to have more than three or four.

Source: Adapted from P. Luidens, personal communication, January 27 and April 9, 2010.

Figure 1.3: Setting high school teacher team collective commitments protocol.

Visit **go.solution-tree.com/commoncore** for a reproducible version of this figure.

Your high school team should keep collective commitments focused on behaviors and practices that will support the collaborative work of your team. Some teams find it useful to post their norms in a conspicuous place as a reminder to each other. Other teams might choose a commitment to highlight at each meeting as a reminder to the commitments of the team. For great advice and insight into collaborative team protocols, go to http://allthingsplc.info under Tools & Resources for additional ideas. Visit **go.solution-tree.com/commoncore** for links to additional resources.

As an example, members of a high school Algebra 2 Team decided their collective commitments would be to: (1) listen to understand, (2) challenge ideas, and (3) keep the focus on teaching and learning. Although the team included most of the same people as the previous year, team members reflected on the previous year and observed that sometimes one or two individuals passionate about their ideas often hijacked the discussions without hearing others' ideas. The collective commitments reflect the collaborative team's dedication to hearing all ideas and respectfully challenging each other.

Each team member has the responsibility to hold one another accountable for the agreed-on commitments in a form of lateral or peer-to-peer accountability. To address team members for not adhering to the norms is a permissible and expected aspect of the team culture. Collaborative teams might find it useful to establish a collective commitment that addresses what happens when a commitment is not honored. The purpose of the collective commitments is to raise the level of professionalism and liberate the team to openly, safely, and respectfully discuss the work at hand. As collaborative teams grow and develop or change membership, collective commitments will likely change. Regardless of whether your collaborative team members change at the semester, you should revisit your collective commitments at the start of each semester every year.

Collaborative Team Leaders

Just as effective staff development doesn't happen without intentional planning and facilitating, collaborative team meetings also need intentional forethought and someone from your team to lead the group. The role of team leader or meeting facilitator might rotate or be delegated to one individual. On one hand, one person assigned team leader for the entire school year might bring continuity to your team discussions and functions. (A team leader may have other responsibilities related to the work of the team in addition to leading the team meetings.) On the other hand, perhaps rotating the role of team leader or meeting facilitator gives more of your colleagues the opportunity to take ownership and develop in their ability to facilitate discussions. To make the most of the collaborative meetings, the team leader's role should involve intentionally maximizing your group's ability to collaborate by inviting diversity of thought and challenging ideas and practices. An effective collaborative team always knows who is driving the meeting agenda and communicating the meeting outcomes. An effective high school mathematics team leader encourages all members to participate and ask each other questions to push for clarity and understanding. An effective team leader will also summarize team questions, understandings, decisions, and actionable items in a timely fashion.

Collaborative Team Agendas and Meeting Minutes

Designing time for mathematics collaborative teams is a considerable commitment of resources in people, money, and time. The payoff occurs when collaboration around teaching and learning mathematics results in professional growth and increased student achievement. Agendas and meeting minutes are tools that lend themselves to a more efficient use of time. The team leader is responsible for seeking input from team members, determining the agenda, and making the agenda public to the team a few days prior to the meeting. Agendas acknowledge that time is valuable and are essential to successful meetings (Garmston & Wellman, 2009). An agenda need not be complicated or long. Figure 1.4 provides a sample agenda from an Advanced Algebra Collaborative Team.

Tuesday, April 5

- Share and analyze results from the exponential unit assessment instrument (test).

  › How did our students do overall?

  › Were the results what we expected?

  › Which learning targets were the weakest overall performers for the students?

  › Did anyone's students do better on the weaker learning targets? What might this teacher have done different than the rest of us?

- Review learning targets for the logarithm unit.

  › Do our learning targets capture the key content concepts?

  › Do the learning targets together represent a balance of higher-level reasoning and procedural fluencies?

- Bring your best ideas for introducing logarithms for student exploration.

  › What have you tried in the past that seems to have worked?

  › Are there ideas, problems, or strategies that you have tried that didn't work?

  › What task or problem might we use to help students understand what a log is and how to better understand the log properties?

Figure 1.4: Sample team meeting agenda.

Visit **go.solution-tree.com/commoncore** for a reproducible version of this figure.

Meeting minutes are beneficial and do not need to be overly detailed. Minutes serve many useful purposes. First, minutes for each meeting capture the actions and decisions that the team has made. Teams have found it helpful to go back to minutes earlier in the year or even to the previous year to recall discussions related to the ordering of content or why they decided to use a particular instructional approach for a concept. Minutes also capture who is responsible for various action steps, such as creating a scoring rubric and key for a quiz or test or arranging for copies of artifacts for all team members.

Notice that the minutes illustrated in figure 1.4 are quick bullet points that communicate the focus of the meeting so team members can come prepared with ideas, data, or other possible resources for the next meeting. Also note that the team leader provides guiding questions for team members to reflect on prior to the meeting. He or she primes the pump of expectations, so to speak. Team members can give prior thought and consideration to the topics, thus making the meeting more productive.

If you are like most high school teachers, you have anywhere from two to four different mathematics courses you teach each year. This means you serve multiple teams—creating a challenge to attend all team meetings. The minutes are also an efficient way to communicate to others what transpired at the meeting. So if you are unable to attend a meeting, you can use the minutes as a resource to see what was discussed and decided. Much like students absent from class, if you are absent from the meeting, you are still expected to know and carry out the decisions of the team. Technology is an effective means by which to make minutes public to others. Minutes can be posted in an email, to a wiki, to a team blog, on a team website, or through cloud sharing.

The minutes also provide one form of communication to the mathematics department chairperson or the school mathematics administrator. The minutes allow school leaders to provide targeted guidance, direction, or resources to support the work of your collaborative team. Figure 1.5 is an example of a Geometry Honors Team's meeting minutes that were posted electronically. Notice how the meeting blends a balance of team procedural issues (when to give the formative cumulative exam based on the calendar) with team instructional issues (discontinuing the lab).

- After today's meeting, we are thinking about doing a variation of Val's social-emotional learning activity after the first quiz for the unit.

- We discussed how to deal with the shortened first-term grading period. We are thinking we should stay with the plan of giving the formative cumulative exam on the Monday after the grading period ends.

- We discussed ways to deal with properties of quadrilaterals rather than doing the lab. We are in favor of no longer doing the lab because it does not mirror the thought process we are trying to develop.

- We decided on partial credit for multiple-choice questions on tests and the formulas to use during all chapter 12 assessments.

- We decided to focus the formative assessment work in this unit on student communication and conjecturing with each other (Mathematical Practice 3).

Figure 1.5: Sample team meeting minutes.

Visit **go.solution-tree.com/commoncore** for a reproducible version of this figure.

Laying the groundwork for collaboration by articulating both the expectations of how your collaborative team will work together (toward constructive discussions and decision making) and the logistics of announcing and capturing your team discussions is essential. Attention to these fundamental team management issues supports deeper and more meaningful discussions that will impact student learning of mathematics. Once expectations have been articulated about collaboration, you and your team can engage in meaningful discussions around teaching and learning mathematics.

Collaborative Team Time

First and foremost, as a high school mathematics teacher, you need adequate time in order to achieve the expectations of ongoing weekly mathematics professional development. Reeves (2009) asserts it is a myth that people love to collaborate. He notes that real and meaningful collaboration takes time and practice and requires accountability: "Schools that claim, for example, to be professional learning communities but fail to provide time for collaboration are engaging in self-delusion" (p. 46). School district leaders sincere in their efforts to create a PLC will help you find creative ways to build time into the schedule for collaboration.

Figure 1.6 provides a few ideas to make your collaborative team professional development time a priority (Bowgren & Sever, 2010; Loucks-Horsley, Stiles, Mundry, Love, & Hewson, 2009).

1. Provide common time by scheduling most team members, if not all, the same period free from teaching during the day.

2. Create an altered schedule for early-release or late-arrival students on an ongoing basis.

3. Use substitute teachers throughout the day to release different collaborative teams for two to three hours at a time.

4. Occasionally release teachers from a teaching duty (such as one class period) or other supervision in order to collaborate with colleagues on a daily basis.

5. Restructure time by permanently altering teacher responsibilities, the teaching schedule, the school day, or the school calendar.

6. Purchase teacher time by providing monetary district compensation for weekends and summer work.

Figure 1.6: Options for scheduling teacher collaboration time.

Visit **go.solution-tree.com/commoncore** for a reproducible version of this figure.

Yet in order for your district or school to make a commitment to time, your school leaders must know that the team time will be focused on high-leverage professional development activities that will result in improved student learning for your course.

High-Leverage Professional Development

Just as students are not empty vessels waiting to be filled with mathematical knowledge and ways of reasoning, you and your team members bring myriad resources to the table—content knowledge, pedagogical knowledge, beliefs about teaching, classroom experiences, and personal experiences (Raymond, 1997). While the impact of these prior knowledge factors cannot be ignored, the team's collaborative efforts can influence some of these attributes in your colleagues. Based on what is known about adult learning and professional growth, professional development programs should emphasize building teachers' pedagogical content knowledge (Loucks-Horsley et al., 2009). You can engage in these programs; however, teachers don't have the authority to create the programs. School and district leaders are responsible for creating on-site professional development learning opportunities for teachers, built around developing and implementing teaching strategies specific to the CCSS content being taught. The collaborative efforts of district and school leaders and teachers will have a positive impact of student learning.

The CCSS Mathematics Standards for High School (see appendix C, page 165) provide a vision and verification tool of the content to be taught that can be used to challenge you and your colleagues as you reflect on your beliefs and practices about teaching mathematics. As you collaborate, your beliefs about teaching and learning become revealed. Through discourse in your teams, you and your colleagues articulate beliefs and expectations and seek to reconcile inconsistency of ideas and practices in the quest to continuously improve student mathematics learning and creating greater equity in the student learning experience. This ongoing process of sharing, questioning, and reconciling ideas culminates in professional learning that in turn brings about more equity and access for all students learning mathematics in the courses you teach.

Collaborative teamwork centered on developing student processes and proficiencies (the CCSS Standards for Mathematical Practice), meaningful student understanding of the content (CCSS content standard clusters within the domains of the high school curriculum), and development of assessment protocols (the CCSS consortia assessment framework expectations) result in ongoing, continuous, and embedded professional learning opportunities for you and your colleagues. Meaningful collaboration is built around high-leverage, high-inquiry collaborative team tasks, such as the ten listed in figure 1.7.

PLC Collaborative Teacher Team Agreements for Teaching and Learning

1. The team designs and develops agreed-on prior-knowledge skills to be assessed and taught during each lesson of the unit or chapter.

2. The team designs and implements agreed-on lesson design elements that ensure students actively engage with the mathematics. Students experience some aspect of the CCSS Mathematical Practices (such as construct viable arguments and critique the reasoning of others or Attend to precision) with the language embedded in the daily lessons of every unit or chapter.

3. The team designs and implements agreed-on lesson design elements that allow for student-led summaries and demonstrations of learning the daily lesson.

4. The team designs and implements agreed-on lesson design elements that include the strategic use of tools—including technology—for developing student understanding.

PLC Collaborative Team Agreements for Assessments Instruments and Tools

1. The team designs and implements agreed-on common assessment instruments based on high-quality exam designs. The collaborative team designs all unit exams, unit quizzes, final exams, writing assignments, and projects for the course.

2. The team designs and implements agreed-on common assessment instrument scoring rubrics for each assessment in advance of the exam.

3. The team designs and implements agreed-on common scoring and grading feedback (level of specificity to the feedback) of the assessment instruments. Two team members together grade a small sample of student work to check on consistency in scoring and grading feedback.

PLC Collaborative Team Agreements for Formative Assessment Feedback

1. The team designs and implements agreed-on adjustments to instruction and intentional student support based on the results of both formative daily classroom assessments and the results of student performance on unit or chapter assessment instruments, such as quizzes and tests.

2. The team designs and implements agreed-on levels of rigor for daily in-class prompts and common high-cognitive-demand tasks used to assess student understanding. This also applies to team agreement to minimize the variance in rigor and task selection for homework assignments and expectations for makeup work. This applies to depth, quality, and timeliness of teacher descriptive formative feedback on all student work.

3. The team designs and implements agreed-on methods to teach students to self-assess and set goals. Self-assessment includes students using teacher feedback, feedback from other students, or their own monitoring and self-assessment to identify what they need to work on and to set goals for future learning.

Figure 1.7: High-leverage actions of high school mathematics collaborative teams.

Visit **go.solution-tree.com/commoncore** for a reproducible version of this figure.

You can use figure 1.7 as a diagnostic tool to measure the focus of the work and energy of your team. The items in the figure can help you determine the level of implementation—high or low—for each of the team actions. Meaningful implementation of the CCSS will require time—time to digest the CCSS Mathematics Standards for High School, time to create a focused and coherent curriculum, and time to design instruction and assessments around the actions listed in figure 1.7.

Collaborative Protocols

Several protocols combine collaboration with a spotlight on the teaching and learning of mathematics. Five structured protocols can be especially beneficial for you and your team. These protocols provide different settings in which you can collaborate and share reflections and beliefs about teaching and learning.

1. **Lesson study:** Lesson study differs from lesson planning. Lesson study focuses on what teachers want students to learn; lesson planning focuses on what teachers plan to teach. A lesson study example is shown in the feature box on page 22.

2. **Peer coaching:** Peer coaching is a kind of partnership in which two or three teachers engage in conversations focused on their reflections and thinking about their instructional practices. The discussions lead to a refinement and formative assessment response to classroom practice. The participants may rotate roles—discussion leader, mentor, or advocate. Teachers who engage in peer coaching are willing to reveal strengths and weaknesses to each other. Peer coaching creates an environment in which teachers can be secure, connected, and empowered through transparent discussions of each others' practice.

3. **Case study:** Case study can be used to address a wide range of topics or problems the collaborative team encounters. The case study presents a story—one involving issues or conflicts that need to be resolved through analysis of available resources leading to constructive plans to address the problem. Typically,

case studies are used to examine complex problems—the school's culture, climate, attendance, achievement, teaching, and learning (Baccellieri, 2010).

4. **Book study:** Book study is a familiar and popular activity for teachers to engage in conversations with colleagues about professional books. It may be a formalized activity for some collaborative teams; however, book study can emerge in any number of ways—from hearing an author speak at a conference, from a colleague's enthusiastic review of a book, or from the mutual interests of teachers who want to learn more about a topic. Book study promotes conversations among faculty and staff that can lead to the application of new ideas in the classroom and improvement of existing knowledge and skills. Book study is a great way to connect with a personal learning network as you blog, tweet, Skype, or use other forms of communication to connect with colleagues outside of your school.

5. **Collaborative grading:** Collaborative grading occurs as your team reaches stages four and five (see table 1.1, page 11) of team collaboration. In this situation, you and your colleagues design a common unit test together and assign point values with scoring rubrics for each question on the exam. Together you grade and discuss the quality of student responses on the assessment instrument and develop an inter-rater reliability for scoring of the assessment tool. Achieving consistency in grading students' assignments and assessments is an important goal for collaborative teams.

From the point of view of instructional transparency and improvement, lesson study is a particularly powerful collaborative tool that merits close consideration. Lesson study has been shown to be very effective as a collaborative protocol with a high impact on teacher professional learning (Hiebert & Stigler, 1999).

Example of a Lesson-Study Group in Action

Typically, teachers choose a content area that data indicate is problematic for students. Consider a lesson-study group that develops a goal related to the CCSS Mathematical Practices (see appendix B, page 161). The teachers select Mathematical Practice 1 as the goal—students will learn to make sense of problems and persevere in solving them. They share ideas about how to help students achieve this goal through the content of the lesson. The teachers select content from the CCSS domains and content standard clusters that presents a particular challenge to students. In this case, the group chooses "understand that polynomials form a system analogous to the integers" (A-APR.1, see appendix C, page 172). The teachers use various resources to learn more about the content and its connections to other mathematical concepts, as well as about information from research about student learning of operations with polynomials. From those resources, the teachers together designed a lesson to address the goal. One team member was asked to teach the lesson and be observed by one or two other members of the team. The teacher who taught the lesson and the observers debriefed the team about their observations and made changes to the lesson design. The revised lesson was taught with a final debriefing of the second instructional episode. By the end of the lesson study, these teachers have increased their knowledge of pedagogy and mathematics content. By contributing to development of the lesson and engaging in discussions of the lesson's strengths and limitations, they have also raised the level of respect and trust among team members. The lessons learned from participating in lesson study extend to the teachers' daily instruction.

Lesson study may seem time and work intensive for a single lesson. Nonetheless, the benefit of lesson study is the teacher professional learning that results from the deep, collaborative discussions about mathematics content, instruction, and student learning. See the lesson-study references listed in the Extending My Understanding section at the end of this chapter (page 24) for more information about this powerful activity for stages six and seven (see table 1.1, page 11).

Looking Ahead

Your collaborative team is the key to all students successfully learning the Common Core Mathematics Standards for High School through effective instruction, assessment, and intervention practices. In subsequent chapters, we'll provide tools to assist you and your colleagues' work to make the vision of the Common Core for mathematics a reality for all students. In regard to the administrator's role in this process, the National Board for Professional Teaching Standards (2010) states:

> Seeing themselves as partners with other teachers, they [administrators] are dedicated to improving the profession. They care about the quality of teaching in their schools, and, to this end, their collaboration with colleagues is continuous and explicit. They recognize that collaborating in a professional learning community contributes to their own professional growth, as well as to the growth of their peers, for the benefit of student learning. Teachers promote the ideal that working collaboratively increases knowledge, reflection, and quality of practice and benefits the instructional program. (p. 75)

Highly accomplished mathematics teachers value and practice effective collaboration, which professional organizations have identified as an essential element to teacher professional development (Learning Forward, 2011; National Board for Professional Teaching Standards, 2010). Teacher collaboration is not the icing on top of the proverbial cake. Instead, it is the egg in the batter, holding the cake together. Your school is a learning institution responsible for educating students and preparing them for the future. Your school is also a learning institution for the adults. The professional learning of teachers is not solely a prerequisite for improved student achievement. It is a commitment to the investment in the professionals, like you, who have the largest impact on students in schools. The process of collaboration capitalizes on the fact that teachers come together with diverse experiences and knowledge to create a whole that is larger than the sum of the parts. Teacher collaboration is *the* solution to your sustained professional learning —the ongoing and never-ending process of growth necessary to meet the classroom demands of the CCSS expectations.

Chapter 1 Extending My Understanding

1. A critical tenet of a mathematics department of a PLC is a shared vision of teaching and learning mathematics.

   - Do you have a shared vision of what teaching and learning mathematics looks like? If not, how might you create one?

   - Does this vision build on current research in mathematics education?

   - Does your vision embrace collaboration as fundamental to professional learning?

2. Graham and Ferriter (2008) identify seven stages of collaborative team development. These stages characterize team development evolving from cooperating to coordinating, leading ultimately to a truly *collaborative* team.

   - Using table 1.1 (page 11), at what stage are your teams operating?

   - What role might you play in helping your team transition to a more advanced stage?

3. Using figure 1.7 (page 21), identify the high-leverage actions your team currently practices extremely well. What is your current level of implementation on a scale of 0 percent (low) and 100 percent (high)? How might you use this information to identify which actions should be your team's priority during this or the next school year?

4. Implementing the CCSS content and Mathematical Practices might seem daunting to some teachers, and as a result, there may be resistance or half-hearted attempts to needed changes in content, instruction, or assessment. Consider leading your collaborative team through a Best Hopes, Worst Fears activity. Give team members two index cards. On one, have them identify their best hopes for implementing the CCSS. On the other card, have team members record their worst fears. Depending on the level of trust and comfort of the team, the team leader might collect the index cards and read the best hopes and worst fears anonymously or individuals can read their hopes and fears aloud to the group. The purpose is to uncover concerns that, left covered, might undermine collaborative teamwork. Team members should talk about how they can support one another to minimize fears and achieve best hopes.

5. Choose a collaborative protocol (pages 21–22) that you are either familiar with or would like to learn more about. How might that protocol be used to engage your collaborative team in a discussion of implementing the CCSS content and Mathematical Practices?

Online Resources

Visit **go.solution-tree.com/commoncore** for links to these resources. Visit **go.solution-tree.com/plcbooks** for additional resources about professional learning communities.

- *The Five Disciplines of PLC Leaders* (Kanold, 2011a; go.solution-tree.com /plcbooks/Reproducibles_5DOPLCL.html): Chapter 3 discusses the commitment to a shared mission and vision by all adults in a school for several tools targeted toward collaborative actions. These reproducibles engage teachers in professional learning and reflection.

- **Chicago Lesson Study Group (www.lessonstudygroup.net/index.php):** This website provides a forum for teachers to learn about and practice lesson study to steadily improve student learning. To learn more about lesson study or other collaborative protocols, see the following resources.

  - *Lesson Study: A Handbook of Teacher-Led Instructional Change* (Lewis, 2002)

  - *Powerful Designs for Professional Learning* (Easton, 2008)

  - *Leading Lesson Study* (Stepanek, Appel, Leong, Managan, & Mitchell, 2007)

  - *Data-Driven Dialogue: A Facilitator's Guide to Collaborative Inquiry* (Wellman & Lipton, 2004)

- **AllThingsPLC (http://allthingsplc.info):** Search the Tools & Resources of this website for sample agendas and activities for collaborative work.

- **The Educator's PLN—the Personal Learning Network for Educators (http:// edupln.ning.com):** This website offers tips, tools, and benefits for starting your own PLN.

- **The Center for Comprehensive School Reform and Improvement (2009; www.centerforcsri.org/plc/websites.html):** This website offers a collection of resources to support an in-depth examination of the work of learning teams.

- **Inside Mathematics (2010b; www.insidemathematics.org/index.php/tools -for-teachers/tools-for-principals-and-administrators):** This portion of the Inside Mathematics website supports school-based administrators and district mathematics supervisors who are responsible for establishing the structure and vision for the professional development work of grade-level and cross-grade-level learning teams or in a PLC collaborative team.

- **Learning Forward (2011; www.learningforward.org/standards/standards .cfm):** Learning Forward is an international association of learning educators focused on increasing student achievement through more effective professional learning. This website provides a wealth of resources, including an online annotated bibliography of articles and websites, to support the work of professional learning teams.

- **The National Commission on Teaching and America's Future (NCTAF, 2006; www.nctaf.org/NCTAFReportNSFKnowledgeSynthesis.htm):** With the support of the National Science Foundation and in collaboration with

WestEd, NCTAF (2006) released *STEM Teachers in Professional Learning Communities: From Good Teachers to Great Teaching*. NCTAF and WestEd conducted a two-year analysis of research studies that document what happens when science, technology, engineering, and mathematics teachers work together in professional learning communities to improve teaching and increase student achievement. This report summarizes that work and provides examples of projects building on that model.

- **Learning by Doing: A Handbook for Professional Communities at Work (DuFour et al., 2010; go.solution-tree.com/PLCbooks/Reproducibles _LBD2nd.html)**: This resource and its reproducible materials help educators close the knowing-doing gap as they transform their schools into professional learning communities.

- **The Mathematics Common Core Toolbox (www.ccsstoolbox.org)**: This website provides coherent and research-affirmed protocols and tools to help you in your CCSS collaborative teamwork. The website also provides sample scope and sequence documents and advice for how to prepare for CCSS for mathematics implementation.

CHAPTER 2

Implementing the Common Core Standards for Mathematical Practice

Reasoning and sense making must become a part of the fabric of the high school mathematics classroom. Not only are they important goals themselves, but they are the foundation for true mathematical competence. Incorporating isolated experiences with reasoning and sense making will not suffice. Teachers must consistently support and encourage students' progress toward more sophisticated levels of reasoning.

—National Council of Teachers of Mathematics

The Common Core Standards for Mathematical Practice have caused a shift in the instructional paradigm for mathematics. This shift means that you must teach standards that require demonstrations of student *understanding* as well as standards for student *proficiency* in mathematical *practice.* The Common Core State Standards Initiative (NGA & CCSSO, 2010) states, "The Standards for Mathematical Practice describe varieties of expertise that mathematics educators at all levels should seek to develop in their students. These practices rest on important 'processes and proficiencies' with longstanding importance in mathematics education" (p. 6). The ultimate goal is to equip your students with expertise that will help them be successful in doing and using mathematics not only across the high school mathematics curriculum but also in their college and career work. College instructors rate the Mathematical Practices as being of higher value for students to master in order to succeed in their courses than any of the CCSS content standards. This was true for mathematics, language, science, and social science instructors (Conley, Drummond, de Gonzalez, Rooseboom, & Stout, 2011).

This chapter provides an analysis of the eight Common Core Standards for Mathematical Practice (see appendix B, page 161). The chapter then provides a description of the elements of lesson design that help you understand and implement the eight CCSS Mathematical Practices in your instruction and includes a lesson-design template for your use. This information is designed to support your work as a high school mathematics teacher working collaboratively within a PLC to answer these questions: (1) How can I design lessons that embed student Mathematical Practices into my daily instruction? and (2) How should I make the pedagogical decisions necessary to create environments in which the Mathematical Practices are enhanced by my instruction for improved student learning?

In high school lesson design, instruction and content are so intertwined it is challenging to address the CCSS Mathematical Practices apart from the CCSS content. To meet the teaching and planning vision of the CCSS for mathematics high school expectations requires a coherent curriculum built on effective and high-yield instructional strategies. Otherwise, it is like having a wonderful menu planned without a good cook. On the other hand, strong instructional practices without a coherent and focused curriculum are like teaching a chef all the skills to prepare a wonderful meal without supplying any of the necessary ingredients.

As you seek to make sense of the Mathematical Practices and the mathematical content standards contained in the Common Core Mathematics, you should take advantage of this opportunity to develop with your colleagues a collective understanding of effective and meaningful teaching of mathematics at your high school. If your school or district has not already embarked on the journey of emphasizing student understanding, reasoning, and sense making, now is the ideal time to embrace the paradigm shift of teaching fewer standards, but with greater depth. The Common Core becomes the catalyst for your work in collaborative teams and asks you to abandon lessons devoid of mathematical reasoning and connected ideas. In addition, your instruction will not only encourage your students to think deeply about the mathematics content but will require them to demonstrate understanding as well. This becomes your personal teaching paradigm shift over the next decade.

As you give deliberate attention to the CCSS Mathematical Practices, the challenge may be to envision these practices as part of instructional planning. As you collaborate with others around instruction, your dialogue will focus specifically on interpreting and implementing lessons that promote the understanding of Mathematical Practices in your students. Altogether, the tasks designed, the questions asked in the classroom, and the discourse in which students participate will serve to advance students' abilities to engage in the CCSS Mathematical Practices. A powerful collaborative team discussion can result by taking each of the eight CCSS Mathematical Practices and asking your team members to identify evidence of the practice as part of their daily lesson design.

The Common Core Standards for Mathematical Practice

The Mathematical Practices describe what your students are doing as they engage in learning the CCSS mathematics content standards. How should your students engage with the mathematics standards and interact with fellow students? Through a classroom culture that extends beyond traditional, teacher-centered instruction, the teacher facilitates student engagement in mathematics related to the CCSS Mathematical Practices. The Mathematical Practices are not a checklist of teacher to-dos. Rather, they sustain an environment in which the CCSS content standards are enacted and framed by the specific expertise you help students develop in order to support their understanding and application of mathematics.

Figure 2.1 provides a framework for the eight Mathematical Practices. Mathematical Practices 1 and 6 encompass all the practices and thus are viewed as overarching and embedded across all of CCSS for mathematics. The remaining practices are grouped to highlight close connections between various Mathematical Practices. The model provides a lens for you to view your collaborative team's curriculum, teaching, and learning and to identify how team members develop and teach the Mathematical Practices.

Overarching Habits of Mind	Reasoning and Explaining
1. Make sense of problems and persevere in solving them. 6. Attend to precision.	2. Reason abstractly and quantitatively. 3. Construct viable arguments and critique the reasoning of others.
	Modeling and Using Tools
	4. Model with mathematics. 5. Use appropriate tools strategically.
	Seeing Structure and Generalizing
	7. Look for and make use of structure. 8. Look for and express regularity in repeated reasoning.

Source: Adapted from McCallum, Black, Umland, & Whitesides, n.d. Used with permission.
Figure 2.1: CCSS Mathematical Practices organization model.

To assist your collaborative team in discussing the eight CCSS Mathematical Practices, we provide three questions in figure 2.2 that you can use on a unit-by-unit basis. In this chapter, we provide resources that answer the first two questions. The third question is left to you and your collaborative team to explore and answer.

1. What is the intent of this CCSS Mathematical Practice, and why is it important?
2. What teacher actions develop this CCSS Mathematical Practice?
3. What evidence is there that students are demonstrating this CCSS Mathematical Practice?

Figure 2.2: Key questions used to understand the CCSS Mathematical Practices.

The explanations and examples of Mathematical Practices in appendix B (page 161) will help you and your team reflect on your practice and answer the questions in figure 2.2. During your collaborative conversations, you can generate ideas for how to support the Mathematical Practices in your daily lesson and weekly unit design and analyze ways to assess your students' interactions using the practices. As a result of your team discussions and efforts to modify your instruction, you may be interested in tracking your progress in implementing the Common Core mathematics. The Common Core Look-Fors Mathematics app (http://splaysoft.com/CCL4s/Welcome.html) for the iPad or iPhone is an example of one tool that tracks the growth of a teacher's transition through the implementation of the Common Core State Standards. A tool for teachers and teacher leaders, this app provides for informal peer observation and is a source for data analysis related to teaching. The app's *crowd-sourcing* feature allows users to access the online resources that other educators have shared, evaluated, and tagged to the Common Core content standards.

Overarching Habits of Mind

Mathematical Practices 1 and 6 speak to fundamental dispositions that are developed in mathematical thinkers early in grade school and reinforced and threaded throughout a student's K–12 mathematical experiences. These two practices connect to your current classroom problem-solving efforts.

Mathematical Practice 1: Make Sense of Problems and Persevere in Solving Them

The first step in exploring CCSS Mathematical Practice 1, "Make sense of problems and persevere in solving them," is to provide a clear definition of what a problem is as it specifically relates to mathematics instruction (NGA & CCSSO, 2010, p. 6). A *problem* is defined as a *situation*, be it real or contrived, in which a challenge (question or unknown) that requires an appropriate response (such as an answer, solution, explanation, or counterexample) is presented and for which the person facing the challenge does not have a readily accessible appropriate response (Kantowski, 1980). That is:

> To solve a problem is to find a way where no way is known, to find a way out of a difficulty, to find a way around an obstacle, and to attain a desired end that is not immediately attainable, by appropriate means. (Hatfield, Edwards, Bitter, & Morrow, 2008, p. 100)

Students do not always initially see a viable solution pathway and sometimes will need multiple attempts to successfully solve the problem. This inherently means that problems can vary regarding topics, contexts, structure, and so on, and it means that teaching problem solving is not about teaching specific problems or memorizing problem types but about teaching students how to use their knowledge, skills, attitude, and resources to successfully respond to problems (Pólya, 1957).

What Is the Intent of Mathematical Practice 1, and Why Is It Important?

Problem solving is one of the hallmarks of mathematics and is the essence of doing mathematics (NCTM, 2000). When your students are engaged in problem solving, they are drawing on their understanding of mathematical concepts and procedures with the goal to reach a successful response to the problem. Although problem solving is a critical element of school mathematics, you may sometimes find that problem solving is a source of frustration for your students.

According to results of *The TIMSS Videotape Classroom Study* (Stigler, Gonzales, Kawanka, Knoll, & Serrano, 1999), teachers typically "design lessons that remove obstacles and minimize confusion [where] procedures for solving problems would be clearly demonstrated so students would not flounder or struggle" (p. 137). Lessons planned from this perspective—that students need protection from struggle—do not support the perseverance aspect of this CCSS Mathematical Practice, and they deny students the opportunity to develop meaningful mathematical understandings (Stein, Remillard, & Smith, 2007).

What Teacher Actions Develop Mathematical Practice 1?

You, as a high school teacher, play a critical role in supporting your students' ability to make sense of problems and persevere in solving them. The first of these roles is the presentation of appropriate problems or rich mathematical tasks for students to solve. While it seems that *appropriate* is subjective, figure 2.3 highlights six questions to discuss within your collaborative team when planning lessons to assess the quality of a problem or mathematical task.

---

1. Is the problem interesting to students?

2. Does the problem involve meaningful mathematics?

3. Does the problem provide an opportunity for students to apply and extend mathematics?

4. Is the problem challenging for students?

5. Does the problem support the use of multiple strategies?

6. Will students' interactions with the problem reveal information about students' mathematics understanding?

Figure 2.3: Six planning questions that promote CCSS Mathematical Practice 1.

Examining students' interactions with a problem (for example, students' work, discourse, and processes) should provide information about how their thinking is hindered or evolving by interacting with the problem or task. This list is not exhaustive, but it is a step toward examining problems that will potentially benefit students' mathematical learning. Successful problem solving does not mean that your students will always conclude with the correct response to a problem but rather that they will undertake a genuine effort to engage in the problem-solving process, drawing on resources, such as appropriate tools, prior knowledge, discussion with others, and questions to aid in the process.

You can also help students understand that the answer is not the final step in problem solving. A great deal of mathematical learning can happen when students are guided to explain and justify processes and check the reasonableness of solutions. In many instances, students can learn about other solutions for the problem and other ways of solving the problem, and they can make mathematical connections to other problems and content. Students can examine and change variables in the problem and hypothesize what might change in the process of solving the new problem and how the answer might change.

In figure 2.4, students are asked to determine the probability that a point randomly chosen in the square lands in each of the shaded regions (see N-Q.3, page 167, and S-CP.1, page 190, in appendix C). Visit **go.solution-tree.com/commoncore** for an expanded version of this figure.

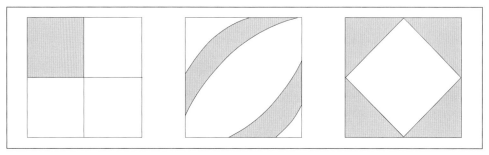

Figure 2.4: Sample geometric probability problem.

Visit **go.solution-tree.com/commoncore** for a reproducible version of this figure.

You support problem solving when you allow students to make sense of the problem and develop strategies to solve the problem. Using more open-ended problems (tasks) that have multiple entry points to highlight student solution strategies—both strategies that work as well as those that do not work—helps your students to learn and develop perseverance. Your role as the teacher is to acknowledge problem solving as a learning process that has stops and starts. As your collaborative team designs rich tasks to be used during the unit of instruction, discuss in what ways students might struggle with this problem.

For example, will some students want to use rulers to measure as they solve the geometric probability problem shown in figure 2.4? Will students get stuck with the unfamiliar shaded area in the middle square? Do some students want to use a formula for finding the area, or can some of the students demonstrate an understanding of what area means as a measure of so many square units of surface? Without providing too much of a lead to the solution, what types of advancing or assessing student thinking questions might you ask students who are stuck? And what will be the expected precision of student response regarding both the explanation of their answer and the computation format of their answer? In the first square, are 25%, ¼, one out of four, or 1:4 acceptable student responses? Attending to precision becomes an important habit of mind to develop in your students.

Mathematical Practice 6: Attend to Precision

Inherent in learning mathematics is the need to be precise. Precision is not just about the accuracy of a solution but also about being precise in the way teachers and students communicate about mathematics. Terms used in mathematics have intentional and rich definitions. When your communication in the mathematics classroom veers from the use of correct vocabulary and from encouraging students to use accurate mathematical language, opportunities for learning are often missed. Precise use of mathematical vocabulary supports students' development of the critical nuances of mathematical ideas within content-specific terms. Attention to precision is about clear student communication with the teacher and peers, using accurate mathematical vocabulary, and appropriately using labels as the means to support and articulate mathematical reasoning.

What Is the Intent of Mathematical Practice 6, and Why Is it Important?

CCSS Mathematical Practice 6, "Attend to precision," refers to the need for students to communicate precisely and correctly (NGA & CCSSO, 2010, p. 7). Student communication will involve developing and using definitions properly; using symbols appropriately, most notably the equal sign; specifying units, along with the associated quantities; and including clear and concise explanations when describing solutions or task pathways. Additionally, an expectation of CCSS Mathematical Practice 6 is that students will be accurate and appropriate with procedures and calculations. Accuracy is self-explanatory, but appropriateness as it relates to precision is a bit more elusive. Part of solving problems provided in context involves determining the level of precision that is necessary. Sometimes an estimate is sufficient. If that is the case, how close of an estimate is warranted or acceptable? The same is true with measurement. The level of accuracy for measurements is often determined by the context of the problem.

What Teacher Actions Develop Mathematical Practice 6?

Students often emulate their teachers when they are not precise with definitions, general language, and ideas related to mathematics. You want to be careful concerning the messages you send your students at all times through mathematics instruction. Reaching agreement on language usage is an appropriate use of your time during lesson planning in your collaborative team. Consider student or teacher work that might look like the following. In the course of a lesson on logarithms, a student might write the following on the board:

$$ln(x + 1) = 2 = (x + 1) = e^2 = x = e^2 - 1 = 6.389$$

While the string of equal signs might represent the student's spoken explanation of her solution process, it also indicates that $ln(x + 1) = 6.389$, when the actual equivalent equation is $x = 6.389$. That is not a precise or accurate use of the equal sign and must be avoided. Instead, students should represent their written explanation as follows.

$$ln(x + 1) = 2$$
$$x + 1 = e^2$$
$$x = e^2 - 1$$
$$x \cong 6.389$$

This representation models the appropriate use of symbols while simultaneously representing the student's thinking related to the problem. As the teacher, you want to attend to precision with the vocabulary, symbols, and explanations you use in the classroom so that students do not learn unintended and inaccurate mathematics but rather are provided a model of attending to precision.

Reflecting back on figure 2.4 (page 32), precision appears as your students learn and use "sample space" appropriately and accurately. The example also addresses the question of the unit of measure that makes the most sense, as well as the level of acceptable precision of calculations for area. Asking students to measure and use units of square centimeters may be appropriate, but then a level of precision to the nearest hundredth would seem unnecessary. These types of content precision issues should be part of the discussion agenda with your collaborative team. See p. 35 of *What Principals Need to Know About Teaching and Learning Mathematics* (Kanold, Briars, & Fennell, 2012) for a computational model for mathematics problems and tasks.

When students are given opportunities to explain and justify their mathematical ideas, they become engaged in Mathematical Practice 6. Similarly, you should expect your students to include appropriate units with quantities when sharing solutions to problems involving linear, quadratic, polynomial, area, and volume measurements as well as other solutions to problems provided in context.

Students engaged in Mathematical Practice 6 are:

1. Using careful, accurate definitions

2. Including units with quantities as necessary

3. Performing calculations carefully and appropriately

4. Describing the procedures they used accurately

Thus, mathematical precision is important not simply for accuracy of calculations but also for communication. Mathematical terms are often rich with meaning. As you model and then encourage students to communicate with accuracy and precision, students develop a richer understanding of the complexity and nuances of mathematical ideas embodied in the language. Furthermore, modeling and encouraging students to communicate with specificity and precision provides you with much greater insight into actual student thinking and mathematical understanding.

Mathematical Practices 1 and 6 should cross all high school courses as an integral part of students learning mathematics. Sharing ideas for how to develop the overarching habits of mind should be an ongoing part of your collaborative team time as you establish precise language for your course.

Reasoning and Explaining

Mathematical Practices 2 and 3 are about how students communicate their mathematical reasoning and sense making to you and to other students. These Mathematical Practices emphasize the need for students to quantify, contextualize, and decontextualize mathematics. As they do so, students learn to justify their reasoning and critique others' mathematical justifications as they learn the content together.

Mathematical Practice 2: Reason Abstractly and Quantitatively

In mathematics, we want students to be able to take specific situations and learn to make them more generalized or abstract so that they can reason about the mathematical properties and ideas without the details of the situation. Students who are able to reason abstractly and quantitatively view mathematics as a way to make sense of the world around them.

What Is the Intent of Mathematical Practice 2, and Why Is It Important?

Reasoning in mathematics is the means by which students try to make sense (by thinking through ideas carefully, considering examples and alternatives, asking questions, hypothesizing, pondering, and so on) of mathematics so it is usable and useful (NCTM, 2000). Hence, the role of Mathematical Practice 2, "Reason abstractly and quantitatively," is critical to students' engagement in every area and at every level of the mathematics curriculum (NGA & CCSSO, 2010, p. 6). According to Ball and Bass (2003), "Mathematical reasoning is something that students can learn to do" (p. 33). In fact, these authors suggest two very important benefits of reasoning: (1) it aids students' mathematical understanding and ability to use concepts and procedures in meaningful ways, and (2) it helps students reconstruct *faded knowledge*—that is, knowledge that is forgotten by your students but can be restored through reasoning with the current content.

What Teacher Actions Develop Mathematical Practice 2?

Classroom discourse that promotes reasoning is talk that involves teacher-to-student communication as well as student-to-student communication as essential elements of your daily classroom lesson planning. Your teacher-to-student communication includes questions you pose that probe students' thinking beyond their suggestions of an answer. You consider students' answers, whether right or wrong, so that opportunities to stretch their thinking beyond the answer are realized. In addition, teacher-to-student communication can and should involve discussions emerging from students' hypotheses about a mathematical concept or procedure and students' propositions on how mathematics works. Peer-to-peer explanations and debates support student-to-student communication when students are required to provide justification for their thinking.

These statements are examples that help elicit and promote discourse in the mathematics classroom.

- "Explain to a partner how Lindsay's and Brandon's strategies are similar and different."

- "Explain why Kevin's strategy will or will not always work on these types of problems."

- "Create a problem and a rubric for scoring the problem that could be used on a quiz or test for this Mathematical Practice."

Additionally, you can do the following to promote discourse.

- Give students a *solved* problem containing errors. Ask students to identify the errors and indicate how to correct accordingly.

- Provide students a problem from prior experience, and then expand the problem to include new discoveries or extensions of the mathematical structures involved.

In addition, students working collaboratively to engage in mathematics can fuel student-to-student discourse by sharing their mathematical thought and making decisions about routes for their thinking in order to arrive at sensible conclusions. Inferences about students' ability to reason can also be determined through carefully analyzing student work, discussions with peers, and performance on rigorous in-class and shared mathematical tasks.

When your students are engaged in Mathematical Practice 2, they are sharing and justifying their mathematical conceptions and adjusting their thinking based on mathematical information gathered through discussions and responses to questions. Mathematical reasoning must be a continuous expectation for students as they learn to *do* mathematics, whether while working in groups or during whole-class discussion or after school working on homework. To facilitate discourse well takes advanced planning and intentional work.

Mathematical Practice 3: Construct Viable Arguments and Critique the Reasoning of Others

In order for students to authentically engage in the learning of mathematics, it is imperative they articulate their reasoning through the use of logical reasoning and argumentation. In their communication of ideas, students develop the ability to construct justifications based on mathematical definitions, properties, and conceptual understandings. As they listen to one another, students can distinguish well-thought-out explanations from arguments that lack specificity or accuracy.

What Is the Intent of Mathematical Practice 3, and Why Is It Important?

Students engaged in Mathematical Practice 3, "Construct viable arguments and critique the reasoning of others," are making conjectures based on their analysis of given situations (NGA & CCSSO, 2010, p. 6). Students explain and justify their thinking as they communicate to other classmates and to you. Classmates listen to explanations and justifications and judge the reasonableness of the claims based on the explanations' clarity and precision combined with demonstrated understanding of tasks' or problems' mathematics. The successful facilitation of this standard is based on the social learning environment of the classroom. As Rasmussen, Yackel, and King (2003) state:

> Every class, from the most traditional to the most reform-oriented, has social norms that are operative for that particular class. What distinguishes

one class from another is not the presence or absence of social norms but, rather, the nature of the norms that differ from class to class. (pp. 147–148)

When students justify their strategies and critique the strategies of other students, they are making sense of the mathematics in meaningful ways. The teacher is no longer seen as the sole authority of mathematical knowledge, but rather the teacher facilitates the student construction of knowledge.

What Teacher Actions Develop Mathematical Practice 3?

In a high school classroom in which students are expected to construct arguments and critique others' reasoning, students should:

- Provide explanations and justifications to one another as part of their solution processes

- Attempt to make sense of their classmates' solutions by asking questions for clarification

- Communicate when they don't understand or don't agree with solutions others present by spurring discourse between and among students

- Respect all ideas and be open to challenging them, including the teacher's ideas

Eventually, these discussions become a natural part of the classroom discourse and can occur in an organized way without your direction. However, this type of student discourse will require well-established norms through a process of negotiation in which you make your expectations clear but involve students in the process of implementing the norms (Yackel & Cobb, 1996). These sorts of expectations help support communication of what effective mathematics learners do. Mathematics learners make conjectures, test those conjectures, and discuss their implications within a community that is receptive to such discussions. Your role as the teacher is to establish a classroom environment in which students are safe to present and challenge ideas without ridicule. Your lesson plan must also require you to read and address the sometimes subtle signals of tone and body language between peers. Following are some possible norms that support and encourage students to engage in discourse involving constructing viable arguments and critiquing the reasoning of others:

- Every student is responsible for sharing ideas and reasoning about problems or tasks.

- Each student respectfully listens to others.

- Students ask another student before asking the teacher.

- Students understand that mistakes are opportunities and part of the process of learning.

- Students understand that sharing and discussing reasoning and justification are critical components and expectations of learning in the mathematics classroom.

Emphasis should be placed on the need to include mathematical reasoning as part of the solution. As you plan your lesson, include opportunities for students to make and evaluate conjectures within meaningful mathematics discussions. A teacher's level of specialized content knowledge supports the development of cognitively complex problems to elicit conjectures and arguments and to guide discussions around important mathematical ideas. The collective content knowledge and experiences of your collaborative team can be great assets to create or identify such tasks. In the classroom, when there is disagreement regarding a solution, the student making the claim explains his or her thinking. The student critiquing the claim makes sense of the argument and then provides clarification, including another justification.

In the sample problem in figure 2.5, students are asked to make a conjecture about a Wikipedia claim that could be used as a common team task during a unit that is addressing certain standards from the Number and Quantity conceptual category (see N-Q.1, and N-Q.3, page 167, in appendix C). Students are expected to work together in teams and to use their mathematical knowledge and understanding to justify their solution. In the process, students must be clear about the units they are using for representing various quantities, such as people, restaurants, or meals. Your role is to facilitate the conversations in the classroom so students are respectfully critiquing each other's claims and justifications. If students are unaccustomed to challenging others' thinking, your collaborative team should develop questions to ask students, such as, "Can you replicate the work of your peer? If not, what additional questions do you have for the student presenter?"

Wikipedia reports that 8 percent of all Americans eat at McDonald's every day. Data reveal approximately 311 million Americans in 2012 and 12,800 McDonald's restaurants in the United States.

Make a conjecture as to whether or not you believe the web release to be true, and then create a mathematical argument that justifies your conclusion.

Figure 2.5: Sample conjecture about a Wikipedia claim.

Visit **go.solution-tree.com/commoncore** for a reproducible version of this figure.

Mathematical Practice 3 should become a daily part of your instructional planning. Your collaborative team must be prepared to provide students with explicit instruction as to what this Mathematical Practice requires of them as they become actively engaged students responsible for each other's learning. Your collaborative team should work together to develop a collective understanding of how this looks and sounds in your classroom.

Modeling and Using Tools

Mathematical Practices 4 and 5 combine to capture the essence of how students use mathematics and appropriate and varied tools in order to reason and make sense of the content.

Mathematical Practice 4: Model With Mathematics

Just as students need to be able to generalize or reason abstractly, mathematically proficient students are able to use their knowledge of mathematics to model various phenomena or mathematical ideas. Modeling involves the ability to see mathematics as a way to make sense of both the world around us as well as the world of mathematics.

What Is the Intent of Mathematical Practice 4, and Why Is It Important?

Students engaged in CCSS Mathematical Practice 4, "Model with mathematics," solve real-world problems by applying known mathematics (NGA & CCSSO, p. 2010, p. 7). This practice is often misinterpreted as representing mathematical concepts by using manipulatives exclusively because of the word *model*. While manipulatives and other representations can be used as instructional tools to make sense of real-world problems, that is just one element of this Mathematical Practice. In this practice, students might use tools such as diagrams, tables, graphs, expressions, equations, graphing calculators, and area or volume models to make sense of the mathematics. More generally, students use symbols and tools to represent real-world situations and move fluidly between different representations based on what questions they are trying to answer. The ways students model and represent situations will evolve as students learn more mathematics. A goal is for students to model mathematics in order to become more mathematically proficient.

This standard serves to connect CCSS Mathematical Practices 1 and 2, with its focus on mathematizing real-world problems. Students must first be given the opportunity to explore real-world problems or situations and then encouraged to represent those problems mathematically. Once students represent the problems with mathematics, they solve the problems and interpret their results within the context of the problem. All this depends on the students being provided the opportunity to solve problems that arise from everyday life. These sorts of experiences will prepare students for expectations related to reasoning mathematically in high school (NCTM, 2009).

What Teacher Actions Develop Mathematical Practice 4?

Your role is to provide opportunities for students to explore and share solutions to real-world situations that present themselves in and out of daily school life. The classroom environment must be conducive to the sorts of discourse that are described in Mathematical Practice 3.

The McDonald's Wikipedia problem presented in figure 2.5 is an example that can be expanded or altered to lend itself to modeling of mathematics. Students might be given data about the consumption of meals at McDonald's for several years and asked what they predict might be the American consumption of meals at McDonald's in 2020 (see F-BF, page 177, in appendix C). In such a problem, your collaborative team anticipates strategies and questions students might develop and determines how much scaffolding to provide students. You could also give students the problem task in figure 2.5 and ask them to explore related questions that might require the development of a mathematical model to predict future trends. Visit **go.solution-tree.com /commoncore** for the full problem.

Students engaged in this Mathematical Practice will not only check for reasonableness of the computations but will extend sense making to determine if the solution is appropriate given the original problem context. You will need to support this practice by asking students if their answers are reasonable, facilitating the classroom discourse that allows students to learn from each other, and ensuring that students make sense of their answers according to the context of the problem.

By providing opportunities for students to develop real-world contexts to correspond to mathematics equations and then to check to make sure the correspondence is accurate, teachers are facilitating students' sense making relative to modeling mathematics. In order for you and your colleagues to be comfortable in this role, you will need to explore such representations within your collaborative team.

One such student problem task involves using functions to model world population data, using linear, quadratic, and exponential growth functions (see the Functions conceptual category in appendix C, pages 176–179). Students can use a graphing calculator or a software tool (for example, Fathom or Geogebra) to examine a set of data and determine the best-fitting model from a list of familiar functions.

Consider the world population (in millions) from 1960 through 2011, as shown in table 2.1. Your students could create a scatterplot of the data and then use the regression capabilities of the graphing calculator or computer software to determine the best-fitting model for the data.

Table 2.1: Predicting World Population

Year	1960	1965	1970	1975	1980	1985	1990	1995	2000	2011
Population (millions)	3,039	3,345	3,707	4,086	4,454	4,851	5,279	5,688	6,083	7,000

Source: U.S. Census Bureau, 2011.

Visit **go.solution-tree.com/commoncore** for a reproducible version of this table.

The world population reached seven billion on October 31, 2011. Students could use their models to predict the year that the world population will reach eight billion (currently predicted as 2027) and the implications of that population figure and then answer questions about whether the world population rate is staying the same, slowing, or increasing over the next fifty years.

As your team develops or identifies problems that require students to model contextual problems and construct viable arguments to support their reasoning, you work together to anticipate what students will do, to determine what constitutes a viable argument, and to teach students how to use a tool (such as a graphing and statistics tool) strategically.

Mathematical Practice 5: Use Appropriate Tools Strategically

Mathematical tools come in all shapes and sizes. Regardless of the tool, what is important is the way in which students use these tools to reason and learn mathematics. The decisions you make about the choice of tool and how the tool is used in the context of instruction have long-term implications for how students view and effectively use these tools in a meaningful way.

What Is the Intent of Mathematical Practice 5, and Why Is It Important?

The nature of mathematics facilitates the use of a variety of tools enabling hands-on, active, and concrete learning that support this Mathematical Practice. Every mathematics classroom should be equipped to accommodate CCSS Mathematical Practice 5, "Use appropriate tools strategically" (NGA & CCSSO, 2010, p. 7). Tools go beyond calculators and visual diagrams. Hiebert et al. (1997) define tools as "oral language, physical materials, written symbols, and skills students already have acquired" (p. 53). Tools provide ways to record, communicate, and develop mathematical thinking that is particularly powerful when meaning is developed together as a class. How and when a student uses a tool is critical. Specifically, this Mathematical Practice is about students experiencing the opportunity to develop an understanding by engaging in applications involving mathematics. For students, this standard is not about watching you demonstrate various tools. In fact, some high school mathematics conceptual categories, such as algebra, functions, and statistics, cannot be sufficiently explored unless students have access to proper tools.

What Teacher Actions Develop Mathematical Practice 5?

You should have a plan for acquiring or providing access to tools and a system for students to use those tools. As Hiebert et al. (1997) state, "What seems to be important is not which tool a teacher chooses to introduce into the classroom, but rather that the teacher thinks carefully about the way in which students' thinking might be shaped by using particular tools" (p. 63). Once your students have access to various tools, you can guide them in selecting appropriate tools for a particular mathematics activity. By allowing students to choose the tools to use, you provide space for them to make hypotheses, try new ways of studying mathematics, and have a context for comparing how different tools can either be useful or a hindrance for studying the specific mathematics.

You can use these four questions to help students select the most appropriate tool (technology or otherwise) to do the mathematics.

1. Is the tool necessary?
2. Is the tool easy to use?

3. Is the tool efficient for the problem or task presented?

4. Will the tool facilitate learning the mathematics or support your proficiency and development in the Mathematical Practices?

You may find that it is very enjoyable to teach mathematics with a variety of tools. However, the real issue is whether student learning is supported by tool use—tools should not be used for the sake of using tools. If your students use tools to engage in mathematics and walk away from the experience with little or no understanding of the mathematics, then the use of the tools was ineffective. You will want to continually ask challenging questions and probe students' thinking before, during, and after using a tool to be certain that students are learning mathematics, not merely how to push buttons on a calculator or manipulate algebra tiles without any reasoning about the content.

The following area model in figure 2.6 is an example of a tool. Students come to develop an understanding of area and how the area of each part can be added to find the total area. The area model can be extended to multiply and divide polynomials. Figure 2.6 is an area model used to multiply a binomial into a quadratic polynomial (see A-APR.5, page 172, in appendix C). Students use the model to find the area of each piece and then total all the components.

	$3x^2$	$-5x$	8
$2x$	$6x^3$	$-10x^2$	
-1	$-3x^2$		

Figure 2.6: Sample area model.

The model can be further extended to find the remainder when dividing polynomials as well as a tool when completing the square of a quadratic (see A-SSE.3, page 172, in appendix C).

Technology as a tool can be especially powerful in advancing student mathematical thinking. In particular, technology can effectively be used to develop students' conceptual understanding of abstract mathematical concepts. NCSM (2011a), in its position paper on technology in the mathematics classroom, highlights several benefits of technology on student mathematics learning, including greater student participation and engagement. Teachers can use technology to:

- Display student solution strategies for discussion and validation

- Illustrate multiple mathematical samples—leading to efficient student discovery within a dynamic environment

- Highlight multiple representations for solution paths that will verify student results and develop deeper understanding
- Collect and disseminate formative assessment data from students and student teams, and use the data to make decisions about next steps in class
- Enhance student collaborative learning and discussions

Discussing effective technology and tool use with your students as they reason mathematically is an integral part of your collaborative team's discussions and decisions about tasks selection. Using technology as a tool to support student development of Mathematical Practice 4 can be a powerful teacher weapon for expanding students' learning experiences well beyond paper and pencil (see figure 4.7, page 109, in chapter 4 for an example with solving square-root inequalities). Your students can model population growth using a spreadsheet and at the same time explore the impact of that growth on natural resources as well (see F-IF, page 176, and F-BF, page 177, in appendix C). Spreadsheets are an integral part of every market and job sector, so experience with these will contribute to your students' career readiness.

Seeing Structure and Generalizing

Mathematics Practices 7 and 8 are about the inherent beauty and power of mathematics. Helping students develop proficiency toward seeing the structure of mathematics will increase their ability and disposition to do mathematics.

Mathematical Practice 7: Look For and Make Use of Structure

When students are mathematically proficient, they seek to make connections to prior learning and to other mathematical ideas. These comparisons are made when students use patterns as a tool for learning and discovering structure. In their evolving understanding of mathematical concepts, students see the similarities and the differences that exist across topics.

What Is the Intent of Mathematical Practice 7, and Why Is It Important?

A major contribution to the beauty of mathematics is its structure. Structure exists all across the mathematics curriculum. For example, there is structure in geometry (every square is a rhombus), in basic operations (an even number plus an even number always results in a sum that is an even number), and in numerical patterns (the second set of differences of consecutive outputs between corresponding consecutive inputs of a quadratic function will always be a constant). Structure helps your students learn what to expect in mathematics. If students learn how mathematics works and why it works the way it does, they then begin to notice, look for, and make use of structure to solve problems—they become engaged in what it means to do mathematics.

What Teacher Actions Develop Mathematical Practice 7?

There are several actions you can take to support students in their development of looking for and making use of structure in mathematics. Students may or may not recognize structure in mathematics. For your students who do not readily recognize structure in mathematics, it is important they be encouraged to look for the structure. You can do this by presenting examples that are conducive to exploring structure and then providing students opportunities to create examples of structure of their own to share and discuss with each other. Encourage students to wonder by asking questions: "If every square is a rhombus, is every rhombus a square?" or "If an even number plus an even number always results in a sum that is even, does the same property hold true for multiplication?"

Students can benefit from acknowledging structure when studying across the high school mathematics curriculum. After your students are confident in recognizing structure, you can model for students the mathematical power that comes from using structure in mathematics.

An excellent example of a problem about structure is found on pp. 38–40 in *Focus in High School Mathematics: Reasoning and Sense Making* (NCTM, 2009). In this problem, students are moved strategically through a series of questions that allows them to discover structure in mathematics. Beginning with a simple sequence of numbers (3, 7, and 11) generated by the linear function $f(x) = 4x - 1$ (at $x = 1, 2,$ and 3), students go on a journey that reveals a cubic function $g(x) = x^3 - 6x^2 + 15x - 7$ that yields the same first three terms but predicts a different fourth term. More importantly, students then discover there is a reason $g(x)$ works as it does by examining the factored form of $h(x) = g(x) - f(x)$, and they eventually discover a connection between the visual representation of these functions and the structure of a polynomial expression of the form $4x - 1 + k(x - 1)(x - 2)(x - 3)$, in which k is any real number as an expression that will yield a sequence of 3, 7, 11 but with variant predicting fourth terms and beyond. The key to your success with rich mathematical tasks such as this is to provide proper advancing and assessing questions through the problem, as students attend to the structure discovery.

Mathematical Practice 8: Look For and Express Regularity in Repeated Reasoning

As students learn mathematics, they are constantly looking for patterns as a way to reason about and make sense of the mathematics. Looking for and being able to express regularity is one way students use patterns to generalize mathematical concepts.

What Is the Intent of Mathematical Practice 8, and Why Is It Important?

When engaged in CCSS Mathematical Practice 8, "Look for and express regularity in repeated reasoning," students move beyond solving problems to finding ways to generalize the methods they use to determining *efficient methods* for those procedures

(NGA & CCSSO, 2010, p. 8). With their desire to simplify students' learning pathways and minimize confusion (Stigler et al., 1999), high school teachers are often tempted to provide students with efficient procedures for algebraic computations too early. When this occurs, students miss the opportunity to look for and express regularity in repeated reasoning. Instead, teachers should provide students with opportunities to make sense of problems and to look for the regularity in the calculations. This practice helps students to develop the skills and dispositions to abstract and generalize mathematical concepts. This practice interacts with Mathematical Practice 1, requiring that students develop perseverance to make sense of the repeated reasoning.

What Teacher Actions Develop Mathematical Practice 8?

The examples you provide and the questioning techniques you employ help students notice if calculations repeat. Asking your students to describe the processes they use and to look for repetition in those processes provides the scaffolding necessary for high school students to begin to make sense of the process of determining general methods for calculations. You will need to consider multiple examples—as well as their progression—to help students move from seeing the repeated reasoning of a single example to being able to build a general method. Consider the following example (see A-CED, page 173, in appendix C).

> Your grandma wants to help you begin a savings account for college. She will give you $100 to open the account and then increase the amount by 5% each month. How much money will you have in the account after 1 month? 2 months? 10 months? x months?

As students complete a table, they begin to see the pattern in the repetition of multiplying each successive amount by 1.05 leading to the general exponential model for any number of months. See table 2.2 for an example.

Table 2.2: Sample Exponential Table

Month	Amount in Account
0	$100
1	100(1.05)
2	(100(1.05))(1.05)
3	((100(1.05)(1.05))(1.05)
4	((100(1.05)(1.05)(1.05))(1.05)
5	((100(1.05)(1.05)(1.05)(1.05))(1.05)
10	$100(1.05)^{10}$
x	$100(1.05)^{x}$

Once again, the classroom environment and expectations you establish related to social interactions in the classroom set the stage for students to engage in this practice. If there is an expectation that students will make conjectures related to what they notice in the pattern of calculations they complete, students are more likely to look for and make sense of those generalizations. Your role is to create and maintain the social norms for this type of discovery to take place in your classroom. In classrooms with the expectation that students will create generalizations and then defend them, as well as consider potential counterexamples, students have the opportunity to create general methods for repeated reasoning. Thus, Mathematical Practice 8 is closely linked to Mathematical Practice 3, Construct viable arguments and critique the reasoning of others.

Lesson-Design Elements That Reflect the Common Core Mathematical Practices

Typically in preservice training, high school teachers are taught lesson-design elements. This lesson design is usually quite extensive and several pages long, serving the intended purpose of allowing the professor or cooperating teacher the opportunity for meaningful feedback. However, in actual practice, limited time and experience make this practice cumbersome. Nonetheless, the preservice lesson plans often contain important and useful elements, including connection to state standards, the lesson goal or objective, student prerequisite knowledge, lesson details (for example, warm-up or bell ringer, end-of-lesson summary), and an assessment strategy. At some point, usually early in their careers, teachers make their lesson plans much more abbreviated. Whereas teachers typically give consideration to key components of the lesson, these considerations are often not recorded or tracked. Yet without a way to document critical elements of the lesson plan and the teacher thinking that went into its creation, collaborative dialogue with your colleagues around meaningful instruction is challenging, if not impossible.

In many high schools, the details and specifics of the overall lesson design often vary widely from teacher to teacher in the same mathematics department. Is that the case in your department or team? Nevertheless, certain design elements are known to be essential in the creation of mathematics lessons that ensure each student is engaged in the expectations of learning the CCSS for mathematics throughout the class period.

Your lesson-design elements should also be based on instructional strategies that research has shown to have a positive impact on student achievement. In his book *Qualities of Effective Teachers*, Stronge (2007) captures a synthesis of such significant research. In short, lecturing can overwhelm students with too much information, whereas hands-on learning strategies and instruction focused on meaningful conceptualization have been shown to increase student achievement. Furthermore, Stronge (2007) notes, "Effective teachers recognize that no single instructional strategy can be used in all situations" (p. 69). Rather, highly effective high school teachers develop a toolbox of various methods to be used to create a blend of whole-group and small-group discourse instruction during all phases of class.

Table 2.3 combines essential elements of effective instruction (Smith & Cartier, 2007, as cited in Smith & Stein, 2011; Marzano, 2007; Stronge, 2007) and draws from the collective expectations of the CCSS Mathematical Practices as well. It provides general guidelines and questions that your collaborative teams can use as you work together to create unit lesson designs that reflect the spirit and intent of the CCSS for mathematics.

Table 2.3: Elements of an Effective High School Mathematics Classroom Lesson Design

	Probing Questions for Effective Lesson Design	Reflection
1. Lesson Context: Learning Targets Procedural Fluency *and* Conceptual Understanding Balancing	What is the learning target for the lesson? How does it connect to the bigger focus of the unit?	
	What evidence will be used to determine the level of student readiness and prior knowledge for the learning target?	
	Are conceptual understanding and procedural fluency examples and tasks appropriately balanced?	
	Is the mathematics lesson primarily skill based and aimed at building procedural fluency (a *how-to* lesson)?	
	Is the mathematics lesson concept or generalization based (a *what* lesson)?	
	How will you formatively assess student conceptual understanding of the mathematics concepts and of the procedural skill?	
	Which CCSS Mathematical Practices will be emphasized during this lesson?	
2. Lesson Process: High-Cognitive-Demand Tasks Planning Student Discourse and Engagement	What tasks will you use to create an a-ha student moment and leave "mathematical residue" (insights into the mathematical structure of concepts) regardless of content type at a high-cognitive-demand level?	

continued ▸

	Probing Questions for Effective Lesson Design	Reflection
Planning Student Discourse and Engagement	How will you ensure the task is accessible and meaningful to all students while still maintaining a high-cognitive demand for students?	
Formative Assessment Through Small Group Discourse	What strategic mathematical tools will be used during the lesson?	
	How will you present and sequence each lesson example to build mathematical reasoning and sense making connected to student prior knowledge?	
	What are the advancing and assessing questions you might ask during guided, independent, or group practice? What are anticipated student responses to the examples or tasks?	
	How will students be engaged in self-reflection and action about their own learning toward the learning targets?	
	What strategies will be used to collect data (formal or informal) about each student's progress toward the learning target and to provide students with formative feedback? What student misconceptions might need to be addressed?	
	How might technology and student attention to precision play a role in the student lesson experience?	
3. Introduction, Daily Review, and Closure	What activity will be used to immediately engage students at the beginning of the class period?	

	Probing Questions for Effective Lesson Design	Reflection
3. Introduction, Daily Review, and Closure	How can the daily review be used to provide brief, five-minute meaningful feedback on homework?	
	How will the students summarize the lesson learning target and key vocabulary?	
4. Homework	How does the collaborative team–developed unit homework assignments provide variety and meaningfulness to the students—including long-term review and questions—that balance procedural fluency with conceptual understanding?	

Visit **go.solution-tree.com/commoncore** for a reproducible version of this table.

Table 2.3 highlights four essential lesson-design components for your team planning and discussion. These guidelines for effective mathematics lesson-design elements are meant as a framework you can use with your collaborative team as you discuss how best to implement Common Core expectations in meaningful and enriching ways. The lesson design elements are not intended for use as a checklist, nor is it practical to incorporate all the elements in every daily lesson. You can use the guiding questions to lead your collaborative team in a dialogue centered on critical lessons that get at the heart of a standard's instruction. The process of teacher discussion and reflection on lesson design—success and failure—is an integral part of the five-step teaching-assessing-learning cycle discussed in chapter 4.

Design Element One: Lesson Context

The lesson-design process begins with identifying the lesson context for the standards to be taught. Key elements of the standard should be established prior to delving into the intricacies of the actual classroom activities used to process students through the standard. You should be explicit about the mathematical concepts and skills needed to guide the lesson.

Identifying Learning Targets

The context of the lesson is the driving force for the entire lesson-design process. The lesson context centers on clarity of the mathematical content (including the understanding standards) and the skill processes students are to learn. The crux of the lesson rests on your collaborative team identifying and determining the learning targets that align with the content standard clusters for the unit. The learning target articulates for students what they are to learn and at the same time begins to give insight as to how students will be assessed. Although learning targets might be developed as part of curriculum writing or review, your collaborative team should take time during lesson design to make sure that the learning targets your team writes for the lesson clearly communicate to students the key content and level of reasoning on which they will be assessed (Stiggins, Arter, Chappuis, & Chappuis, 2007).

Your collaborative team must also discern how the learning target for each lesson is connected to and leads toward a bigger content standard cluster goal or focus. For example, a team may have a learning target that states, "Students will be able to represent a linear function as a table, ordered pairs, graph, or equation." Your collaborative team must be able to explain how this learning target might fit into a larger CCSS domain, such as Linear, Quadratic, and Exponential Models (F-LE). To ensure students make connections across content and to the overarching concepts, you must make those connections for the students. A more comprehensive discussion of learning targets, clusters, domains, conceptual categories, and enduring understandings is found in chapter 3.

How often have students asked you, "When am I ever going to need this?" Teachers know all too well that today's students are inundated with all sorts of distractions, leading to a struggle in the classroom to maintain student interest and engagement in mathematical tasks or activities. Explicitly telling students how a learning target might be relevant helps them put context to what they are about to learn and prepares them to better connect new knowledge in ways that are meaningful and more engaging.

Before an architect can begin to draw out the specifics of a blueprint, he or she must have a vision of the end product. Similarly, Ainsworth (2007) asserts that to best impact instruction, your collaborative teams must design end-of-unit assessment instruments reflecting the intended outcomes of a unit of instruction prior to planning the details of each lesson. That is, as part of the initial stages of lesson design, your collaborative team has a vision of the assessment instruments that demonstrate learning of the outcomes. This process is part of step one in the teaching-assessing-learning cycle described in detail in chapter 4 (page 100). How will you know when students have achieved the learning target? What evidence will be used to determine what progress a student has made toward the intended learning? What probing questions will students be asked? A shared understanding and agreement of what student learning looks like and sounds like leads to greater coherence in the instruction and expectations of mathematical learning by all students of the course as well as by every teacher for the course.

Procedural Fluency and Conceptual Understanding Balancing

In the United States, the mathematics primarily taught in high schools is focused on procedures and cursory knowledge of mathematical content (Hiebert et al., 1999). For several years, a war of sorts raged as to whether teaching mathematics should emphasize procedural fluency *or* conceptual understanding. This controversy is not an *either/or* proposition. It is an *and* requirement that is at the heart of the instructional paradigm shift in mathematics. Both have a place in meaningful mathematics teaching and learning (Brown, Seidelmann, & Zimmermann, 2006). NGA and CCSSO (2010) and NCTM (2000, 2009) agree that procedural fluency is important but must be developed with understanding, reasoning, and critical thinking. In general, procedural fluency should be a result of conceptual understanding. NCTM has long been a proponent of students learning mathematics with understanding and reasoning (1989, 2000). In *Principles and Standards for School Mathematics* (NCTM, 2000) and *Focus in High School Mathematics: Reasoning and Sense Making* (NCTM, 2009), NCTM strongly advocates that students learn mathematics in a thoughtful and deliberate manner by which they engage in using the Process Standards and Reasoning Habits. The Mathematical Practices, the Process Standards, and the Reasoning Habits are different, yet related. Together they speak to how students should learn, reason, and communicate about mathematics.

All lesson-design roads lead to a new era of teaching high school mathematics with reasoning and sense making, regardless of whether the learning target of the lesson is the mastery or demonstration of procedural skills or the development of conceptual knowledge. If the main purpose of the lesson is how to develop procedural fluency, your collaborative team must determine what problems or questions to include in the lesson that will reveal student understanding of the underlying mathematical concepts. By the same token, if the main focus of the lesson is about developing and building conceptual knowledge, your collaborative team must choose applications and context that will hook students and draw them into the lesson while at the same time allowing them to make sense of the mathematics.

Design Element Two: Lesson Process

According to Siegler (2003), analytical thinking leads to purposeful engagement and vice versa. In other words, when students are asked to make sense of something, they engage, and when students engage, they are trying to make sense of something. Student interaction with the content and processes is vital to learning, and through the interaction between the teacher, students, and the content, meaning is made of mathematical knowledge and ways of reasoning (Cobb, Yackel, & Wood, 1992). Fundamental to mathematics instruction is carefully choosing tasks that support and encourage students' reasoning about the content. Collaborative teams are obligated to design "worthwhile mathematical tasks" that engage students to "make connections and develop a coherent framework for mathematical ideas" (Martin, 2007, p. 32). Tasks need to highlight problem solving and mathematical reasoning in ways that "do not separate mathematical thinking from mathematical concepts and skills" (Martin, 2007, p. 33).

Selecting Common and High-Cognitive-Demand Tasks

Stein, Smith, Henningsen, and Silver (2009) define the cognitive demand of a task as "the kind and level of thinking required of students in order to successfully engage with and solve a task" (p. 1). They further identify low-level cognitive demand tasks as memorizing or applying procedures without connections. High-level cognitive demand tasks are procedures with connections, or what the authors call *doing mathematics*, whereby students engage in more complex reasoning, analyzing, and problem solving. The learning target of the lesson dictates the cognitive level of task. If the learning target is for students to develop fluency, low-level cognitive demand tasks are appropriate. However, if students only work through tasks of low-level cognitive demand, they do not develop the connected and deep mathematical understanding needed to apply their knowledge in new situations. As Stein et al. (2009) state, "Students also need opportunities on a regular basis to engage with tasks that lead to deeper, more generative understandings regarding the nature of mathematical processes, concepts, and relationships" (p. 5).

Hiebert et al. (1997) talk about carefully choosing sets of tasks that are related and connected so as to leave meaningful and relevant *mathematical residue* or insights into the mathematical structure of concepts. When students engage in high-cognitive-demand tasks your team selects to connect and build to prior student knowledge, the students become involved in thinking critically, reasoning mathematically, and making sense of what they are learning about the knowledge they are acquiring. Tasks that have multiple entry points and can be solved in multiple ways not only result in richer student discourse but also allow all students access to the mathematics.

When your collaborative team creates common tasks that are rich, multifaceted, and leave mathematical residue, you engage students in Mathematical Practice 1, Making sense of problems and persevere in solving them. In the process of problem solving around carefully constructed and chosen high-cognitive-demand tasks, your students analyze problems seeking patterns and relationships. They develop strategies, assess the effectiveness of those strategies, and change their approach if necessary. More information on high-cognitive-demand task development is provided for you in the collaborative strategies sections of chapter 3 (pages 85–91).

Planning and Implementing Student Discourse and Engagement

Common high-cognitive-demand tasks do not guarantee high-cognitive-demand thinking. Your role in facilitating discourse is the key to eliciting high-cognitive thinking. As the National Board for Professional Teaching Standards (2010) states:

> Accomplished teachers deliberately structure opportunities for students to use and develop appropriate mathematical discourse as they reason and solve problems. These teachers give students opportunities to talk with one another, work together in solving problems, and use both written and oral discourse to describe and discuss their mathematical thinking and understanding. As students talk and write about mathematics—as they explain their thinking—they deepen their mathematical understanding in powerful ways that can enhance their ability to use the strategies and thought processes gained through the study of mathematics to deal with life issues. (p. 57)

The manner in which high school teachers facilitate discourse is critical in creating and supporting a classroom learning environment that values reasoning and sense making. You decide what thinking to share and whose voices are to be heard. Your position and practice on this issue have a profound impact on how knowledge is shared and created as well as who plays a role in the knowledge sharing and creation. As the National Council of Teachers of Mathematics (1991) state, "Teachers, through the ways in which they orchestrate discourse, convey messages about whose knowledge and ways of thinking and knowing are valued, who is considered able to contribute, and who has status in the group" (p. 20).

Discourse required to meet the expectations of CCSS Mathematical Practice 3 supports student learning in several ways. Student cognitive processes are made public, and the collective thinking of the group that is shared and discussed results in richer and more varied ideas (Bruer, 1994, as cited in Cazden, 2001). Additionally, articulating one's reasoning is cognitively demanding and requires higher-level thinking.

Small-group classroom discourse provides a window into student reasoning about mathematics. As you observe the students talking, you see and hear the connections they make, the questions they ask, and the obstacles or misconceptions that can hinder conceptual understanding. You are in a better position to make formative assessment decisions and implement strategies to support learning and push the level of reasoning and problem solving expected in CCSS Mathematical Practice 1, Make sense of problems and persevere in solving them. The subsequent peer-to-peer dialogue creates a community of learners who collectively build their mathematical knowledge and proficiencies.

Smith and Stein (2011) identify five key actions to make discourse-focused instruction more manageable and effective by moderating the degree of improvisation teachers require. You and your collaborative team can use Smith and Stein's framework to develop deep discussions and classroom practices that support student discourse. The five actions are the following.

1. **Anticipating:** Once you have determined the instructional goal and selected appropriate tasks, you can anticipate likely student responses to the task. You should consider the various strategies the students might use to approach and solve the task, along with how you would respond to each strategy and which strategies would best serve to accomplish the learning target.

2. **Monitoring:** The practice of monitoring happens during the lesson as you watch and listen to observe how students are solving the problem.

3. **Selecting:** From monitoring students during lessons, you and your team have likely anticipated most of the responses and discussed which student responses to select and attend to during whole-class discourse. Your collaborative team decides which anticipated responses will be most helpful to support student progress toward the lesson's learning target.

4. **Sequencing:** The learning target also guides the sequencing of responses or strategies. No longer do students who volunteer to present their solutions control the classroom discussion. Rather the relevancy of the mathematics being presented and the learning target are the guides that help you implement the

most productive student strategies. The deliberate and careful selection and sequencing of student work reinforces students as the creators of mathematical ideas rather than the teacher.

5. **Connecting**: This practice focuses on how you help students make connections among the strategies and concepts that have emerged during the discourse.

The intent of the five actions is to give teachers more control over the cognitive demand of the task by controlling the content discussed. When these practices are incorporated as part of instructional delivery in class, you have more time to diagnose students' thinking. In turn, these practices provide more time to plan appropriate questions and instructional moves during class. Much of the design of these practices takes place during *lesson planning* and provides your collaborative teams with a framework around which to collaborate about content and pedagogy.

The application of the Smith and Stein (2011) framework may not be feasible for every lesson. However, when your team uses the framework as an embedded part of your lesson planning, you will regularly anticipate student responses, sequence tasks and problems to intentionally build and connect, monitor student responses and work, and emphasize student voices in creating knowledge, reasoning, and making sense of the mathematical learning targets.

Figure 2.7 illustrates how you can utilize various strategies that support student involvement and engagement in small-group and whole-class discourse.

- Have a student paraphrase or summarize a student response or strategy and ask others to verify the first student's summary.
- Direct a student question to the class or another student to respond.
- Ask another student or team if they agree or disagree with the statement of a student or team and why.
- Ask a student or student team to explain something in a different way and ask them to defend the response.

Figure 2.7: Strategies for student engagement during discourse.

Formative Assessment Through Small-Group Student Discourse

If the only experience students have in the high school mathematics classroom is working independently without collaborating with their peers, they will not be able to realize the vision of any of the eight CCSS Mathematical Practices. Through the discourse and the articulation of one's thinking, students create meaning and make connections. Students who listen to each other's strategies and critique each other's reasoning learn more. When students are working together to learn, the collaborative effort "enhances problem solving and reasoning to a greater degree than working independently would achieve" (Wood, Bruner, & Ross, 1976, as cited in Siegler, 2003, p. 298).

Forman (2003) asserts that when students work together to reason, problem solve, and communicate about mathematics, it has a "profound influence on children's learning processes and outcomes . . . includ[ing] motivational, affective, normative factors and involves beliefs about learning and goals for learning" (p. 347). Although there is a place for independent practice and learning, when students work together in a learning environment around carefully chosen tasks centered on meaningful mathematics, they develop shared and complex understandings of ideas, concepts, vocabulary, and symbols contained within the CCSS for mathematics.

More importantly, however, is the formative assessment opportunity provided to you, as the small-group student work takes place. In-class formative assessment is the means by which you measure the effectiveness of your instruction and the level to which students have achieved the learning target. According to the National Board for Professional Teaching Standards (2010), *accomplished* mathematics teachers use formative assessment to inform instruction so as to best meet the needs of each student:

> Teachers know how to observe and listen to students' interactions in order to blend instructional goals for the lesson with the learning goals of students. Teachers constantly reflect on the interaction between the purpose of the lesson and the requirements of the student to effectively satisfy both. Teachers use these observations to differentiate their instruction by providing different entry points to the same assignment with different skill sets. (p. 44)

Furthermore, formative assessment strategies should include ways for students to reflect on their own learning, identifying any possible gaps in their knowledge and understanding during the class period. See chapter 3, collaborative strategy four (page 90), and chapter 4, step one (page 100), for full details as how to use in-class formative assessment practices as part of the teaching-assessing-learning cycle.

Design Element Three: Introduction, Daily Review, and Closure

Hiebert and Stigler (1999) affirm the excessive amount of high school class period instructional time lost to noninstructional issues. Great classroom teachers, like you, take advantage of every moment of precious instructional time. Designing activities for immediate student use at the beginning of the class period can be an efficient method for student engagement. Your collaborative team should discuss the goal and purpose for the opening activity. The activity could be used as a hook to grab the attention and curiosity of students about the upcoming lesson. Your chosen activity might assess prerequisite knowledge for the day's lesson or assess what your students know about a previous learning target. The initial activity might be used as a quick practice of standardized testing strategies or problems. Regardless of the goal of your opening activity, the idea is to immediately engage students in doing mathematics. The opening activity can also be a time for teachers on the collaborative team to differentiate activities to best meet the needs of students in their respective classes.

A common practice in U.S. classrooms is to spend a significant portion of the instructional period going over homework (Hiebert & Stigler, 1999). Usually at some point in the beginning of class, the teacher provides homework answers for students to check their homework. Hands begin to go up with questions about various problems. Before long, at least half of the class period passes. The teacher then rushes to get through new material in less time. Students leave class with incomplete understanding. The next day, students come in with several questions about the homework, and the cycle repeats itself. To avoid this counterproductive cycle, homework review should be brief and focused, providing students with meaningful feedback about students' progress. Johnson (1990) provides specific ideas for limiting the amount of time spent reviewing homework—no more than five minutes as part of the formative assessment process for student action.

One way homework can be handled expeditiously is to choose one key problem to check as students work on a warm-up problem or group activity. Some teachers choose to collect homework so as to provide specific feedback to students. If you anticipate one or two problems are likely to generate a lot of student questions, choose one or two students to prepare quick presentations of solutions ahead of time as the class is also doing the warm-up activity.

Be sure to ask yourself, "Who is doing all of the work during the *going over* moments of class—going over homework, a test or quiz, a problem or task, or a key practice problem?" If you are the one doing all of the work while the students listen and watch, then you need to restructure the activity. For example, you could plan student-centered activities, such as small-group discussion, to redirect the students' attention to what they should be learning as the selected task is reviewed.

Whether the instructional period is thirty-two or ninety minutes, some type of *student-led* closing to the lesson is crucial to summarize and highlight key concepts or ideas from the lesson. The bell is about to ring, and students are already thinking about meeting their friends in the hallway or worrying about the test next period in biology. The end of the period is a last opportunity for students to reflect on the key concepts and processes emphasized during the lesson, make connections to overarching themes, and reflect on their own learning. The closure can be as simple as asking students to share their thoughts about new ideas or how the day's lesson connects to lessons previously taught. Whether the closure is a whole-class question, a group reflection, or an individual task, an end-of-lesson summary refocuses students on important conceptual understandings and Mathematical Practices. Teachers and students each need to reflect on whether students met the learning target that was set for that lesson. You might simply ask students what they learned in the lesson and what questions they have about the lesson's learning target. Asking students to solve a quick problem (or exit slip) that reflects the learning target enables them to receive immediate feedback about their progress toward the learning target. The exit slip also gives you valuable formative data about where student learning is at the end of the instructional period.

Design Element Four: Homework

There are several schools of thought about the role and extent of homework. Marzano (2007) finds that homework at the high school level results in positive student achievement. To have positive effect, homework should have a clear purpose that is communicated to students. The purpose of homework may be to deepen students' conceptual understanding, enhance procedural fluencies, or even to expose students to new content. Your team should intentionally consider and choose each problem based on the learning target.

Completing homework is an opportunity for students to reflect on their learning while developing strategies to problem solve and persevere. (In chapter 4, the value of student self-reflection, goal setting, and action is presented as a formative process for student learning.) The mathematics is visible in the process of how the student worked through the problem. Answers do little to reveal the extent of student understanding or misconceptions.

There are many advantages to providing students the homework answers as part of a unit-by-unit common formative assessment experience for all students in a course. When students are only expected to provide an answer for homework (and not show all work), the message communicated is that the problems' solutions are valued over the *process* used to arrive at the solution.

When teachers provide students with answers to the homework problems, students can check their solutions against the answers, and if their end result does not match the provided answer, they can rework the problem to find their error. In other words, students receive immediate and formative self-assessed feedback of their work. Moreover, a compelling reason to provide students the answers to the homework in advance of the assignment is the time saved reviewing the homework during the class period. Time is no longer needed to display answers as the expectation has been developed in students that it is their responsibility to check those answers and identify what they understand or what help they will need prior to entering class the next day. Visit **go.solution-tree .com/commoncore** for sample collaborative team–developed unit homework assignment sheets.

The Mathematical Practices Lesson-Design Tool

As discussed in chapter 1, effective mathematics instruction rests in part on careful planning (Morris, Hiebert, & Spitzer, 2009). Ensuring that the CCSS Mathematical Practices are an important component of mathematics lessons will require significant and careful planning by your collaborative team. Collaborative teams are uniquely structured to provide the time and support they need to interpret the CCSS for mathematics, focus on the essence of these practices for students, embed the Mathematical Practices into daily mathematics lessons, and reflect together on the effectiveness of implementation. A lesson-planning tool, such as the one provided in figure 2.8 (page 58), should support the vision of instruction for your school or district. This tool can be useful to you and your collaborative team as you discuss daily lesson construction that will include the design elements described in table 2.3 (page 47).

Unit:	Date:	Lesson:	

Learning target: As a result of today's class, students will be able to _____

Formative assessment: How will students be expected to demonstrate mastery of the learning target during in-class checks for understanding?

Probing Questions for Differentiation on Mathematical Tasks	
Assessing Questions	**Advancing Questions**
(Create questions to scaffold instruction for students who are "stuck" during the lesson or the lesson tasks.)	(Create questions to further learning for students who are ready to advance beyond the learning target.)

Targeted Standard for Mathematical Practice:

Which Mathematical Practice will be targeted for proficiency development during this lesson?

Tasks (Tasks can vary from lesson to lesson.)	**What Will the Teacher Be Doing?**	**What Will the Students Be Doing?** (How will students be actively engaged in each part of the lesson?)
Beginning-of-Class Routines How does the warm-up activity connect to students' prior knowledge?		
Task 1 How will the students be engaged in understanding the learning target?		
Task 2 How will the task develop student sense making and reasoning?		
Task 3 How will the task require student conjectures and communication?		
Closure How will student questions and reflections be elicited in the summary of the lesson? How will students' understanding of the learning target be determined?		

Figure 2.8: CCSS Mathematical Practices lesson-planning tool.

Visit **go.solution-tree.com/commoncore** for a reproducible version of this figure.

The template provides an intentional focus on differentiated instructional planning, Mathematical Practice development, and building the lesson around meaningful student tasks that are engaging and require student communication. Regardless of the textbook or course materials, the lesson content, or unit standards, this template provides consistent planning for the teacher and student actions of the lesson, focused on the CCSS Mathematical Practices. The intention is for this planning tool to be used in conjunction with your other lesson-planning tools and the instructional vision of your district as well. (Visit **go.solution-tree.com/commoncore** for sample teacher team lesson-design plans using the CCSS Mathematical Practices planning tool.)

Student Motivation: A Benefit of the Mathematical Practices

High school teachers have long lamented students' lack of motivation as a reason for minimal student engagement and less-than-stellar mathematics achievement results. *Motivation* is treated rather like a substance in students' brains. Some students have a lot of it, and others don't. When students fail to learn, teachers tend to blame it on motivation. At the other extreme, if students don't learn, teachers are blamed for not being sufficiently good motivators. There is another way to think about motivation—not as a cause but as a consequence of achievement (Wiliam, 2011). Similarly, Middleton and Spanias (2002) find that student motivation depends on how students interpret their success and failures. They also posit that teachers can influence student motivation by focusing instruction on learning goals, designing instruction that is inquiry oriented (thereby supporting the notion that the teacher's way is not the only way), and defining success by hard work and not by ability. Learners tend to view themselves in one of two mindsets: (1) fixed mindset or (2) growth mindset (Dweck, 2006). Learners with a fixed mindset believe intelligence is fixed, and one is either mathematically inclined or not. A learner who has a growth mindset believes that hard work pays off. One can learn from effective effort and making mistakes. Learners with fixed mindsets shut down when confronted with new challenges and see mistakes as failures, whereas learners with growth mindsets welcome new experiences that push their thinking.

Adults can have fixed or growth mindsets, just like students. Teachers who tend toward a fixed mindset hold the belief that mathematics is a gatekeeper and that some students are *naturally* better at mathematics than other students. Teachers who have a growth mindset believe that all students with access to high-quality curriculum and instruction can learn mathematics. How are you supporting a growth mindset in your classroom? When you praise students for their effort, the strategies they use to solve problems, their perseverance, and the progress they have made, you are supporting a growth mindset. Do not praise students for being *smart*. Give students challenging problems and feedback on what they are doing well and where they need improvement with suggestions how to improve. Writing "Try harder" or drawing a smiley face on the paper does little to communicate what is expected of students.

Teachers can influence students' mindsets by the way they provide feedback and recognize effort (Dweck, 2006). When students are aware of learning expectations and are taught that effective effort (trying something different when doing the same thing over and over doesn't work) positively impacts their learning, they are motivated to challenge themselves, problem solve, and persevere. Collaborative teams that communicate to students the learning targets and the high dividends of effective effort develop the Mathematical Practices in their students.

Looking Ahead

Although the Mathematical Practices are not content, but rather ways of interacting with the content, they cannot exist without the CCSS content standards. Planning must therefore simultaneously involve careful consideration of the mathematical content goals of instruction and how the practices can be implemented during the lesson to aid students in developing deep understanding of the content standards. Chapter 3 will examine the unique characteristics and essential features of the CCSS for mathematics content standards, and chapter 4 will examine ways you can further assess the development of both the CCSS Mathematical Practices and the content of the Mathematics Standards for High School.

Chapter 2 Extending My Understanding

1. In figure 2.2 (page 29), we pose three questions to better understand the Mathematical Practices. The third question—What evidence is there that students are engaged in this CCSS Mathematical Practice?—was generally left for your team to discuss. Take each of the Mathematical Practices, and in your collaborative team, identify the evidence you might see that students are engaged in the Mathematical Practice.

2. With your collaborative team, take an application problem from your textbook and eliminate the scaffolding.

   ○ Does the problem meet the suggested criteria in figure 2.3 (page 31)? If not, how might your team change the problem?

   ○ Discuss the approaches students may take and what support teachers might provide without doing the problem for the students.

   ○ Which Mathematical Practices might your team emphasize in the problem?

3. Creating classroom norms is a critical component of creating a classroom culture, whereby students reason abstractly and quantitatively as well as construct viable arguments and critique the reasoning of others (Mathematical Practices 2 and 3). How will you create expectations for students about their role in explaining, justifying, and critiquing mathematical reasoning? How will you "celebrate" missteps and mistakes as learning opportunities?

4. Smith and Stein (2011) identify *Five Practices for Orchestrating Productive Mathematics Discussions*. The first practice is to anticipate student responses to

the task and plan instructional moves based on the student response. In your collaborative team, identify a high-cognitive-demand task, and work together to discuss anticipated student responses as well as possible instructional moves a teacher might use.

5. The lesson-design components in table 2.3 (page 47) are detailed and extensive. A collaborative team development of a lesson involving all components of the lesson design would involve rich, meaningful dialogue about mathematics teaching and learning. Your collaborative team should begin lesson planning together by using a few of the components. Choose two of the components around which your collaborative team might begin to plan a lesson together.

6. Communicating a growth mindset to students is a key motivational factor. Teacher words and actions have an impact on whether students perceive a classroom culture that emphasizes a growth or fixed mindset. What are ways that you convey a growth mindset to students?

Online Resources

Visit **go.solution-tree.com/commoncore** for links to these resources.

- **Resource Roundups (PBS Teachers, n.d.; www.pbs.org/teachers /resourceroundups):** This website includes a list of possible questions and teaching tips for developing mathematical thinking in the classroom.

- **Discourse: Questioning (National Council of Teachers of Mathematics, 2011a; www.nctm.org/resources/content.aspx?id=6730&itemid=6730& linkidentifier=id&menu_id=598):** NCTM provides several resources to examine and support questioning strategies.

- **Mathematics Questioning Strategies (Standards Management System, n.d.; http://sms.sdcoe.net/SMS/mas/mathQuestionStrategy.asp):** The San Diego County Office of Education offers a resource on the art of questioning in mathematics.

- **Common Core Standards for Mathematical Practice (Inside Mathematics, 2010a; http://insidemathematics.org/index.php/common-core-standards):** This site provides classroom videos and lesson samples designed to illustrate the Mathematical Practices in action.

- **Standards for Mathematical Practice (Common Core State Standards Initiative, 2011; www.corestandards.org/the-standards/mathematics /introduction/standards-for-mathematical-practice):** This site links the text of the eight Mathematical Practices and the selection on "Connecting the Standards for Mathematical Practice to the Standards for Mathematical Content."

- **NCTM Lessons (http://illuminations.nctm.org):** Illuminations provide standards-based resources that improve mathematics teaching and learning for all students. These materials illuminate the vision for school mathematics set forth in *Principles and Standards for School Mathematics*, *Curriculum Focal Points for Prekindergarten Through Grade 8 Mathematics*, and *Focus in High School Mathematics: Reasoning and Sense Making*.

- **Handheld Graphing Technology in Secondary Mathematics (http://education .ti.com/sites/UK/downloads/pdf/References/Done/Burrill,G.%2520%282002 %29.pdf):** This resource synthesizes and provides peer-reviewed, published research on the implications for classroom practice regarding the relationship between graphing calculator technology and improved student mathematics achievement.

- **Tools for the Common Core Standards (http://commoncoretools.wordpress .com):** Follow Bill McCallum's blog about tools that are being developed to support the implementation of the CCSS.

- **Common Core Math Initiative (Maine West Mathematics Department, n.d.; https://sites.google.com/a/maine207.org/mw-math-department/home /common-core):** The Maine West Mathematics Department offers a collection of resources, articles, and blogs to support the CCSS for mathematics vision.

- **Adlai E. Stevenson High School District 125 mathematics department (www.d125.org/academics/mathematics.aspx):** This website provides up-to-date collaborative team artifacts, including unit-by-unit homework assignments, quizzes, tests, goal-setting worksheets, projects, calendars, and more.

CHAPTER 3

Implementing the Common Core Mathematics Content in Your Curriculum

The high school portion of the Standards for Mathematical Content specifies the mathematics all students should study for college and career readiness. These standards do not mandate the sequence of high school courses. However, the organization of high school courses is a critical component to implementation of the standards.

—National Governors Association Center for Best Practices & Council of Chief State School Officers

In a professional learning community, you and your colleagues work together to ask and answer the critical question, "What is it we want all students to know and be able to do?" In this chapter, you will analyze the content language, design, and organization of the Common Core Mathematics Standards for High School. The chapter also provides several implementation strategies necessary for you and your colleagues to meet the expectations of the CCSS Mathematics Standards for High School (see appendix C, page 165).

In an effective PLC culture, a clearly articulated curriculum provides the vision for what students should know and be able to do at the completion of each course in your mathematics program. The Common Core Mathematics Standards for High School describe that vision of standards for your high school curriculum. Successful implementation of the CCSS will require you and your colleagues to close the gap between the current reality of the content taught in your department and the CCSS vision for that content.

As the National Governors Association Center for Best Practices and the Council of Chief State School Officers (2010) state:

> These standards are not intended to be new names for old ways of doing business. They are a call to take the next step. It is time for states to work together to build on lessons learned from two decades of standards-based reform. It is time to recognize that standards are not just promises to our children, but promises we intend to keep. (p. 5)

The last sentence in the quote bears restating: "It is time to recognize that standards are not just promises to our children, but promises we intend to keep" (NGA & CCSSO, 2010, p. 5). It is important to note that whether intentional or unintentional, there is a reason much of the expected content and practices for the delivery of an effective high school mathematics curriculum have failed to be implemented. Several factors contribute to the inequity that often exists in a high school mathematics curricular program. The factors are the following.

- **Teacher isolation:** Some teachers prefer to (intentionally) remain apart from their colleagues teaching the same course or others in the mathematics department. Such behavior creates problems in communication and consistency of instruction. Modifying learning targets in isolation or using teaching strategies that have not been agreed on as a team can result in a very different mathematics learning experience for the students simply based on the teacher a student was assigned. If any collaborative team member works in isolation, the team's effectiveness in creating equity for all students is diminished because universal support for desired learning targets or teaching strategies will be lacking.

- **Teacher independent decision making:** Decisions about what topics to leave out or not teach for depth of knowledge and understanding should be made collaboratively. You and your colleagues make many decisions in the classroom on a daily basis as lessons unfold and students make progress toward the learning targets. However, the district curriculum, aligned with the Common Core, identifies the expected learning for all students. When your district clearly articulates the curriculum and pays attention to the curricular flow in the design process, you and your team know exactly what content must be taught and what students should be able to do as a result of their learning. Without such clarity of expectations, the omission of targets or lack of attention to the depth of learning also creates an inequitable experience for students.

- **Widely variant district-level interpretation of state standards in curricula documents:** Without clear district- or school-level communication about expectations for implementing the standards, teachers can be left to interpret the curriculum in their own way. The interdependent nature of the teachers in your collaborative team helps create a greater level of understanding regarding the intent and interpretation of state and local standards.

- **Hidden messages about student mathematic ability:** Individual teachers may hold contrasting views about student ability to learn mathematics—belief that some students are not capable of learning mathematics (a fixed mindset) versus belief that all students are capable of learning mathematics if they persist in their efforts with appropriate support (a growth mindset). When your team members collaborate to identify learning targets and address required supports for student learning as a team, you can help each other identify ways to ensure the mathematical learning and development of all students. A focus on every student demonstrates a commitment to equity and continued learning.

The efforts of your collaborative team will ensure the promises of the CCSS for mathematics will be kept. In a PLC, you and your team members analyze your actual implemented curriculum through an *equity lens*: What is best for all students of this course, not just the students I teach? When your collaborative team works interdependently to achieve the learning goals for a course, you jointly commit to resisting the temptations that a lone teacher may not be able to avoid. These temptations may include decisions about who does or does not belong in a course, overemphasis of certain topics, intentional slowing of the curriculum, omission of content, and all issues of equity and access. The CCSS Mathematics Standards for High School will require you and your colleagues to embrace positive beliefs for curriculum implementation and enter into a new era with determination and clarity regarding that implementation. The strength and focus that a collaborative team offers will provide for greater equity and learning for all students.

A primary focus of your team is to ensure the alignment of the local curricula to the Common Core Mathematics Standards for High School. When your collaborative team works to implement the designed curriculum based on the CCSS for mathematics, your team members must be able to address how to ensure alignment of the local curriculum framework with the processes inherent in a PLC (goals, collaboration, data, and continuous improvement) as you purposely revisit the curriculum on a unit-by-unit basis each year. Your course content alignment effort should begin with an understanding of the language and the intent of the Mathematics Standards for High School.

The Mathematics Standards for High School Content

Since 1989, NCTM has been a leader in the development of curriculum standards. The council's landmark *Curriculum and Evaluation Standards for School Mathematics* (NCTM, 1989) influenced the development and realignment of state mathematics standards throughout the United States. NCTM's *Principles and Standards for School Mathematics* (NCTM, 2000) updated the *Curriculum and Evaluation Standards* and served as the blueprint for revised state standards throughout the 2000s, and *Focus in High School Mathematics: Reasoning and Sense Making* (NCTM, 2009) focused the teaching and learning of high school mathematics content on student *understanding*.

The CCSS for mathematics call on all K–12 students to practice mathematical ways of thinking real-world issues and challenges as they prepare to think and reason mathematically. The standards set a rigorous definition of college and career readiness, not by expecting an excessive number of topics, but by demanding that students develop a depth of understanding for the content that must be taught.

The Mathematics Standards for High School Content Design

To develop your own understanding of the Common Core Mathematics Standards for High School, you should begin with an examination of the differences between the K–12 content expectations within the *Principles and Standards for School Mathematics* (PSSM; NCTM, 2000) and the Common Core State Standards (NGA & CCSSO,

2010). One initial difference is the descriptive language used to define the standards. The CCSS content areas are referenced as *domains* rather than *content topics* or *strands*. Also note that while the PSSM content topics are the same across all grades K–12, the content domains within the CCSS differ according to grade level, with, for instance, Counting and Cardinality appearing only at the kindergarten level and Number and Operation–Fractions having a three-year focus from grades 3–5, while Modeling as a conceptual category appears only at the high school level. An analysis of the domain headings (see table 3.1) reveals a comparison of what is important at and across particular grade levels and how they are connected as a progression K–12.

Table 3.1: Mathematics Content—*Principles and Standards for School Mathematics and the Common Core State Standards*

PSSM—Content Topics Grades PreK–12	CCSS—Content Domains Grades K–5	CCSS—Content Domains Grades 6–8	CCSS—Conceptual Categories High School
Number and Operations	Counting and Cardinality (K only)	Ratios and Proportional Relationships (Grades 6–7)	Number and Quantity
	Number and Operations in Base Ten	The Number System	
	Number and Operations—Fractions (Grades 3–5 only)		
Algebra	Operations and Algebraic Thinking	Expressions and Equations	Algebra
Geometry	Geometry	Geometry	Geometry
Measurement		Functions (Grade 8 only)	Functions
Data Analysis and Probability	Measurement and Data	Statistics and Probability	Statistics and Probability
			Modeling

At the K–8 level, NCTM released *Curriculum Focal Points* in 2006, right before the CCSS emerged. *Curriculum Focal Points* was intended to serve as a discussion document for states, school districts, and local schools as they began a conversation around the more important or focus topics at particular grades for levels K–8. Many states saw the Focal Points as an opportunity for their school or school district to identify areas of curricular focus within particular grades and also to provide the grade-by-grade essentials for all students. In many ways, the Focal Points became a precursor to the Common

Core State Standards for grades K–8 and have increased the expected learning and readiness standards for high school mathematics.

Like the K–8 standards, the high school conceptual categories are organized into domains and content standard clusters. The clusters are organized into twenty-two *domains* of content for high school, and the domains are organized into the six *conceptual categories* of Number and Operations, Algebra, Functions, Modeling, Geometry, and Statistics and Probability. (For the full CCSS Mathematics Standards for High School, see appendix C, page 165.) As the National Governors Association Center for Best Practices and the Council of Chief State School Officers (2010) state:

> Conceptual categories portray a coherent view of the high school mathematics; a student's work with functions, for example, crosses a number of traditional course boundaries, potentially up through and including calculus. Modeling is best interpreted not as a collection of isolated topics but in relation to other standards. (p. 57)

Thus, modeling becomes an integrated aspect of your teaching preparation that permeates the entire curriculum. More importantly, the conceptual categories represent a body of knowledge for students to obtain during high school. On the surface, these conceptual category names should seem very familiar to you. However, as you dig deeper and unpack the standards inside these categories, you will observe a more robust and deeper expectation for student demonstrations of understanding.

Figure 3.1 (page 68) highlights how to read and understand the format of the Mathematics Standards for High School. This example is from the Algebra conceptual category (see appendix C, page 169).

As another example, consider the domain Similarity, Right Triangles, and Trigonometry (G-SRT) under the Geometry conceptual category. The G-SRT domain has four content standard clusters, which contain eleven standards (NGA & CCSSO, 2010; see appendix C, pages 185–186):

1. Understand similarity in terms of similarity transformations.
2. Prove theorems involving similarity.
3. Define trigonometric ratios and solve problems involving right triangles.
4. Apply trigonometry to general triangles. (p. 57)

Making sense of these standards at the collaborative team level, fully understanding what it means to teach these learning targets with modeling, and deciding when to teach these learning targets (what year—grades 9, 10, 11, or 12—and what course) within your high school mathematics courses will be the responsibility of your district mathematics curriculum team. It will be your collaborative team's responsibility to implement the agreed-on course scope and sequencing. Your team will need to take a deeper look at each content standard cluster for the high school standards. For example, under the content standard cluster *Define trigonometric ratios and solve problems involving right triangles* are the following standards:

Standards define what students should understand and be able to do.

Clusters summarize groups of related standards. Note that standards from different clusters may sometimes be closely related because mathematics is a connected subject.

Domains are larger groups of related standards. Standards from different domains may sometimes be closely related.

Conceptual categories are the main topics of study for high school mathematics.

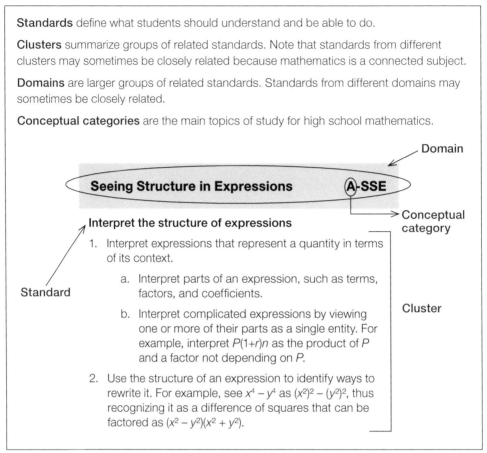

Source: Adapted from NGA & CCSSO, 2010, pp. 5 and 64.
Figure 3.1: How to read the high school standards.

Visit **go.solution.tree.com/commoncore** for a reproducible version of this figure.

6. Understand that by similarity, side ratios in right triangles are properties of the angles in the triangle, leading to definitions of trigonometric ratios for acute angles.

7. Explain and use the relationship between the sine and cosine of complementary angles.

8. Use trigonometric ratios and the Pythagorean Theorem to solve right triangles in applied problems. (NGA & CCSSO, 2010, p. 77)

Notice the verbs used to describe these standards: *understand, explain,* and *use.* Notice too the reference to *applied problems,* which indicates a level of mathematical modeling. Each of these standards represents and expects students to be *doing* mathematics. Your team will need to have robust discussions about what it means to teach students to *understand similarity, explain relationships,* or *use trigonometric ratios* as each learning target or standard surfaces during your course content scope and sequence of learning standards.

Additionally, Mathematics Standards for High School include *plus* standards—(indicated by a (+) symbol. These are standards necessary to prepare for advanced courses.

Although the plus standards will not be part of the state assessment content, you and your team need to determine how teaching many of the plus standards can and should be part of each course in your high school curriculum. Three standards in the G-SRT domain in the fourth content standard cluster *apply trigonometry to general triangles* are for more advanced course preparation:

9. (+) Derive the formula $A = \frac{1}{2}\,ab\,\sin(C)$ for the area of a triangle by drawing an auxiliary line from the vertex perpendicular to the opposite side.

10. (+) Prove the Laws of Sines and Cosines and use them to solve problems.

11. (+) Understand and apply the Law of Sines and the Law of Cosines to find unknown measurements in right and non-right triangles (e.g., surveying problems, resultant forces). (p. 77)

As you examine each of the domains and content standard clusters for the Mathematics Standards for High School, you will realize that the number of standards necessary for you to teach in any given year is now about two-thirds of past expectations. This allows you additional time that will be needed for delivering on the expectations for mathematical modeling, problem solving, and the development of deeper student understanding.

The Mathematics Standards for High School Content Paradigm Shift

The *content* paradigm shift of the CCSS is *less is more* with fewer standards to be taught in each course for high school. Thus, *less* (fewer standards) provides an opportunity to meet the expectations of *more* (focused and deeper rigor with understanding) at every high school grade level and in every course. As you begin full implementation toward the CCSS learning targets, there should no longer be a "race to the finish in April" feeling for state assessment preparation.

The content paradigm shift for you, as a high school teacher, is to implement the Common Core Mathematics Standards for High School not by teaching an excessive number of learning targets or topics—a standard a day—but by demanding your students develop the ability to demonstrate *a depth of understanding* for the content standards. You and your team can and should approach a content *grain size* consisting of each unit of instruction of roughly four to six content standards over a period of fourteen to eighteen days of instruction and assessment.

According to Popham (2011a), grain size describes the nature of how narrow or broad, how complex or demanding, a body of knowledge is. High school mathematics lesson and assessment design has generally been built on a grain size of several disconnected lessons; for example, one standard each and one day in length and measure. This small grain size fails to address actual learning target progressions and development during a unit or chapter of study. Thus, eight to ten units or chapters per year consisting of four to six connected learning targets per unit of study represent the right grain size for the PLC teaching-assessing-learning cycle to be discussed in chapter 4.

How do you know if a particular building block of content and the learning targets within that content progression is worthy of your collaborative team formative assessment time and effort? Popham (2011b) provides some guidelines on how to judge the worthiness of the learning targets in the building block. Your collaborative team should answer the following four questions on a unit-by-unit basis:

1. Is this target's curricular aim a cognitive skill—one that would take more than a class session to teach?

2. Will this skill be applicable to a wide range of subsequent situations, in or out of school?

3. Is this skill a foundation for future learning in this course or subsequent courses?

4. Is mastery of this skill something students must display on a subsequent high-stakes assessment?

For a unit of content to be an effective size, your collaborative team (the Algebra Team, the Precalculus Team, the Ninth-Grade Mathematics 1 Team, Tenth-Grade Mathematics 2 Team, and so on) must first determine that the learning targets chosen within a chapter or unit progression are all worthy of student understanding and mastery for proficiency. To do so, you must make sure every learning target (content standard) for the chapter or unit is able to pass the Popham test.

For the Common Core content, the paradigm shift includes standards that expect:

1. An extensive emphasis on mathematical modeling throughout the year, in each high school course

2. An extensive emphasis on student *understanding* and learning targets for instruction that require student demonstrations of proficiency in the understanding of mathematical content throughout the year, in each high school course

3. An increased emphasis and use of statistics integrated with content during the first three years of high school (not treated only as a separate course) to analyze empirical situations, understand them more fully, and make sound decisions

4. The use of higher-cognitive-demand tasks in each unit of instruction that weave mathematical topics together into an integrated whole and address the dual nature of learning both content and process

5. An increased emphasis on the concepts of congruence, similarity, and symmetry as understood from the perspective of geometric transformation

6. An increased use of technology to aid in the investigation and problem-solving aspect of each high school course (technology becomes a valuable and expected tool for student use)

Finally, you can further develop an understanding of the expectations for the CCSS high school content by consulting the PARCC (www.parcconline.org) or the SBAC (www.smarterbalanced.org) websites. Both consortia provide extensive information about their respective *curricular framework* plans for implementation of the CCSS Mathematics Standards for High School at each grade level.

You can also use the next section of this chapter to help you answer questions such as:

1. What is the expected high school mathematical content of the CCSS for each grade level?

2. How might the Mathematics Standards for High School be different from previous curricular expectations for a robust high school mathematics curriculum?

3. Are there particular content standards that will need greater attention on a unit-by-unit basis?

4. Are there CCSS content standards that appear to be a struggle for our students each year?

5. What will curriculum pacing and course sequencing look like with the CCSS?

6. Most importantly, how will your mathematics department and collaborative teams implement the expectations of the CCSS Mathematics Standards for High School?

The Mathematics Standards for High School Content Analysis

One way to better understand the Common Core content expectations is to examine the structure from a macroscopic and microscopic view. At a macroscopic view, you see six conceptual categories and twenty-two domains, and at a microscopic level, you can see multiple content standard clusters within each domain of the Mathematics Standards for High School. You will need an intentional plan to help all stakeholders develop a better understanding of the CCSS language and content intentions.

This Mathematics Standards for High School content analysis begins with a look at the broad scope and understanding of the coherence-building nature of the CCSS conceptual categories and progresses to an extensive analysis of each of the domains, clusters, and standards. In the end, the development of specific student learning targets aligned to the standards within the clusters will provide the course-level teams in your district with the coherence and clarity necessary for implementation. Moving directly to learning targets without the needed attention to the overall structure may lead to a curriculum that lacks focus and connections across all conceptual categories.

Conceptual Categories Analysis

What are the similarities and differences between the content expectations within the *Principles and Standards for School Mathematics* (NCTM, 2000) and the Common Core State Standards (NGA & CCSSO, 2010)? One slight difference is the descriptive language used to define the standards. As mentioned previously, the CCSS content areas are referenced as *conceptual categories* rather than content *topics* or *strands*. As a beginning look at mathematical content expectations, an analysis of the conceptual category headings (see table 3.2) provides a starting point in thinking about what's important at and across the high school grades and mathematics program courses. Table 3.2 provides an opportunity for a comparative team discussion of what *was* versus what will now *be* the content focus for your collaborative teams. The discussions will reveal either comfort or discomfort with the CCSS conceptual categories and will help you determine your professional development content needs for the various CCSS conceptual categories.

Table 3.2: Mathematics Content—PSSM and CCSS

PSSM—Content Topic Grades PreK–12	CCSS—Conceptual Categories High School
Number and Operations	Number and Quantity
Algebra	Algebra
Geometry	Geometry
Measurement	Functions
Data Analysis and Probability	Statistics and Probability
	Modeling

Your collaborative team should examine the detail of the CCSS Mathematics Standards for High School conceptual categories by reading the overview sections for each conceptual category (see appendix C, pages 165, 169, 174, 179, 181, and 187) and use the comparison chart in table 3.2 to ask the questions contained in figure 3.2.

1. Why is Number and Quantity used in the CCSS instead of Number and Operations as in the PSSM? Compared to your current practice, what is different about the reference to *quantity*, and what is the same in the Number and Quantity overview (see appendix C, page 165)?

2. Why are Algebra (appendix C, page 169) and Functions (appendix C, page 174) listed as separate conceptual categories (when they were not separate in the PSSM)? How do the CCSS Mathematics Standards for High School treat these conceptual categories differently?

3. How is the Geometry conceptual category (appendix C, page 181) different from typical practice in a high school geometry course? Why is there a renewed emphasis on transformations, for example?

4. What are the expectations of the four domains of the CCSS Statistics and Probability conceptual category (appendix C, page 187)? How will these content domains be integrated into the current mathematics program? How prepared are teachers to design classroom experiences that will allow students to learn this content?

5. Where in your current curriculum pacing guides do we intentionally integrate the conceptual category for Modeling (appendix C, page 179)? How does your current curriculum reflect the modeling cycle description in the CCSS? How prepared are

teachers to design classroom experiences that will allow students to learn this content?

6. How do the expectations for the development of Mathematical Practices interact with the development of content? Is there interplay between proficiency with certain practices and the timing of specific content?

7. How is the Modeling conceptual category integrated as part of the Mathematical Practices, as well as part of the high school standards indicated with a ★? How will modeling become part of your unit design and development?

Figure 3.2: Questions to compare PSSM and CCSS.

Visit **go.solution.tree.com/commoncore** for a reproducible version of this figure.

Digging deeper into the conceptual categories helps develop your awareness of the various content domains for the Mathematics Standards for High School. (You can use the questions in appendix A, pages 156–157, and tables A.1 and A.2, pages 156 and 157.) The next natural level of inspection then, is the domain level, which will in turn reveal insight into the content standard clusters as well.

Domain Analysis

As described in chapter 1, your collaborative team works together to develop a shared understanding of the content to be taught because, among other reasons, it develops consistent curricular expectations between you and your colleagues, serving equity goals for the course as well as creating ownership among all teachers (DuFour et al., 2006). As your team examines the content domains within the high school conceptual categories, you and your colleagues begin to develop this shared understanding. You can use the following three questions to guide your study of the CCSS content at the domain level.

1. What is familiar to us in the content standard clusters for each domain?

2. What expectations appear to be new for the standards and clusters for each domain?

3. What might be challenging in each domain for students or for teachers?

The example in table 3.3 (page 74) provides a tool to analyze one specific high school content domain and its corresponding content standard clusters within the conceptual category Geometry (appendix C, page 181). Geometry, and more specifically the domain Similarity, Right Triangles, and Trigonometry (G-SRT), was chosen for this example because it is a significant shift from the current approach to teaching Euclidian geometry in high school. The use of a transformational approach will require professional learning on the part of many teachers. As your team encounters new content within various courses, it should be expected that your professional development and team discussions may address the specific nature of the content as you do some of the mathematics together. Your team will need to address how the transformational approach is connected to the more familiar content of Geometry.

Table 3.3: Domain Analysis Tool for the CCSS

Content Standard Cluster	Which Standards in the Cluster Are Familiar?	What's New or Challenging in These Standards?	Which Standards in the Cluster Need Unpacking or Emphasis?
Similarity, Right Triangles, and Trigonometry (G-SRT)			
Understand similarity in terms of similarity transformations.			
Prove theorems involving similarity.			
Define trigonometric ratios, and solve problems involving right triangles.			
Apply trigonometry to general triangles.			

Source: NGA & CCSSO, 2010.

Visit **go.solution-tree.com/commoncore** for a reproducible version of this table.

The domain-level analysis tool provided in table 3.3 should be viewed as a beginning stage for your discussions and the work that takes place in your collaborative team to develop a shared understanding of the differences between current district standards and the vision of the CCSS for mathematics. It may also help identify specific areas of continued learning for your team members.

As you plan for or seek professional development linked to a step-by-step domain analysis, your collaborative team should assess its level of confidence teaching the domains' content standard clusters and discuss your reactions about the content as a team. Your team can then examine transition issues across the high school grades in order to ensure coherence from year to year for the students. Teams will also need to determine how to address the more advanced content or (+) standards identified for their course.

Use table 3.3 as an analysis tool for making sense of the details of the four content standard clusters within the Geometry domain. Complete the table, identifying the content in the domain that is familiar to you and your team, the content that is new and challenging, or the content that you believe needs emphasis. After each team member completes the table, the team should engage in a discussion to identify common needs across the team and design a professional development plan to ensure that everyone is ready to teach the content at the required level. The check for consistency, patterns, and agreement across a team will provide a more equitable experience for all students in the course. See appendix C, pages 185–186, for the complete listing of the content standards under the domain Similarity, Right Triangles, and Trigonometry (G-SRT).

Table 3.4 provides an example of how your collaborative team might complete the cells of the table as teachers make sense of—unpack—the clusters.

Table 3.4: An Example of Unpacking a CCSS Domain

Content Standard Cluster	Which Standards in the Cluster Are Familiar?	What's New or Challenging in These Standards?	Which Standards in the Cluster Need Unpacking or Emphasis?
Similarity, Right Triangles, and Trigonometry (G-SRT)			
Understand similarity in terms of similarity transformations.	I am completely comfortable with the definition of *similarity*. We have taught dilations as a transformation before, but we never took the time to connect it to similarity.	Using similarity transformations (new) Verifying properties experimentally (new) Using the properties of similarity transformations to establish the AA criterion for two triangles to be similar	I need to review what is meant by *transformations*. I have not taught these before. I did learn about them in a college geometry course, so I will need to review them. Also, I am not sure if I recall how they are connected to similarity.
Prove theorems involving similarity.	A criterion for two triangles to be similar Using congruence and similarity criteria to solve problems	Prove theorems about triangles: a line parallel to one side of a triangle intersects the other two proportionally (side-splitter theorem) and the Pythagorean Theorem.	I know that I am rusty on these particular items. We have not proved the Pythagorean Theorem in our geometry classes before, and now we must design experiences so that the students will be able to prove it using similarity. What will this look like? Are our students ready for proofs like these?
Define trigonometric ratios, and solve problems involving right triangles.	Defining and using trigonometric ratios as a result of similarity Examining and using the sine and cosine ratios is very familiar to me. Solving right triangles in applied problems has long been a part of our curriculum.	There is nothing new in this cluster for our team.	It will be exciting to hear about the applications my team members think we should use in this cluster.

continued →

Apply trigonometry to general triangles		All three of these standards are (+) standards and have not been a part of our course previously. I am most concerned with proving the Law of Sines or the Law of Cosines as I know I have not done that before.	I know I will have to learn about ways to teach these topics. I have to learn them first and then our team can look for ways to help our students learn them!

Visit **go.solution-tree.com/commoncore** for a reproducible version of this table.

Digging deeper into the domains helps develop your awareness of the content standard clusters for the Mathematics Standards for High School. The next natural level of inspection, then, is the content standard clusters, which reveal the high school content at the standards level as well.

Content Standard Cluster Analysis

While unpacking the standards is crucial to understanding the intent of the standards, keep in mind that the standards are intentionally grouped within a content standard cluster. Daro, McCallum, and Zimba (2012) emphasize their intentionality (as CCSS for mathematics writers) of the standards within a cluster:

> Fragmenting the Standards into individual standards, or individual bits of standards, erases all these relationships and produces a sum of parts that is decidedly less than the whole. Arranging the Standards into new categories also breaks their structure. It constitutes a remixing of the Standards. There is meaning in the cluster headings and domain names that is not contained in the numbered statements beneath them. Remove or reword those headings and you have changed the meaning of the Standards; you now have different Standards; you have not adopted the Common Core.

How your district design teams, high school mathematics departments, and collaborative teams unpack the domains' content standard clusters is an important consideration. It will help you to better understand and know the content to emphasize at a particular time (for example, a two- to three-day lesson on the standards in the cluster and where the mathematics of the cluster may occur within the instructional year—first half of the year, early in the year, or so on).

You will also need careful attention and support in your collaborative team for the learning progressions built within the Mathematics Standards for High School. James Popham (2007) describes a learning progression as a "carefully sequenced set of building blocks that students must master en route to mastering a more distant curricular aim" (p. 84). Learning progressions are sophisticated ways of thinking about big ideas that will reasonably follow one another as students are learning.

Table 3.5 and table 3.6 (page 78) each provide a sample learning progression for two of the conceptual categories in the Mathematics Standards for High School. They depict a development of the Mathematics Standards for Functions and for Statistics and Probability, respectively, over a four-year mathematics experience. These learning progression tables, provided by the Phoenix Union High School District mathematics program, highlight one district's choice for the learning progression of various content standard clusters, based on the domains for each conceptual category. The first column of each table lists the domain, and the cells represent the progressions of the CCSS high school content standard clusters by grade level, regardless of the name or the type of course for that grade level.

Table 3.5: Sample High School CCSS Learning Progression for Functions

Domain	Grade 9	Grade 10	Grade 11	Grade 12
Conceptual Category: Functions				
Interpreting Functions (F-IF)	Understand the concept of a function, and use function notation. Relate the domain of a function to its graph. Be proficient with these ideas as they apply to linear and quadratic functions.	Interpret functions that arise in applications in terms of the context. Analyze functions using different representations. Become proficient with these functions: linear, absolute value, quadratic, exponential, step, piecewise, and logarithmic.	Analyze functions using different representations (rational functions).	
Building Functions (F-BF)	Understand the concept of a function, and use function notation. Relate the domain to its graph. Compare properties of two functions each represented in a different way.	Analyze functions using different representations. Build new functions from existing functions.	Interpret functions that arise in applications in terms of the context.	

continued →

Linear, Quadratic, and Exponential Models (F-LE)	Build a function that models a relationship between two quantities.	Construct and compare linear, quadratic, and exponential models, and solve problems.	Model inverse functions. Interpret expressions for functions in terms of the situation they model.	
Trigonometric Functions (F-TF)			Model periodic phenomena with trigonometric functions. Extend the domain of trigonometric functions using the unit circle. Prove and apply trigonometric identities.	

Source: Used with permission from Phoenix Union High School District.

Table 3.6: Sample High School CCSS Learning Progression for Statistics and Probability

Domain	Grade 9	Grade 10	Grade 11	Grade 12
Conceptual Category: Statistics and Probability				
Interpreting Categorical and Quantitative Data (S-ID)	Summarize, represent, and interpret data on a single count or measurement variable. Interpret linear models.	Use statistics appropriate to the shape of the data distribution to compare center and spread of two or more different data sets. Summarize, represent, and interpret data on two categorical and quantitative variables.		
Making Inferences and Justifying Conclusions (S-IC)	Decide if a specified model is consistent with results from a given data-generating process.	Understand and evaluate random processes underlying statistical experiments. Make inferences and justify conclusions from sample surveys, experiments, and observational studies.		
Conditional Probability and the Rules of Probability (S-CP)		Understand independence and conditional probability and use them to interpret data. Use the rules of probability to compute probabilities of compound events in a uniform probability model.		

Using Probability to Make Decisions (S-MD)	Calculate expected values, and use them to solve problems. Use probability to evaluate outcomes of decisions.			

Source: Used with permission from Phoenix Union High School District.

Analyzing learning progressions (the sequencing of the content standard clusters across grades) is a sophisticated way of keeping in mind the big ideas that will reasonably follow one another across courses as students advance though high school. By keeping an eye on this big picture of the vertical scope and sequence, while daily tending to the CCSS content standards, there is a greater chance your collaborative team will be able to adhere to the benefits of the vertical coherence features of the Common Core Mathematics. The content standard cluster analysis and the natural questions that arise for the high school course scope and sequence of the content lead to several implementation strategies you and your team can use for the CCSS Mathematics Standards for High School. (Visit **go.solution-tree.com/commoncore** for more learning-progression examples of the Number and Quantity, Algebra, and Geometry conceptual categories.)

The Mathematics Standards for High School Content Implementation

In order for you to address the complex nature of the CCSS Mathematics Standards for High School, the work of implementing a CCSS-based high school curriculum begins by first understanding three implementation design principles. Adapted from Marzano (2003), those principles are:

1. Seek to understand the enduring and supporting knowledge of the CCSS.

2. Seek to establish opportunities to learn.

3. Seek adequate time to teach the CCSS content.

These three guiding principles will support your transition to the CCSS content expectations.

Principle One: Seek to Understand the Enduring and Supporting Knowledge of the K–12 CCSS

In 2009, NCTM released *Focus in High School Mathematics: Reasoning and Sense Making* to provide further guidance to you as a secondary mathematics teacher. The Common Core Mathematical Practices described in chapter 2 are built solidly on the NCTM recommendations to develop mathematical reasoning and engage in tasks that promote sense making as your team develops and implements the local mathematics programs of study. The Mathematical Practices provide guidance on *how* to lesson plan for the core content of the high school standards so that students will develop the expected Mathematical Practices proficiencies over time.

Figure 3.3 provides a sample high school Advanced Algebra Team unit plan that highlights intentional planning for CCSS Mathematical Practice 1, Make sense of problems and persevere in solving them, as part of the unit content standard learning targets and goals.

Unit 2: Quadratics

Learning target A: Use quadratic functions to model real-world situations. (F-IF.4, 5, and 6 and SMP4)

Learning target B: Graph quadratic functions. (F-IF.7a)

Learning target C: Write the equation of quadratic functions. (F-IF.4)

Learning target D: Solve quadratic equations using the factoring, completing the square or quadratic formula. (A-REI.4b)

Learning target E: Simplify and approximate square roots. (A-REI.2)

Process learning target: Problem solving (Mathematical Practice 1)—

- Build new mathematical knowledge through problem solving.
- Solve problems that arise in mathematics and in other contexts.
- Apply and adapt a variety of appropriate strategies to solve problems.
- Monitor and reflect on the process of mathematical problem solving.

Source: Adapted from Stevenson High School (http://sites.google.com/site/shsadvancedalgebra).

Figure 3.3: Unit content that includes Mathematical Practice 1 as a process learning target.

The CCSS also reinforce the importance of your collaborative team incorporating *increasingly complex learning tasks* that reflect the content standards as student progress through high school coursework for the year. As you and your team collaborate to develop worthwhile mathematical tasks (in chapter 4 this is described as a "start of unit" expectation for your team), you should also encompass student proficiency with the Mathematical Practices. This will help your students learn the mathematical content with a deeper understanding that undergirds the development of content skill acquisition.

For example, under the conceptual category Functions and the Building Functions (F-BF) domain is the cluster *Build new functions from existing functions* (appendix C, page 178). The fifth standard within this content standard cluster is, "Understand the inverse relationship between exponents and logarithms and use this relationship to solve problems involving logarithms and exponents" (appendix C, page 178). It is important to note that the opening verb in this student standard is *understand*.

Your teaching and assessing of this standard requires your students to demonstrate understanding of the inverse relationships as well as demonstrate procedural fluency in using the relationship. This duality of learning expectations and outcomes— understanding and procedural fluency—becomes an implementation goal of your collaborative team. The challenge with this content standard cluster for many teams will be teaching students to perform specific actions pertaining to inverse functions in addition to building an understanding of how inverse functions are connected to the bigger and more enduring picture of relationships in mathematics.

When is a standard an enduring standard versus when is it supportive knowledge? When planning for the flow (scope and sequence) of the Common Core Mathematics Standards for High School content, your collaborative team should take into account the new foundational knowledge that your students will eventually possess as they enter high school. As the CCSS-based curriculum is taught in K–8, a ninth-grade student will start high school and will have already learned about radicals, integer exponents, simultaneous linear equations, congruence, volume, and patterns in bivariate data. In addition, the student will have experienced several years of focus and progress in developing proficiency toward the CCSS Mathematical Practices.

As your collaborative team designs lessons that provide all students with access to important mathematics, developing concepts from the informal to the formal (Smith & Stein, 2011) can help all students remain engaged in the learning process as you meet their diverse needs. For example, when teaching a standard in the content standard cluster *Reasoning with equations and inequalities* (see A-REI, page 173, in appendix C), students may demonstrate a depth of understanding through their responses to common team-designed tasks that require them to solve a system of equations. Some students may rely completely on their knowledge of graphing and attempt to solve all systems by graphing, while others may show various levels of sophistication through algebraic methods. Ongoing formative assessment, as outlined in chapter 4 in the teaching-assessing-learning cycle, will allow you and other support personnel to provide students with the formative feedback they need to master the learning targets as part of their enduring knowledge.

Providing needed interventions through a positive and required response to intervention (R^2TI) system (see chapter 5) can also help all students reach the goal of college and career readiness as they progress through the curriculum and develop enduring knowledge through the grades.

Figure 3.4 highlights several fundamental algebra 1 content shifts of typical high school standards to grades 6–8. This is a result of the grades 6–8 CCSS content standards. Thus, the grades 6–8 CCSS content standards are expected to prepare students for the increased rigor of the high school standards and the expected enduring knowledge needed for high school mathematics.

CCSS Content Standards in Grades 6–8

Solve and graph simple absolute-value equations and inequalities (grade 6) (6.EE).

Compute simple probability with and without replacement (grade 7) (7.SP).

Communicate real-world problems graphically, algebraically, numerically, and verbally (grade 7) (7.EE).

Figure 3.4: High school algebra 1 content shifts.   continued →

Evaluate algebraic expressions, including radicals, by applying the order of operations (grade 8) (8.EE).

Apply the laws of (integral) exponents and roots (grade 8) (8.EE).

Solve problems involving scientific notation, including multiplication and division (grade 8) (8.EE).

Describe the effects of parameter changes, slope, or y-intercept on graphs of linear functions and vice versa (grade 8) (8.EE).

Calculate slope given two points, the graph of a line, or the equation of a line (grade 8) (8.EE).

Using slope, determine whether two lines are parallel, perpendicular, or neither (grade 8) (8.EE).

Write equations in slope-intercept, point-slope, and standard forms given two points, a point and y-intercept, x- and y-intercepts, a point and slope, the graph of a line, or a table of data (grade 8) (8.EE).

Solve multistep equations and inequalities with rational coefficients numerically (from a table or guess and check), algebraically (including the use of manipulatives), and graphically using technology (grade 8) (8.EE).

Solve systems of two linear equations numerically (from a table or guess-and-check), algebraically, graphically, or technologically (grade 8) (8.EE).

Distinguish between functions, nonfunctions, and relations by inspecting graphs, ordered pairs, mapping diagrams, or tables of data (grade 8) (8.F).

Determine domain and range of a relation from an algebraic expression, graph, set of ordered pairs, or table of data (grade 8) (8.F).

Source: Adapted from NGA & CCSSO, 2010, pp. 46–57.

Your collaborative team should work together to write unit-by-unit plans that capitalize on the prior knowledge that is now a part of the grades 6–8 curriculum. Charting the high school path through the five conceptual categories and twenty-two domains will require your collaborative teams to understand the student's *prior knowledge* and the *depth of knowledge* learned in the grades 6–8 standards and in the subsequent newly redesigned mathematics courses for each grade level of your high school mathematics program. As students progress through the K–8 CCSS expectations, you can strengthen the opportunities you provide them to successfully learn the Mathematics Standards for High School by connecting to their prior knowledge.

Principle Two: Seek to Establish Opportunities to Learn

After your team has developed an understanding of the enduring and supporting knowledge needed for a full implementation of the Common Core mathematics in your course, your team must now engage in discussions about *how* to teach the content. Considering the content together with the Standards for Mathematical Practice, how will your team design the necessary learning experiences for the students? Chapter 2 provided great insight and advice on lesson design. When the new content is analyzed at the depth described in this chapter, it will be important for your team to discuss what the teaching of the content will look like, what common and core tasks you will use, and how those opportunities for learning will connect to each other across the course and across each year of high school.

As noted briefly on page 68, one of the challenges associated with high school curriculum design for the CCSS is the inclusion of plus standards, content identified as needed "in order to take advanced courses such as calculus, advanced statistics, or discrete mathematics" (NGA & CCSSO, 2010, p. 57). Within the conceptual category Number and Quantity, there are eighteen topics identified as needed for advanced study (see pages 167–169 in appendix C). These standards fall primarily in the area of The Complex Number System and Vector and Matrix Quantities. As students progress through the high school curriculum, you must pay attention to the development of these standards to ensure that options are open for students to move beyond the standards without a (+) for college and career readiness—even though the standards without a (+) will be the focus of the state testing consortia for the CCSS.

In some schools, the challenge will be how to ensure *all* students are prepared for future opportunities while resisting the urge to create tracked classes that only meet the minimum expectations of the CCSS. While avoiding homogeneously grouped classes, schools with heterogeneously grouped classes must design curriculum and feedback systems as part of their unit-by-unit work that will allow every student to master the necessary learning goals, whether they are planning to take advanced courses immediately after high school or at a later time in their life. Your collaborative teams will need to determine how to best ensure all students have access to opportunities to be fully prepared for future learning and college experiences, including opportunities to learn many of the plus standards.

Principle Three: Seek Adequate Time to Teach the CCSS Content

As your district, school, or collaborative teams begin the task of identifying the content to be taught in each high school course, the theme *less is more* becomes apparent. That is, there are fewer standards per year, about two-thirds of typical high school course expectations—from ninety standards per year to about sixty standards per year, depending on how the CCSS curricular frameworks unfold for your state or district. This will allow for the needed time to develop a deep understanding of the mathematical content and attend to the secure development of the Mathematical Practices.

However, many of the standards require your students to drill deeper into the content as the grain size of a unit of instruction is no longer at the traditional "standard a day" level or pace, as mentioned earlier in the chapter. You will now have a certain freedom to plan units of study that develop conceptual understanding over time rather than the mere accumulation of discrete skills found in a textbook chapter.

Figure 3.5 provides a sample high school district design team's assignment and pacing calendar for a unit on quadratics in a third-year mathematics course, such as an advanced algebra or a mathematics 3-type course.

September				
Monday	Tuesday	Wednesday	Thursday	Friday
				10 02_01: Product of Linears Learning Target A (F-IF.4, 5, 6, Mathematical Practice 4)
13 02_02: Quadratic Graphing task Learning Target B (F-IF.7a)	14 02_03: Quadratic Graphing task Learning Target B (F-IF.7a)	15 02_04: Quadratic Graphic task Learning Target B (F-IF.7a)	16 Late Arrival 02_05: Quiz	17 02_06: Quadratic Equation Writing Learning Target C (F-IF.4)
20 02_07: Quadratic Solving Investigation Learning Target D (A-REI.4b)	21 02_08: Quadratic Solving method choice Learning Target D and E (A-REI.4b, A-REI.2)	22 02_09: Quadratic (Formula) Solving common task Learning Target D and E (A-REI.4b, A-REI.2)	23 02_10: Quadratic (Formula) Solving Learning Target D and E (A-REI.4b, A-REI.2)	24 02_11: Quadratic (Formula) Solving Learning Target D and E (A-REI.4b, A-REI.2)
27 02_12: Quadratic Modeling tasks Learning Target A (F-IF.4, 5, 6, Mathematical Practice 4)	28 02_13: Quadratic Modeling tasks Learning Target A (F-IF.4, 5, 6, Mathematical Practice 4)	29 02_14: Preassessment	30 02_15: Review and student goal setting	1 02_16: Unit 2 Test

Figure 3.5: Advanced algebra or mathematics 3 pacing calendar for unit two— Quadratics.

Recall in figure 3.3 (page 80) how the second unit on quadratics for this course had five learning targets with standards for the unit. Notice in figure 3.5 the pacing calendar this collaborative team uses to ensure all teachers on the team receive the necessary time to teach the content—and to ensure all students learn, reflect, and take action on the content for this cluster of standards before the teacher team uses final common assessment instrument for this unit of study.

Notice how twelve days of instruction (during days of instruction and assessment) are used to unfold the depth of the standards (including quadratic modeling) for these five learning targets of the unit. This collaborative team has effectively planned for the time necessary to ensure student understanding by using common tasks that build on prior knowledge, developing the student Mathematical Practices, providing formative feedback, and unpacking important details of understanding for each learning target from the various clusters.

Per the guiding principles, the questions you and your colleagues should answer as you transition to the Common Core mathematics for high school are:

1. How will we ensure every teacher understands the enduring and supporting knowledge of the CCSS?

2. How will we ensure all students have an opportunity to learn the core knowledge of the Mathematics Standards for High School, as well as additional and more advanced mathematics?

3. How will we ensure adequate time, on a unit-by-unit basis, to teach the Common Core Mathematics Standards for High School content toward the understanding and depth required in each high school course?

As your team responds to these questions, you and your colleagues will engage in the important work of teaching in the 21st century. Collaborating with peers to investigate and respond to these questions is the work of an exceptional and *professional* learning community. As you work together to ensure all students master the learning outcomes, your PLC commitment to continuous growth will rely on the professionalism of you and your colleagues and the recursive nature of ongoing inquiry.

Based on these three design principles, there are four collaborative work expectations that, if honored, will ensure everyone on your team will successfully implement the Common Core Mathematics Standards for High School. These four collaborative strategies are (1) clearly articulated learning targets, (2) specified teaching strategies, (3) identified common unit tasks, and (4) common formative assessments that provide feedback to students and monitor progress individually and collectively toward the learning targets.

Collaborative Strategy One: Clearly Articulate Learning Targets

As your collaborative team develops unit-by-unit or chapter-by-chapter learning targets, you and your colleagues will need to pay attention to the *depth of knowledge* (DOK) that each target will require (Webb, 1997). Webb and his colleagues identify four levels to describe the depth of knowledge: (1) recall, (2) skill and concept, (3) strategic thinking, and (4) extended thinking. You can visit http://facstaff.wcer.wisc.edu/normw for the descriptions of each of the four DOK levels.

The CCSS curriculum should address learning at all depths of knowledge. Table 3.7 highlights a sample concept unit from algebra 1 and its connections to five specific high school CCSS content standards across two conceptual categories and several domains. In your collaborative team, you can use Webb's descriptors to identify the depth of knowledge for each learning target in table 3.7.

Table 3.7: Sample Algebra Unit on Equations and Inequalities

CCSS Standard	CCSS Standard Description	Student-Friendly Learning Target (Derived From Unwrapping the Standards)	Technology Expectations
N-Q.1	Use units as a way to understand problems and to guide the solution of multistep problems; choose and interpret units consistently in formulas; choose and interpret the scale and the origin in graphs and data displays.	I can use units (centimeters, seconds, grams, and so on) appropriately through the problem-solving process. I can understand units that are used in graphical displays.	• Use a graphing calculator to solve a single variable equation by setting each side equal to y. • Use a graphing calculator to explore algebraic structure and equivalence. • Manipulate the settings of the calculator to show answers to the appropriate level of accuracy, including scientific notation. • Graph a linear equation and analyze for solutions to real-world problems.
N-Q.2	Define appropriate quantities for the purpose of descriptive modeling.	I can identify the correct type of measurement to represent a real-life situation.	
N-Q.3	Choose a level of accuracy appropriate to limitations on measurement when reporting quantities.	I can estimate to an appropriate level of accuracy and communicate the process of estimation accurately to others.	
A-SSE.1	Interpret expressions that represent a quantity in terms of its context.	I can understand the vocabulary of the parts of an algebraic expression.	

CCSS Standard	CCSS Standard Description	Student-Friendly Learning Target (Derived From Unwrapping the Standards)	Technology Expectations
A-SSE.1 *(continued)*	a. Interpret parts of an expression, such as terms, factors, and coefficients. b. Interpret complicated expressions by viewing one or more of their parts as a single entity. For example, interpret $P(1 + r)^n$ as the product of P and a factor not depending on P.	I can understand the meaning of the algebraic structure within those expressions.	
A-CED.1	Create equations and inequalities in one variable and use them to solve problems. Include equations arising from linear and quadratic functions and simple rational and exponential functions. (Limit functions to linear, quadratic, and exponential with integer inputs only.)	I can set up an equation to solve a real-world problem with one unknown variable. I can solve the equation to find the answer to the real-world problem context.	

You can use table 3.7 as a sample tool for identifying the actual Common Core Mathematics Standards for High School being addressed during the unit, the student-friendly language that articulates the expected level of understanding, and the technology expectations tied to the unit. Once the learning targets for the unit or chapter of study are identified, the specific teaching strategies for teaching the targets become part of the discussion work for your team. Notice how this sample concept unit contains standards across two domains.

Collaborative Strategy Two: Specific Teaching Strategies

Chapter 2 described several specific teaching strategies that may be used to elicit the level of desired learning. If your collaborative team identifies the unit learning targets, such as those in table 3.7, but fails to identify the teaching strategies for those content standards, your team is left without the guidance needed to support meaningful learning for understanding. While individual teachers on your team may be able to design lessons with a stated target in mind, in order for your collaborative team to engage in the collective inquiry that is expected in a PLC, a set of identified teaching strategies that nurture the expected student behaviors on the eight CCSS Mathematical Practices is needed to help exemplify the student understanding and the desired learning of the content standard.

For example, consider the verbs used in the content standards from table 3.7: *interpret* complicated expressions, *understand* the parts of vocabulary, *understand* problems, and *choose* a level of accuracy. These action verbs each require various teaching strategies that reflect the CCSS Mathematical Practices for student action. Designing student-engaged strategies, such as those provided by Smith and Stein (see chapter 2, page 53–54), becomes a component of the real work of your collaborative team for CCSS implementation. *How* your students experience learning about the content standard is as important as the standard itself. This is best done through extensive planning for student engagement with peers in Common Core tasks that represent the content learning target, as you monitor and provide formative feedback to the small group student-led team discussions (see chapter 2, pages 54–55).

Collaborative Strategy Three: Identified Common Unit Tasks

As students progress through a curriculum, they will learn mathematics by engaging in *worthwhile mathematical tasks* and engaging in discourse that the teacher expertly orchestrates (Hiebert et al., 1997). The common tasks your team uses during the unit should engage students and provide common experiences that can be drawn on to continue learning at various points throughout the curriculum. A core team task is a common activity your team uses to teach specific content. These core tasks are designed by the team with explicit ties to the standards identified for the unit. For example, using the Geometry cluster from table 3.3 (page 74), the curriculum may include a specific right triangle modeling application that all students complete at a specific point in the learning process. The student results on this task are used to foster collaborative discussion about the progress of all students in the course and the students of individual teachers. These common tasks provide the requisite data for team members' informed decision regarding teaching methods, student progress, common expectations, the use of technology, and expectations for successful student achievement.

The identified core tasks for the unit provide your collaborative team the opportunity for rich, engaging, and professional discussions regarding student performance around that task. That is, the identified core tasks in a curriculum unit provide important points of departure for conversations about student learning. They also provide an opportunity for your team to do mathematics together.

Recall table 2.1 (page 40), which offers a problem about world population. Table 2.1 provides an example of a common and core team task that is appropriate to the learning targets described in the content unit from table 3.7 (page 86). Visit **go.solution-tree .com/commoncore** for the complete problem and expected student actions for this common collaborative team task. Common tasks better gauge teacher team progress toward the learning targets, as every team member requires his or her students to engage in the task.

When your collaborative team members can immerse themselves in sharing examples of student work from table 2.1, using both qualitative and quantitative data from those common student experiences, they can identify a focus for how to improve the learning for all students in the course. Members of your collaborative team engaged in sharing information with each other regarding the core and common student tasks such as these can hone their effective feedback to students. In the case of table 2.1, there are many nuances and subtle ways you can extend the task and design open discussions of what it means for students to demonstrate understanding for the task. Collaborative team discussions about student performance on these common in-class problems or tasks allow for improved teacher feedback to students and eliminate the inequity in learning when some teachers use the task and others do not.

Visit **go.solution-tree.com/commoncore** for another sample unit design for a second-semester algebra or mathematics 1 class for ninth-grade students. In this case, the unit of study focuses on statistics and matrices. This unit includes two conceptual categories—Number and Quantity and Statistics and Probability—and three domains—Vector and Matrix Quantities (N-VM), Interpreting Categorical and Quantitative Data (S-ID), and Making Inferences and Justifying Conclusions (S-IC). There are five clusters of learning targets for the unit. Also, note that four of the standards are (+) standards, and your collaborative team should plan to address those standards as well in the college preparatory course, even though they are considered additional content beyond college readiness content.

Your collaborative team decides the nature of the tasks to be used for each standard and decides on some common tasks to be used with students by all members of the team. Once you've determined the learning target's scope and sequence for the unit, and once your collaborative team has agreed on essential strategies for teaching the standards, then it is the next natural step to dig into robust discussions and decisions about the types of mathematical tasks that will reflect the intent of the learning target. For example, in the unit described in appendix F, one of the Common Core unit learning targets is S-ID.6, Represent data on two quantitative variables on a scatter plot, and describe how the variables are related (appendix C, page 189). How does your collaborative team *choose* the mathematical *tasks* that are best for this standard? Failure to choose common unit tasks as a team can create deep inequities among student learning opportunities.

Collaborative Strategy Four: Common In-Class Formative Assessment

In addition to identified common unit tasks, members of your collaborative team will actively seek data as they pertain to agreed-on checkpoints of student learning. As your collaborative team discusses the learning targets for an upcoming unit, you should also agree on how to assess that learning as a team. Then, as you and your team members design your lessons for that unit, the common points of in-class formative assessment processes are used to gather data to provide feedback to students and to the team. This process will be explored further as part of the teaching-assessing-learning cycle in chapter 4.

The embedded formative assessment opportunities are a natural outgrowth of the discussions within your collaborative team and allow for immediate feedback for both students and teachers as part of the common tasks. Without these common in-class formative moments, you and your collaborative team members do not have the information needed to know whether or not all students are learning and understanding at the desired level. As described in chapter 2, using figure 2.8 (page 58), your team should prepare both the *advancing* (enhancing concepts beyond the common task) and the *assessing* (scaffolding the concept for differentiation) formative assessment questions for you and your students to use during the in-class activities designed for the task.

Table 3.8 provides a formative assessment planning tool for the CCSS learning targets from the domain Similarity, Right Triangles, and Trigonometry. The tool asks you to identify specific teaching strategies, common unit tasks, and common in-class formative assessments that provide feedback to students and monitor progress individually and collectively toward the learning targets. Your collaborative teams could use a tool similar to table 3.8 to engage in discussions around the four collaborative strategies for any of the content standard learning targets.

Table 3.8: Learning Target Formative Assessment Development Tool

Learning Target	Teaching Strategies	Core Tasks	Common Formative Assessment Points
State the properties of a dilation given by a center and a scale factor (G-SRT.1).	Cooperative learning exploration and reporting out	Dilation lab: students learn the properties of dilations.	Can all students state the properties in writing and to their peers?
Verify the properties experimentally (G-SRT.2).	Using both hand-drawn triangles and dynamic geometry software	Use the electronic file in the team's geometry materials folder.	Can the student verify the properties across settings?

Learning Target	Teaching Strategies	Core Tasks	Common Formative Assessment Points
Determine if two triangles are similar (G-SRT.3).	Triangle lab in small groups	Students should construct similar triangles using a pencil and paper and dynamic geometry software.	Can students correctly identify proportional relationships after identifying two triangles as similar?
Prove the theorems about triangles (G-SRT.4).	Cooperative learning with some whole-class guidance	Use district materials resource 5 the district math team developed for this unit.	Can students work in pairs to explain and justify the theorems regarding triangle similarity, highlighting necessary steps and validating their reasons with precise language?
Solve problems using similarity (G-SRT.6).	Small group practice		
Identify the trigonometric ratios in right triangles (G-SRT.8).	Students in pairs: quiz-quiz-trade?	Have first trigonometry lab in district materials.	Can students demonstrate to their peers the relationship between sine, cosine, and similar triangles?
Explain the relationship between sine and cosine of complementary angles (G-SRT.7).		Have second trigonometry lab in district materials.	Can students state the relationship and justify their reasoning?
Use trigonometric ratios with the Pythagorean theorem to solve triangles (G-SRT.8).	Applied problem-solving situations	Have third trigonometry lab in district materials.	Can students solve one-step and multistep problems?

Looking Ahead

In this chapter, we've provided a number of tools to support the work within your collaborative team as you determine and analyze the Mathematics Standards for High

School content. The chapter was intended to help your collaborative team begin content discussions regarding the transition to the Common Core mathematics expectations as part of the high school curriculum redesign effort. You can then determine the depth desired for the analysis of the content and when and how your team will engage in strategies for implementing the content of the high school Common Core.

The ultimate goal will be for each member of your collaborative team to develop a clear understanding of the important mathematics impacting current courses—to realize that what's provided within the CCSS is somewhat different content from what you have experienced, to recognize those differences, and to understand that the CCSS provide opportunities to dig deep and to make less (fewer expectations) become more (provide a depth of understanding).

Finally, there are several critical planning questions to ask within your collaborative team. Your professional development efforts related to the mathematical conceptual categories, domains, and content standard clusters of the CCSS could include, but are not necessarily limited to, the following:

1. How many content standard clusters will you be able address in each high school course or grade level?

2. What is your collaborative team plan for the amount of time to dedicate for each content standard cluster of each year?

3. Is there a clear understanding of the conceptual category content progression from year to year? Has there been a content accommodation for the (+) standards?

4. Do you have the instructional tools to accomplish your proposed CCSS implementation plan? If not, what materials or tools do you need?

5. How will your students develop the Mathematical Practices through their experiences in Number and Quantity, Algebra, Functions, Modeling, Geometry, and Statistics and Probability?

This chapter contains several resources to guide your collaborative team's professional development efforts in thinking about, analyzing, and unpacking the conceptual categories, domains, and content standard clusters for the Mathematics Standards for High School expectations. It will be the responsibility of your collaborative team to take responsibility for implementing the vision for the Common Core mathematics and, as chapter 4 will suggest, ultimately the assessment of those standards for successful student attainment.

Chapter 3 Extending My Understanding

1. Examine a specific CCSS domain.

    ○ How do the standards and clusters within this specific domain develop over a student's high school mathematics experience? Refer to table 3.6 (page 78) for an example.

> Conduct a side-by-side comparison with your current mathematics curriculum standards, spending time unpacking and looking for emphasis. Refer to the table 3.5 (page 77) for an example.

> Identify the familiar, new, or challenging content. How might this impact your implementation plan?

2. Examine a specific cluster in the CCSS.

> What are the specific learning targets that are expected of students at each level of curriculum? Refer to table 3.7 (page 86).

> What mathematical tasks could be used to assess student understanding of the standards within this cluster?

> What Mathematical Practices are developed within this specific cluster of standards?

> Refer to table 3.8 (page 90) to create an alignment between the specific learning targets, teaching strategies, core tasks, and assessments for the specific cluster.

3. Examine the instructional materials you currently use to support your mathematics curriculum. Determine the extent to which these materials are aligned with the CCSS by using the Mathematics Curriculum Materials Analysis Project tools discussed in the additional resources. How will you use this information to guide planning, delivery of instruction, and effective assessment?

Online Resources

Visit **go.solution-tree.com/commoncore** for links to these resources.

- **CCSS Mathematics Curriculum Materials Analysis Project (Bush et al., 2011; www.mathedleadership.org/docs/ccss/CCSSO%20Mathematics%20 Curriculum%20Analysis%20Project.Whole%20Document.6.1.11.Final .docx):** The CCSS Mathematics Curriculum Analysis Project provides a set of tools to assist K–12 textbook selection committees, school administrators, and teachers in the analysis and selection of curriculum materials that support implementation of the CCSS for mathematics.

- **Illustrative Mathematics Project (http://illustrativemathematics.org):** The main goal for this project is to provide guidance to states, assessment consortia, testing companies, and curriculum developers by illustrating the range and types of mathematical work that students will experience in implementing the Common Core State Standards for mathematics.

- **Progressions Documents for the Common Core Mathematics Standards (Institute for Mathematics and Education, 2007; http://math.arizona.edu /~ime/progressions):** The CCSS for mathematics were built on progressions— narrative documents describing the progression of a topic across a number of grade levels informed by research on children's cognitive development and by the logical structure of mathematics. The progressions detail why standards are sequenced the way they are, point out cognitive difficulties and provide pedagogical solutions, and provide more detail on particularly difficult areas of mathematics. The progressions documents found here are useful in teacher preparation, professional development, and curriculum organization, and they provide a link between mathematics education research and the standards.

CHAPTER 4

Implementing the Teaching-Assessing-Learning Cycle

An assessment functions formatively to the extent that evidence about student achievement is elicited, interpreted, and used by teachers, learners, or their peers to make decisions about the next steps in instruction that are likely to be better, or better founded, than the decisions they would have made in absence of that evidence.

—Dylan Wiliam

The focus of this chapter is to illustrate the appropriate use of ongoing student assessment as part of an interactive, cyclical, and systemic collaborative team *formative process* on a unit-by-unit basis. You and your collaborative team can use this chapter as the engine that will drive your systematic development and support for the student attainment of the Common Core mathematics content and instruction as described in chapters 2 and 3.

When led well, ongoing unit-by-unit mathematics assessments—whether in-class, during the lesson or the assessment instruments, tests, quizzes, or projects—serve as a feedback bridge within the teaching-assessing-learning cycle. The cycle requires your team to identify core learning targets or standards for the unit, create cognitively demanding common mathematics tasks that reflect the learning targets, create in-class formative assessments of those targets, and design common assessment instruments to be used during and at the end of a unit of instruction.

To embrace the student assessment and learning expectations within the Common Core, you and your students will constantly need to collect evidence of student learning and respond to that evidence (decide and *act* on what to do next) using rich, descriptive, and immediate corrective feedback as part of a formative decision-making process.

A Paradigm Shift in High School Mathematics Assessment Practices

Think about the current assessment practices and processes you, your team members, and others in your mathematics department use. What are they like? How would you know with any certainty if those assessment practices are of high quality and represent a process that will significantly impact student achievement?

Until recently, student assessment has largely been considered an isolated high school teacher activity that served the primary summative purpose of grading. Thus, assessment instruments (mostly quizzes, tests, and projects) primarily serve as an *ends*, not as a *means*, to support and advance student learning. Generally, when used as an end, assessment instruments do not result in student motivation to persevere (Mathematical Practice 1) and continue learning.

If you use each quiz, test, or chapter assessment instrument as a summative evaluation moment for the student, often there is little, if any, opportunity for the student to take action and respond to the evidence of learning the assessment provides. In this limited vision of how you and members of your team use assessment instruments (as ends), each teacher on your team would give a quiz or test to the students, privately grade the test questions right or wrong—based on a personal scoring rubric determined in isolation for colleagues—and then pass back student scores (grades) for the test and for the current class grade.

You return the assessment instrument to your students who in turn either file away the test or turn it back in to you. Typically, you file away the results and move on to the next chapter or unit of teaching—while also responding to the students who failed to take the test on time. For the most part, student learning on the previous unit stopped at this point, because the unit had ended. Do any of these isolated assessment practices seem familiar to you, either in the past or perhaps today, to your colleagues?

Now, with the Common Core mathematics, the fundamental purpose and process for the ongoing unit-by-unit student assessment in mathematics is undergoing a significant change. In a professional learning community, mathematics assessment functions as a multifaceted evidence collecting process by which you gather information about student learning and your teacher practice in order to inform teacher *and* student daily decision making, and to adjust the focus of instruction and learning accordingly.

Today, collaborative teams will use robust assessment processes grounded in the ongoing retrieval and analysis of information about the depth and rigor of student tasks, the effective learning of those mathematical tasks, and the creation of a learning environment in which "error is welcomed as a learning opportunity, where discarding incorrect knowledge and understandings is welcomed, and where participants [teachers and students] can feel safe to learn, re-learn, and explore knowledge and understanding" (Hattie, 2009, p. 239). In this new paradigm, your appropriate use of ongoing student assessment becomes part of an interactive, cyclical, and systemic collaborative team *formative* process for both you and your students.

James Popham (2011b) states the case for a formative assessment process that gathers evidence in a variety of ways, moving from

> traditional written tests to a wide range of informal assessment procedures. Recent reviews of more than four thousand research investigations highlight that when the (formative assessment) process is well-implemented in the classroom, it can essentially double the speed of student learning

producing large gains in students' achievement; at the same time, it is sufficiently robust so different teachers can use it in diverse ways and still get
great results with their students. (p. 36)

As a high school teacher or teacher leader, one of your key collaborative responsibilities becomes ensuring that your collaborative team implements formative assessment
processes into your unit-by-unit work. In this new paradigm, you understand that school
mathematics assessments are no longer driven by and limited to the traditional *summative* function or purpose of unit or chapter tests and quizzes: assigning grades, scores,
and rankings. Essentially, any traditional school assessment instrument used for a grading purpose is only one part of a much bigger multistep formative process necessary for
teacher learning and student learning (Popham, 2008).

In this era of the CCSS, your course-based collaborative teams will plan for and collaborate on ways in which your unit or chapter quizzes, tests, and benchmark exams
are woven onto the fabric of lesson design and planning and used primarily to help
students self-assess their own understanding for improvement and then act as necessary
to improve.

An important distinction is that formative assessment is not a type of unit or benchmark test students take. Formative assessment processes are different from the assessment instruments used as part of the formative process. Popham (2011b) provides an
analogy that describes and distinguishes the difference between summative assessment
instruments and formative assessment *processes*. He describes the difference between a
surfboard and surfing. While a surfboard represents an important tool in surfing, it
is only that—a part of the surfing process. The entire process involves the surfer pad-
dling out to an appropriate offshore location, selecting the right wave, choosing the
most propitious moment to catch the chosen wave, standing upright on the surfboard,
and staying upright while a curling wave rumbles toward shore. The surfboard is a key
component of the surfing process, but it is not the entire process.

High-quality high school assessment practices then function to integrate formative
assessment processes into your decisive *actions* about shaping instruction to meet student
needs, progress, pacing, and next steps. Similarly, these processes inform your students
about their learning progress and direction, enabling them to become actively involved
and to make decisions and take ownership of their work. You learn more about your
instructional practice and students learn more about how to focus the re-engagement
of their learning by:

1. Using unit-by-unit assessment instruments such as quizzes, projects, and tests
   as tools to support a formative learning process for students and teachers (steps
   one, four, and five of the teaching-assessing-learning cycle)

2. Designing and implementing formative assessment in-class strategies, with
   advancing and assessing questions that check for student understanding during
   classroom instruction and student engaged learning tasks (steps two and three
   of the teaching-assessing-learning cycle)

Wiliam's (2011) epigraph at the start of the chapter reveals the definition of formative assessment used in this book:

> An assessment functions formatively to the extent that evidence about student achievement is elicited, interpreted, and used by teachers, learners, or their peers to make decisions about the next steps in instruction that are likely to be better, or better founded, than the decisions they would have made in absence of that evidence. (p. 43)

Two phrases in Wiliam's definition are key: (1) "evidence about student achievement is elicited" and (2) "[assessment functions to] make decisions about next steps." That is, teacher and students in conjunction with their peers must *act* on the evidence. Otherwise, as Wiliam (2011) describes, the formative process is empty in terms of impact on student learning.

Furthermore, Wiliam (2011) cites five elements that need to be in place, if the intent of your teaching and assessing during the lesson (your daily choice of mathematical tasks used for short-cycle assessments and checks for understanding) and unit (your weekly or monthly choice of assessments instruments such as quizzes and tests) is to improve student learning. The five elements are:

1. The provision of effective feedback to students

2. The active involvement of students in their own learning

3. The adjustment of teaching to take into account the results of assessment

4. The recognition of the profound influence assessment has on the motivation and self-esteem of students, both of which are crucial to learning

5. The ability of students to assess themselves and understand how to improve

The teaching-assessing-learning cycle in figure 4.1 is built on the foundations of these essential assessment elements. The cycle is designed to develop a vision of effective high-quality assessment practice on a unit-by-unit basis for the teachers on your team and in your mathematics department. The process begins as your collaborative team designs mathematical tasks and formative in-class assessments for those tasks, lessons that allow for student engagement into those tasks, and assessment instruments that align with the expected learning targets for a unit or chapter of content. Your team works together to determine how to provide students in the course with formative learning opportunities and strategies on those learning targets as you respond to evidence (or lack thereof) of student learning.

The PLC Teaching-Assessing-Learning Cycle

The PLC teaching-assessing-learning cycle described in figure 4.1 provides a systemic collaborative team process that will recognize any assessment used—from the daily in-class informal checks for understanding with student feedback to the more formal unit assessment instruments—as formative, provided students and teachers use the assessments to make instructional and learning adjustments. Assessments—such as quizzes, tests, and

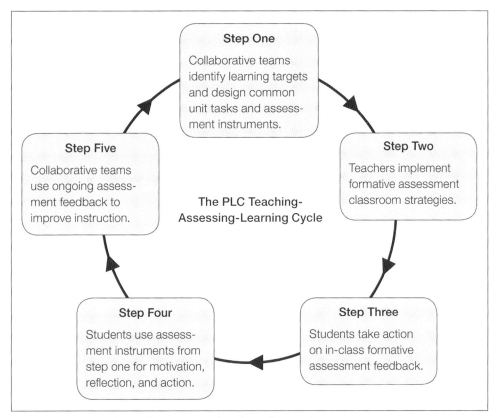

Figure 4.1: The PLC teaching-assessing-learning cycle.

Visit **go.solution-tree.com/commoncore** for a reproducible version of this figure.

projects—that your collaborative team uses strictly for the assignment of grades or mastery scores, not for authentic formative learning opportunities, fall far short of reaching the powerful impact assessment could have on improved student and teacher learning. However, when traditional assessment instruments are used as tools within a robust team assessment plan and process cycle, great things can happen. Great things happen too when in-class formative feedback is part of your teams' lesson design and teaching becomes "*adaptive* to student learning needs" (Wiliam & Thompson, 2008, p. 64).

Moving clockwise in figure 4.1, your collaborative teacher team makes adjustments and moves back and forth in the cycle during a unit as needed, giving feedback to your students and to each other. In step one, you do the hard work of up-front planning and development for the unit: planning for the learning targets, planning the Common Core tasks and formative assessment in-class response to the tasks during instruction, and planning the common assessment instruments to be used throughout the unit.

In steps two and three, teachers use daily formative assessment classroom strategies around the team-designed mathematical tasks from step one and make adjustments as needed during the unit. In step four, students set goals and make adjustments to learning based on all unit or chapter assessment instrument results, at a developmentally appropriate level depending on the grade level (this might be different from the ninth-grade to twelfth-grade high school courses). Students reflect on successes and next-step actions based on evidence of areas of weakness during and after the unit of study as the assessment instrument is used for formative learning.

Ultimately, in step five, you make adjustments to future lesson plans and unit assessment instruments due to individual differences in students and the success of students, as your team collects evidence and data at the end of the unit. At this step, it is important for you to think about *all* students in the course, not just the ones you teach, as you and your team members reflect on student performance during and after the unit of study. You take notes and *share* with colleagues what went well, what changes to make, and so on, for the next unit of instruction.

Step One: Collaborative Teams Identify Learning Targets and Design Common Unit Tasks and Assessment Instruments

In a professional learning community, before the first lesson of the next unit or cluster of mathematics instruction begins, your collaborative course-based team reaches agreement on the design and proper use of high-quality, rigorous common assessment tasks (for formative in-class feedback) and assessment instruments (unit quizzes and tests) for all students during the unit. You can use a lesson-design tool such as the one provided in chapter 2, figure 2.8 (page 58), as you design these common tasks.

However, to do so requires your team to first reach clarity on and understanding of the expected learning targets for the unit as you answer the first of three critical questions for step one.

What Are the Identified Learning Standards?

What are the mathematical *procedural fluency* targets for proficiency in this unit of content? What are the mathematical *understanding* targets for student proficiency? The CCSS define what students should *understand* as well as the skills they must be able to do in their study of mathematics.

Consider the following cluster (one of three) in figure 4.2, under the domain Interpreting Functions (see F-IF, page 176, in appendix C) within the more broad CCSS conceptual category Functions.

The CCSS define what students should *understand* as well as the skills they must be able to do in their study of mathematics. The very nature of the domain Interpreting Functions requires students to show key features of the graphs of functions as part of the learning target assessment. Asking a student to understand something means you must formatively assess whether the student has understood it—and thus the tasks and assessment of the task design must reflect your collective team effort to meet the vision of the CCSS *understanding* aspect of the learning target.

Conceptual category: Functions

Domain: Interpreting Functions (F-IF)

Cluster: Analyze functions using different representations.

Learning targets: Graph functions expressed symbolically, and show key features of the graph, by hand in simple cases and using technology for more complicated cases.

    a. Graph linear and quadratic functions and show intercepts, maxima, and minima.

    b. Graph square root, cube root, and piecewise-defined functions, including step functions and absolute-value functions.

    c. Graph polynomial functions, identifying zeros when suitable factorizations are available, and showing end behavior.

    d. (+) Graph rational functions, identifying zeros and asymptotes when suitable factorizations are available and showing end behavior.

    e. Graph exponential and logarithmic functions, showing intercepts and end behavior, and trigonometric functions, showing period, midline, and amplitude.

Source: Adapted from NGA & CCSSO, 2010, p. 69.

Figure 4.2: Sample domain and cluster in the high school CCSS for mathematics.

Visit **go.solution-tree.com/commoncore** for a reproducible version of this figure.

A collective team discussion on what is intended by the learning targets for the unit, as well as the progression of the learning targets in the unit and to other units, will help the team to better meet the vision of teaching to the CCSS understanding aspect of the standards. Although the specific number of total learning targets has been reduced per year in order to allow greater depth and less breadth, there is a greater expectation for the assessment of student understanding—the conceptual knowledge necessary for developing procedural fluency—which takes time in the unit. As your collaborative team plans the unit calendar and pacing for the learning targets, adequate time should be built in to allow for formative in-class assessment feedback, corresponding instructional adjustments, and the subsequent use of appropriate assessment instruments for student demonstration of understanding the learning targets.

Once your team understands the expected learning targets for the unit, you are ready for the next aspect of step one—identifying the Common Core tasks that will be used to develop student understanding of the learning targets for the unit, which is the second critical question necessary to be prepared for meaningful in-class formative assessment processes.

What Are the Identified Daily Formative Mathematical Tasks?

During step one, members of your collaborative team discuss the cognitive demand of the *mathematical tasks* that will be part of the daily lesson design and used in class as part of the formative feedback process to students (for more on cognitive demand, see chapter 2, pages 51–54). Your lesson-design preparation should take into account both the skill and understanding of the mathematical tasks and problems presented to the students during the unit of mathematical study.

The *Technical Issues in Large-Scale Assessment* (TILSA) project (Wise & Alt, 2005) provides insight into the design and implementation of teacher team–developed local assessment tasks both during and at the end of a unit. Adapted to fit the needs of your teacher team assessment and lesson-design work, you can use figure 4.3 as a resource to guide your collaborative team discussions and evaluate your collaborative teams' readiness to teach, assess, and learn *before* the new unit begins.

---

1. **Student opportunity to learn:** Do all teachers in your course have access to the same content? By the end of the unit, will every teacher have covered the same content with the same rigor?

2. **Depth of knowledge:** Are cognitive requirements between the in-class formative assessment tasks and the learning targets in the unit consistent for each teacher? Is the same complexity of knowledge (and skill) sought and required by all teachers for the mathematics unit?

3. **Range of knowledge:** Is the range of content covered under each of the content clusters for the unit of knowledge similar from teacher to teacher in the course? Do all teachers of the course include daily tasks that prepare students for procedural fluency as well as the conceptual understanding tasks that will be part of the common assessment instruments that all teachers will use?

4. **Balance of representation:** Are learning targets for a particular cluster of standards given the same emphasis on the common assessment instruments?

5. **Source of challenge:** Does student assessment (test) performance actually depend on mastering the learning targets and not on irrelevant knowledge or skills?

Source: Adapted from Wise & Alt, 2005, p. 4.

Figure 4.3: Aligning learning targets with assessment instruments and formative assessment tasks.

Visit **go.solution-tree.com/commoncore** for a reproducible version of this figure.

Your collaborative teams' preparation for the understanding aspects of the content standards is served through the lesson-design expectations of the CCSS Mathematical Practices as described in chapter 2. Common unit mathematical tasks need to be constructed so that student practices, such as construct viable arguments and critique the reasoning of others (Mathematical Practice 3) or use appropriate tools strategically (Mathematical Practice 5), are part of the lesson design. These two student Mathematical Practices would be an important and primary aspect of the student learning experience for the learning target (F-IF.7): "Graph functions expressed symbolically and show key features of the graph, by hand in simple cases and using technology for more complicated cases" (NGA & CCSSO, 2010, p. 69; see appendix C, page 176), as shown in figure 4.2. The CCSS document states it like this:

> One hallmark of mathematical understanding is the ability to justify, in a way appropriate to the student's mathematical maturity, *why* a particular mathematical statement is true or where a mathematical rule comes from. Mathematical understanding and procedural skill are equally important, and both are assessable using mathematical tasks of sufficient richness. (NGA & CCSSO, 2010, p. 4)

Consider the following low-cognitive-demand mathematical task:

Evaluate tan ($^{5\pi}/_6$).

Imagine rewriting the task for a higher-cognitive-demand level.

The tan ($^{5\pi}/_6$) = $^{-1}/_{\sqrt{3}}$. Provide a mathematical argument that verifies this statement is true, and defend your argument with a student partner.

As your team debates the use of a common task, such as the tangent question, step one is the critical place that potentially manufactures inequities in student mathematics learning. If your collaborative team fails to reach agreement on the use of the rewrite of this mathematical task sample or the rigor of other such tasks during the lessons for each unit, then the learning outcomes for students will vary according to the assigned teacher and his or her task selection—the implementation gap only widens. The same will be true if your collaborative team cannot reach agreement on the nature of a viable student response to the tangent question (since there is no longer one unique right answer).

Consider the sample mathematical task in figure 4.4. It does not assess student manipulation (simplifying) to produce the variant forms of the quadratic expression but rather assesses student understanding of the *purpose of the expressions* used in the various, yet equivalent forms. The low-cognitive-demand task to simplify to an equivalent form is written as a higher-cognitive-demand task to understand the purpose of that equivalent form.

Strategic Competence

Question: A street vendor of T-shirts finds that if the price of a T-shirt is set at $\$p$, the profit from a week's sales is $(p - 6)(900 - 15p)$.

Which form of this expression shows most clearly the maximum profit and the price that gives that maximum?

    A. $(p - 6)(900 - 15p)$

    B. $-15(p - 33)^2 + 10,935$

    C. $-15(p - 6)(p - 60)$

    D. $-15p^2 + 990p - 5,400$

Answer: B. Because $(p - 33)^2$ is a square, it is always positive or zero, and it is only zero when $p = 33$. In the expression for the profit, a negative multiple of this square is added to 10,935. Thus, the maximum profit is $\$10,935$, and the price that gives that profit is $\$33$.

Source: Adapted from McCallum, 2005, pp. 4–5.

Figure 4.4: Sample task to assess student understanding of the *purpose of equivalent forms* of an expression.

The same type of task as presented in figure 4.4 could be asked about the other answer choices as well. Such as what does the "form" in answer C represent in the context of this problem (has a purpose of quickly informing the prices that produce zero profit). Interestingly, this type of strategic competence question is rarely asked as part of an in-class mathematical task with the rich student opportunity for formative feedback from peers or teachers.

As your team debates the use of assessment tasks that measure student understanding, step one is the critical first place where inequities in student mathematics learning are potentially manufactured. If some members of your collaborative teams fail to reach agreement on the use of rich mathematical tasks during the lessons and assessments for each unit, then the learning outcomes for students will vary according to the assigned teacher and his or her task selection, and as a result the learning gap only widens for students. The same will be true if your collaborative teams cannot reach agreement on the nature of viable student responses to such questions and the advancing and assessing questions that help to scaffold the learning target expectations for your students.

The collaborative team has a leadership responsibility to ensure the fair implementation of daily mathematical tasks that teach and assess for student understanding. Equity in mathematics education requires your collaborative teams to design instructional lessons that ensure the use of *common* mathematical tasks designed by your team with sufficient richness to engage students in observable mathematical informal discussions that simultaneously serve as a form of ongoing formative assessment with feedback to you and your students (Kanold et al., 2012).

Once the team understands the expected learning targets for the unit and has identified the Common Core tasks that will be used to develop in-class student understanding of those learning targets for the unit, then the discussion and development of the common assessment instruments to be used is the third critical aspect of step one.

What Are the Identified Common Assessment Instruments?

When collaborative teams create and adapt common assessment instruments together, they enhance the coherence, focus, and fidelity to student learning expectations across the school for all teachers. They also provide the hope of greater readiness and continuity for the mathematics the students will experience the following year. The wide variance in student task performance expectations (an inequity creator) from teacher to teacher is minimized when you work collaboratively with colleagues to design assessment instruments appropriate to the identified learning targets for the unit.

Kay Burke (2010) indicates that common formative assessment instruments "must contribute to productive decision making, and they must be high quality. Most importantly, the rigorous common assessments must improve student learning" (p. 28). Thus, based on the identified learning targets for the unit or chapter of study and agreed-on mathematical task, you must monitor the quality of the common assessment instruments —tests, quizzes, or projects—your team will use during each unit of the course.

How do you decide if the unit-by-unit assessment instruments you use are of high quality? Figure 4.5 provides an evaluation tool that your collaborative team can use to evaluate the quality of current assessment instruments, such as tests and quizzes, as well as build new assessment instruments for the course.

Assessment Indicators	Description of Level 1	Requirements of the Indicator Are Not Present	Limited Requirements of This Indicator Are Present	Substantially Meets the Requirements of the Indicator	Fully Achieves the Requirements of the Indicator	Description of Level 4
Identification and emphasis on learning targets	Learning targets are unclear and absent from the assessment instrument. Too much attention is on one target.	1	2	3	4	Learning targets are clear, included on the assessment, and connected to the assessment questions.
Visual presentation	Assessment instrument is sloppy, disorganized, difficult to read, and offers no room for work.	1	2	3	4	Assessment instrument is neat, organized, easy to read, and well spaced with room for teacher feedback.
Time allotment	Few students can complete the assessment in the time allowed.	1	2	3	4	Test can be successfully completed in time allowed.
Clarity of directions	Directions are missing and unclear.	1	2	3	4	Directions are appropriate and clear.
Clear and appropriate scoring rubrics	The scoring rubric is not evident or appropriate for the assessment tasks.	1	2	3	4	Scoring rubric is clearly stated and appropriate for each task or problem.
Variety of assessment task formats	Assessment contains only one type of questioning strategy and no multiple choice. Calculator usage not clear.	1	2	3	4	Assessment includes a variety of question types and assesses different formats, including calculator usage.
Question phrasing (precision)	Wording is vague or misleading. Vocabulary and precision of language is a struggle for student understanding.	1	2	3	4	Vocabulary is direct, fair, and clearly understood. Students are expected to attend to precision in responses.
Balance of procedural fluency and demonstration of understanding	Test is not rigor balanced. Emphasis is on procedural knowledge and minimal cognitive demand for demonstration of understanding.	1	2	3	4	Test is balanced with product- and process-level questions. Higher-cognitive-demand and understanding tasks are present.

Figure 4.5: Assessment instrument quality—evaluation tool.

Visit **go.solution-tree.com/commoncore** for a reproducible version of this figure.

You and your collaborative team should rate and evaluate the quality of current unit or chapter assessment instruments (such as tests or quizzes) using the evaluation tool in figure 4.5 (page 105). The goal is to write common assessment instruments that would score 4s in all seven categories of the assessment evaluation rubric. As Popham (2011) would say, the goal is to create great surfboards for the students to use. Your collaborative team could also create your own agreed-on "Criteria for Assessment Instrument Quality" using figure 4.5 as a starting point based on your local vision for high-quality assessment.

The value of any collaborative team–driven assessment depends on the extent to which the assessment instrument reflects the learning targets, can be used for a student formative process in the aftermath of the assessment, provides valid evidence of student learning, and results in a positive impact on student *motivation and learning*. It is your responsibility to ensure you implement this vision for the use of high-quality assessment processes.

As you and your team complete these three critical planning tasks from step one, you are ready to teach the unit of instruction over the next twelve to sixteen days (recall the unit calendar from figure 3.5, in chapter 3, page 84), and step two of the teaching-assessing-learning cycle begins. You use formative assessment strategies in class to advance and assess observable and formative student discussions and experiences for the unit's learning targets.

Step Two: Teachers Implement Formative Assessment Classroom Strategies

Step two of the teaching-assessing-learning cycle occurs as part of your team members' daily assessment actions during a mathematics unit of study. You intentionally plan for and implement both formal and informal learning structures and design tasks as outlined in chapters 2 and 3 that will provide ongoing student engagement and descriptive feedback around the elements of the learning targets as well as the CCSS Mathematical Practices.

This step highlights the teams' work to design and present the daily common mathematical tasks (designed in step one) in an engaging and formative learning environment and then use appropriate formative assessment feedback strategies to determine student understanding of the intended learning targets.

According to Wiliam (2011):

> When formative assessment practices are integrated into the minute-to-minute and day-by-day classroom activities of teachers, substantial increases in student achievement—of the order of a 70 to 80% increase in the speed of learning–are possible. . . . Moreover, these changes are not expensive to produce. . . . The currently available evidence suggests that there is nothing else remotely affordable that is likely to have such a large effect. (p. 161)

You and your team should not ignore this wise advice.

As discussed in chapters 2 and 3, in-class formative assessments, particularly at the daily-lesson level, should be framed in such a way as to provide you with meaningful feedback about student understanding. For example, you can tell students, "Take five minutes to describe possible solutions to $x = \sqrt{x}$, and share your conjecture with a partner. Determine all possibilities, and be prepared to explain your reasoning as a team." This paired, timed, and engaged mathematical task provides an opportunity for you as a teacher to tour the room, collect evidence, and provide feedback to students that will advance or assess their thinking and their readiness for the next five minutes of class.

Ginsburg and Dolan (2011) and Wiliam (2011) suggest several "informal" strategies of assessment *for* learning and checks for understanding that can provide you valuable insight into the level of student understanding as a lesson unfolds. Some of these strategies are included in figure 4.6. An additional advantage of these formative assessment strategies is that they increase the level of student engagement, a key characteristic of classroom environments that promote high student achievement (Wiliam, 2011). You can use these strategies as implementation structures or boundary markers for team discussion regarding the use of the Mathematical Practices (student practices) as part of your lesson design.

Strategy One: Key Questioning During Whole-Class Discussion

You use preplanned questions during critical points of the lesson to assess student understanding. "These pivotal adjustment-influencing questions must be carefully conceptualized before the class session in which the discussion will take place. . . . Teachers can't expect to come up with excellent adjustment-influencing questions on the spur of the moment" (Popham, 2008, p. 60). The mathematical task should be designed to promote student demonstration of understanding.

Strategy Two: Mini or Large Whiteboard Responses

Supply every student with a mini or large whiteboard. You ask a preplanned question or provide the students with a critical problem to solve. The students then hold up their responses on whiteboards, and you scan the responses to make a decision concerning the students' mastery levels and needed instructional modifications. Students can also rotate to new groups and use the whiteboard to explain their conjecture or solution to others.

Strategy Three: Traffic Lights or Red and Green Disks

You supply students with colored plastic cups—green, yellow, and red—or a CD-sized disk that is red on one side and green on the other. At critical points during the lesson, ask students to display the color of cup or disk that corresponds to their level of understanding (green means that the student understands, while the red—or yellow—cup indicates the student does not understand and that instructional adjustments are necessary).

Strategy Four: All-Student Response Systems

If you have access to SMART Boards and clicker systems in your classroom, you can design key multiple-choice or open-ended questions that students can work on at critical

---

Figure 4.6: Formative assessment strategies for student action.   continued ›

Visit **go.solution-tree.com/commoncore** for a reproducible version of this figure.

points in the lesson and send their answers to you using the clickers. This displays a real-time public chart indicating the class's response to the question and immediately lets you know the level of the class's understanding or common misconceptions (if the multiple-choice options are keyed to common misconceptions).

Strategy Five: Diagnostic Interview Questions

Ask individual students questions to reflect on, articulate, and uncover how they are thinking while working individually or in small groups of two to four. The key is for you to engage in evaluative listening—listening to assess the student's or the student team's understanding in order to modify instruction and provide feedback.

As an example, recall figure 4.2 (page 101), and consider the CCSS learning target (F-IF.7b): "Graph square root, cube root, and piecewise-defined functions, including step functions and absolute value functions" (NGA & CCSSO, 2010, p. 69; see appendix C, page 177), matched with Mathematical Practice 5, Use appropriate tools strategically. Recall too that this learning target is part of a more general CCSS cluster of learning (F-IF.7): "Graph functions expressed symbolically and show key features of the graph, by hand in simple cases and using technology for more complicated cases" (NGA & CCSSO, 2010, p. 69; see appendix C, page 176). How could the formative assessment strategies from figure 4.6 be used on the following mathematical task in order to meet the expectations of this specific learning standard and its process for learning? Consider the following example.

Use a graphing calculator to solve the following equations or inequalities. Show the graph for each solution.

1. $x = \sqrt{x}$
2. $x < \sqrt{x}$
3. $x > \sqrt{x}$

Your collaborative team would discuss how to build in a formative process for observing evidence of student learning and providing in-class formative feedback to student peers by how you break down the problem into parts. Consider the problem as part of an extended process for strategy five in figure 4.6, as your collaborative team seeks to design mathematics tasks that provide evidence of answers to the following formative assessment feedback questions.

1. How do we expect students will express their ideas, questions, insights, and difficulties?

2. Where and when will and should the most significant conversations be taking place (student to teacher, student to student, teacher to student)?

3. How approachable and encouraging should we be as students explore? Do students use and value each other as reliable and valuable learning resources?

Part of the point of step two is for your collaborative team to discuss these strategies in order to enhance the potential of the common mathematical tasks that are part of your ongoing unit-design work. Figure 4.7 is one example of a possible mathematical task

1. Graph the function $y = \sqrt{x}$ using graph paper and pencil.

    a. Why is the graph of $y = \sqrt{x}$ contained in the first quadrant?

    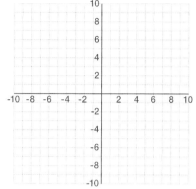

    b. Why is x never negative?

    c. Why is y never negative?

2. Use a graphing calculator tool to solve the following equations and inequalities. Show the graph for each solution.

    a. $x = \sqrt{x}$ b. $x < \sqrt{x}$ c. $x > \sqrt{x}$

3. Describe the potential limits to the graphing calculator solutions in problem 2b.

Figure 4.7: Sample mathematical task.

the entire team could use (and formatively assess student understanding in class) for the learning target (F.IF.7): "Graph functions expressed symbolically and show key features of the graph, by hand in simple cases and using technology for more complicated cases" (NGA & CCSSO, 2010, p. 69; see appendix C, page 176).

Questions one through three in figure 4.7 are designed to check for student understanding of key issues with respect to the functions' domain and range, as well as the strategic use of a calculator tool that, although helpful, could be limiting depending on the "viewing window" used by the students. Under the direction of a skilled teacher, students are able to give and receive formative feedback either from the teacher or their peers that allows them to eventually transfer the visual representation of the solution (for the square root equations and inequalities) to a demonstrated understanding of the nature of those solutions.

By agreeing on the types of mathematical tasks and formative questions to use in class, there will be better in-class teacher adjustments to instruction. Daily demonstrations of student learning in the course will be based on a more coherent *team-based* practice. However, this will not be sufficient. If during the best teacher-designed moments of classroom formative assessment, students fail to *take action* on evidence of continued areas of difficulty (step three), then the teaching-assessing-learning cycle is stopped for the student.

Step Three: Students Take Action on In-Class Formative Assessment Feedback

Do your students learn to take more responsibility for their learning by reflecting long enough on their class work, including various in-class tasks and assessments for learning in order to view mistakes as learning opportunities? This is the goal of step three in the teaching-assessing-learning cycle.

Rick Stiggins et al. (2007), in *Classroom Assessment for Learning: Doing It Right— Using It Well,* state, "Few interventions have the same level of impact as assessment for learning. The most intriguing result is that while all students show achievement gains, the largest gains accrue to the lowest achievers" (p. 37). Thus, you are challenged not only to think and plan beyond the sole use of in-class daily checks for understanding as an accountability measure (assigning points or a grade) but also to think of in-class assessment questions as a way to provide formative learning opportunities and actions for students.

Stiggins et al. (2007) suggest several strategies for student action in figure 4.8. These strategies provide insight into the nature of teacher-designed, but *student-led* formative assessment *actions* that you and your colleagues can use.

Strategy One: Provide a Clear and Understandable Vision of the Learning Target

Share with your students the CCSS content standard cluster, learning targets, and prior-knowledge-understanding expectations in advance of teaching the lesson or unit, giving the assignment, or doing the activity. Provide students with scoring guides written in student-friendly language. More importantly, develop and design scoring criteria and rubrics for problems assigned in class.

Strategy Two: Use Examples and Models of Strong and Weak Work

Use models of strong and weak student work—anonymous student work, work from life beyond school, and your own work. Begin with work that demonstrates strengths and weaknesses related to problems students will commonly experience, especially the problems or tasks that require student demonstrations of understanding. Ask students to discuss with peers the strengths and weaknesses of given solutions or strategies used to obtain a solution to problems posed in class or on a common assessment instrument.

Strategy Three: Offer Regular Descriptive Feedback

Offer descriptive feedback instead of grades on work that is for practice during and after the unit. Descriptive feedback should reflect student strengths and weaknesses with respect to the specific learning targets they are trying to achieve in a given assignment. Feedback is most effective when it is timely and identifies what students are doing right as well as what they need to work on next to act on that feedback.

Strategy Four: Teach Students to Self-Assess and Set Goals

Self-assessment is a necessary part of learning, not an add-on that we do if we have the time or the "right" type of students. Self-assessment includes asking students to do the following:

- Identify their strengths and areas for improvement for specific learning targets throughout the unit

- Offer descriptive feedback to classmates

- Use your feedback, feedback from other students, or their own self-assessment to identify what they need to work on and set goals for future learning and then take action on those goals

Source: Adapted from Stiggins et al., 2007, pp. 42–46.

Figure 4.8: In-class formative assessment strategies for student action.

Visit **go.solution-tree.com/commoncore** for a reproducible version of this figure.

As your team plans mathematics lessons throughout the unit of study, you should discuss the various formative assessment strategies that will ensure students know about their in-class progress. All teachers on your team should design student-led action steps for responding to the formative feedback they receive from you as well as *other students*. As Wiliam (2011) mentions, "Providing effective feedback is very difficult. Get it wrong and the students give up, reject the feedback or choose an easier goal" (p. 119). A key to Wiliam's finding is that feedback functions formatively "only if the information fed back to the learner is used by the learner for improving his or her performance" (p. 120). This gives new meaning and understanding to your responsibility for helping students get "unstuck" in class (without watering down the cognitive demand of the task) while simultaneously helping students to think differently about a problem or its extension as the lesson unfolds.

The strategies listed in figure 4.8 are designed to place much of the in-class feedback response and action onto student ownership. As described in strategy four, self-assessment is a necessary part of learning. Students need to identify their own strengths and areas for improvement (with more teacher guidance and direction in ninth grade versus twelfth grade) and use your teacher feedback, feedback from other students, or their own self-assessment to identify what they need to work on as they set goals for future learning. Assessment then comes to be viewed by the students as something you *do* in order to focus your energy and effort for future work and study. A great time for this type of student reflection is during the closure activities that occur during the class period.

As Wiliam (2007b) indicates, in order to "improve the quality of learning within the system, to be formative, feedback needs to contain an implicit or explicit recipe for future action" (p. 1062). This requires you to think about how daily and weekly feedback from peers or from you as the teacher can be used for student-initiated action and engagement with the feedback.

Thus, students and teachers share the responsibility for successful implementation of the in-class formative assessment practices. Students who can demonstrate *understanding* connect to the learning targets for a unit and can reflect on their individual progress toward that target. Students can establish learning goals and actions they will take in order to reach the targets, and you support students' progress by using immediate and effective feedback not only during the daily classroom conversations but, importantly, as part of the common assessment instrument feedback process used in step four.

Step Four: Students Use Assessment Instruments From Step One for Motivation, Reflection, and Action

The first three steps in the assessment cycle may already be part of your current assessment paradigm if you and your team write common formative assessment tasks and instruments together, design effective formative assessment classroom strategies, and ensure your students take action on the feedback you provide to their classroom performance. However, it is very rare to find high school mathematics teachers or collaborative teams that use common assessment instruments such as quizzes and tests as part of a formative process for learning. It is in this step the old paradigm of testing for grading purposes (an end goal) fades and the new paradigm of using assessment instruments and tools for formative assessment purposes (a means goal) emerges.

Wiliam (2007b) makes the distinction between using assessment instruments for the purposes of (1) monitoring, (2) diagnosing, or (3) formatively assessing. He states:

> An assessment *monitors* learning to the extent it provides information about whether the student, class, school or system is learning or not; it is *diagnostic* to the extent it provides information about what is going wrong, and it is *formative* to the extent it provides information about what to do about it. (p. 1062)

In high school mathematics, the process may look like this. A geometry student studies for and is given an assessment instrument (a test, quiz, or quest—the name is not relevant to the purpose) midway through a unit on the CCSS content standards G-CO.1 and G-CO.9 (page 184, appendix C). Your teacher team has designed a midway assessment instrument tool (quiz) and the scoring rubrics for the tool and decides the assessment tool has a scoring value of 40 points. The student scores 25 out of 40 correct for a score of 62.5 percent. The class score or average is 72 percent. This is the *monitoring* or *grading* assessment function. This function allows the teacher to assign student grades. Furthermore, of the three purposes—monitoring, diagnosing, and formatively assessing —it is the *least useful* for improving and motivating student thinking and achievement toward the identified learning targets for these standards.

As Wiliam (2011) describes:

> [Effective feedback] should cause thinking. It should be focused; it should be related to the learning goals that have been shared with students; and

> it should be more work for the recipient than the donor. Indeed, the whole purpose of feedback should be to increase the extent to which students are owners of their own learning. (p. 132)

At the heart of your feedback to students on such a midunit quiz are some metrics that would allow the assessment instrument to be used beyond the monitoring purpose of assigning a grade. This will require your students to take the time necessary to use the feedback they receive on the assessment instrument to improve their work (Wiliam, 2011). One way to do this is to include exam instrument elements that allow for a diagnostic and then a formative and focused student action.

A collaborative team tool, such as the one in figure 4.9, can be used to help students learn from their assessment and quiz mistakes.

Geometry
Unit 1 Quiz

Name: _____ Reflection date: _____ Period: _____

Chapter 1 student-friendly learning targets:

   *A. I can solve linear and quadratic equations.

   *B. I can identify and demonstrate understanding of points, lines, and planes.

   *C. I can understand when to apply segment addition/bisectors/midpoints rules.

   *D. I can determine the midpoint and distance on the coordinate plane.

    E. I can classify, measure, and construct angles with precision.

    F. I can recognize when to apply angle addition and bisectors rules.

    G. I can identify and demonstrate understanding of special angle pairs.

    H. I can identify, name, and find the perimeters of polygons.

   * Denotes learning targets that were covered on the unit 1 quiz.

Step one: Complete the following table based on your graded quiz.

Problem Number	Learning Target	Correct	Algebra Mistake	Geometry Setup/ Vocabulary Error
1	B	___ /3 pts		
2	B	___ /3 pts		
3	B	___ /4 pts		
4	A	___ /3 pts		
5	A	___ /3 pts		
6	D	___ /3 pts		
7	D	___ /2 pts		

Figure 4.9: Sample geometry student self-assessment goal-setting worksheet.

continued ⟶

Problem Number	Learning Target	Correct	Algebra Mistake	Geometry Setup/ Vocabulary Error
8	D	__ /2 pts		
9	C	__ /5 pts		
10	C	__ /5 pts		
11	C	__ /5 pts		
12	B	__ /2 pts		

Step two: Determine how many points you earned out of the total number of points for each target.

Learning Target A: __ /6	Learning Target B: __ /12
(Questions 4 and 5)	(Questions 1, 2, 3, and 12)
Learning Target C: __ /15	Learning Target D: __ /7
(Questions 9, 10, and 11)	(Questions 6, 7, and 8)

My areas of strength are: _____

My areas of weakness are: _____

To prepare for the unit 1 test, I will (be specific; for example: "I will redo my notes, which cover my areas of weakness; participate in a re-engagement lesson, which cover my areas of weakness; seek help at the learning center; meet with my teacher; and learn the vocabulary"): _____

Visit **go.solution-tree.com/commoncore** for reproducible versions of this figure.

The quiz is scored and returned to the students the next day, not for the primary purpose of a grade (although it does count forty points) but for the express purpose of formative feedback for future action (the unit assessment is in a week or so). Students complete the goal-setting worksheet in figure 4.9 as they identify the problems they completed correctly or incorrectly, type of error that was made, questions that were aligned with each learning target, and learning targets (in this case four of the eight for the unit) that were their weakest or strongest.

By the teacher providing an opportunity to diagnose specific scores by learning target, the student can determine which learning target was the greatest cause for error and the 62.5 percent score. All students use this postassessment goal-setting worksheet to determine future action and as a way to embrace the errors made on the assessment instrument.

As an example, if in the case of the 62.5 percent student response, the student's self-analysis indicates that he or she didn't demonstrate success on learning targets B (*I can identify and demonstrate understanding of points, lines, and planes*) and C (*I can understand when to apply segment addition, bisectors, and midpoints rules*), then it informs the student where to focus re-engagement and learning time.

Thus, a diagnostic assessment is rarely sufficient for the student. Diagnostic assessments do not tell the student what they need to do differently (other than try harder). However, when the student uses specific teacher *or* peer feedback, the assessment result has the potential to be *formative* for the student and improve performance on this essential learning target.

Bennett (2009) notes, "It is an oversimplification to say that formative assessment is only a matter of process or only a matter of instrumentation. Good processes require good instruments and good instruments are useless unless they are used intelligently" (as cited in Wiliam, 2011, p. 40). Your collaborative team will be wise to spend a lot of time designing common unit assessment instruments that can be used intelligently— ensuring all students in a course benefit from both good tests (instruments) and good formative processes that promote student action on the assessment instrument results and feedback. (Visit **go.solution-tree.com/commoncore** for additional samples of student self-assessment feedback and response forms.) However, the assessment cycle is not complete until you and your colleagues work in your collaborative team during the unit of instruction to discuss and decide how to respond to the student assessment evidence you have collected during the unit.

Step Five: Collaborative Teams Use Ongoing Student Assessment Feedback to Improve Instruction

In step five, you and your colleagues use students' assessment results to change your instruction for the next instructional cluster or unit. This allows the test or quiz assessment instruments to become formative for your collaborative team as well. Successes in step five depend on step one—writing and designing common assessment instruments in advance of teaching the next unit of instruction. The collaborative team's assessment has its greatest payoff in this final collaborative step, using the student performance results to make future instructional decisions together.

It will also allow your collaborative team, in hindsight, to evaluate the quality of the assessment questions; indicate improvements for next year; and discuss the quality of the descriptive student feedback, the accuracy of the predetermined student scoring rubrics, and the fidelity of students' grades for the unit. You and your collaborative team can also use the results to identify potential learning targets and assessment questions that may need to be designed for student re-engagement in a learning target mathematical task as part of the next unit of study.

Recall that Wiliam (2011) provides the following definition for formative assessment:

> An assessment functions formatively to the extent that evidence about student achievement is elicited, interpreted, and used by teachers, learners, or their peers to make decisions about the next steps in instruction that are likely to be better, or better founded, than the decisions they would have made in absence of that evidence. (p. 43)

Notice that assessment, then, is in the middle of the PLC assessment cycle, not the end. This is a fundamental shift for high school mathematics teachers. Student learning becomes a *result* of your in-class daily formative assessment work around the mathematical tasks you chose for students, as well as the assessment instruments such as tests and quizzes used by the team, not the other way around. Your team takes future actions that improve teaching, instruction, and learning based on the latest assessment evidence.

Figure 4.10 highlights intentional practices and discussion activities you and your colleagues can use to reflect on performance during and at the end of the unit. Figure 4.10 also highlights questions to guide your lesson-planning and lesson-revision process. As a team, you should reflect on student performance during and at the end of the unit in order to improve instruction for the next unit of learning.

---

1. How much of the lesson and material was approached through student investigation of cognitively demanding tasks or preplanned student questioning (instead of teacher-centered lecture and demonstration)?

   What evidence is there of a climate of mutual respect as students participate in mathematical discussions and provide meaningful feedback and critique the reasoning of other students?

   How will students make and test predictions, conjectures, hypotheses, and estimations with the teacher and with one another?

2. What kinds of in-class formative assessments did the teacher use to reflect on the effectiveness of the lesson?

   What descriptive feedback did the teacher provide to students? How did students show they were engaged in the lesson? Did the lesson design develop student interest and motivation to learn the content? How?

   Did the teacher seek evidence of student understanding?

   Did students have an opportunity to reflect on their learning as it relates to the learning target?

3. Which CCSS Mathematical Practices did the teacher develop for student use in order to learn the mathematics content standards?

   What evidence is there that students were part of a learning community?

   How did students communicate their ideas to one another and the teacher?

   How did the teacher's questions elicit student thinking and other students' respectful critiquing of that reasoning?

   Was there evidence students developed proficiency in the targeted CCSS Mathematical Practice for this unit?

4. What kinds of student-generated questions and conjectures were proposed in the lesson, and what type of student-led tasks were used to assess student understanding and learning?

Source: Adapted from Kanold et al., 2012.

Figure 4.10: Critical lesson-planning questions.

Visit **go.solution-tree.com/commoncore** for a reproducible version of this figure.

By using the critical lesson-planning questions (a formative assessment process for your team) in figure 4.10 as part of your team reflection and feedback, you have a greater chance of gathering data during and after the unit that will inform aspects of the next unit of instruction throughout the year as well as inform practice for a similar unit next year. Working with your collaborative team, you may redesign lessons for improved student re-engagement several times during future units of study, based on the formative feedback collected during these team discussions.

The five-step assessment cycle has a powerful impact on student achievement and learning. More than just becoming a master of teaching content, you also become a master at using varied assessment tasks and tools, especially in-class formative assessment strategies (as identified in step three and figure 4.6, page 107) for students to take greater ownership of their learning.

As the mathematics unit comes to an end, students who have received formative feedback (allowing them to correct errors *before and after* the final unit assessment on the cluster of learning targets) perform at significantly improved rates of learning (Wiliam, 2007b). After a unit's instruction is over, the teacher and the student must reflect on the results of their work and be willing to use the unit assessment instruments to serve a formative feedback purpose. For you, this means a commitment to understanding one of your most *powerful* assessment weapons—using grades as a form of feedback to *motivate* student learning and effort.

Summative Moments in the Formative Feedback Paradigm

For many high school students, traditional mathematics teacher grading practices destroy student motivation and learning. As Alfie Kohn (2011) dryly indicates:

> You know it's ironic: A lot of us [students] are less interested in learning —and therefore won't do as well—precisely because you've made it all about grades. Hey, I guess you can say you've earned our lack of motivation. (p. 28)

Furthermore, Wiliam (2011) notes, "As soon as students get a grade the learning stops" (p. 123). *The student learning stops.*

Think about the last time you handed back a test. Think about the student who achieved the 62.5 percent on the geometry quiz. Did assigning that grade cause (motivate) the student to learn the 37.5 percent of the quiz that was not correct or proficient? This is the old paradigm: the unit or chapter is over—in some cases, more than a week ago or more—by the time the assessment is returned with a grade. The class and the students have already moved on. The student looks at his or her grade and files it away. If it is a D or an F, it is tossed as quickly as possible. A feeling of failure sets in. There is no future action. The next unit has begun anyway.

However, there is hope. In a PLC, you and your collaborative team can overcome the great demotivator of using common assessment tools only to assign grades. That hope lies squarely in you and your team's ability to shift to a new assessment paradigm about grading—grading that serves primarily as a form of effective feedback to students and to enhance the teaching-assessing-learning cycle.

Reeves (2011) establishes this primary purpose of grading as a form of student feedback to improve their performance. Guskey (2000) notes, "In fact, when students are rewarded only with feedback on their [assessment instrument] performance and are not subjected to a grade, their performance is better than when they are graded" (as cited in Reeves, 2011, p. 105). Perhaps the challenge for you and your collaborative team is to determine how long into a semester you could go without assigning any grades to students. Imagine only using your quiz and test instruments as formative tools for student ownership and action on weak learning targets in need of continued attention and learning progress action. Yet the high school world you live in demands grades. However, in a PLC, your collaborative team can choose to structure those grades within certain boundaries that support the use of the assessment instruments (that are graded) primarily as formative tools for learning as described in step four of the cycle.

Thus, your collaborative team discusses whether your *collective* grading practices act as feedback to students in such a way that motivates continued and improved effort and performance. Can your team develop students' mathematical *habits of mind* in which every assessment opportunity is viewed as a formative learning moment?

Think about the current grading practices your collaborative team or your department uses. How do you know whether your current grading practices are effective?

Reeves (2011) provides four boundary markers as a basis to frame and measure your current grading practices. In a PLC culture, grading is viewed as a form of effective feedback to students, based on the following four characteristics.

1. **Grades must be accurate:** Do grades on your tests, quizzes, or projects reflect actual student knowledge and performance on the expected learning targets?

2. **Grades must be specific:** Do grades provide sufficiently specific information to help parents and students identify areas for improvement (formative and not just diagnostic) with student action long before the final summative grade is assigned?

3. **Grades must be timely:** Do grades on tests, quizzes, or projects provide a steady stream of immediate and corrective teacher feedback to students?

4. **Grades must be fair:** Do grades on tests, quizzes, or projects reflect solely on the student's work and not other characteristics of the student? Or some form of student comparison such as assigning grades on a curve, based on other students' performance in the class?

These boundaries on your assessment practices act as part of an effective feedback process and address deeply held, time-honored paradigms about grading. Your team should ensure that all teachers' grading practices reside within these four essential boundaries. Most importantly, any assessment instrument used for determining a student's grade should also provide an opportunity for the student to improve his or her grade.

Grading Feedback Must Be Accurate

Unless your team has made this issue an intentional effort for focus, your grading practices on any graded assessment create a major *inequity*. When assessments are graded in isolation, fidelity to the grading process and indicators for what a grade means are nonexistent.

The intent of accurate feedback on an exam is to give students *information* about their mathematical understanding of the learning targets for the exam. As described in step one (figure 4.1, page 99), you and your collaborative team can ensure greater accuracy to your grading by looking at the expectations for student work (protocols) and the collaborative scoring of the mathematical tasks on the common unit assessments. As you discuss each task, learning targets associated with tasks, and the requirements of each task, your team will identify student successes and misconceptions. These rich conversations also shape your shared content knowledge of the mathematical concepts as you articulate how students should be graded on various concepts and skills.

As a collaborative team, you can improve the *accuracy* of your grading feedback on the team-designed common assessments by using team time to:

1. Establish agreed-on scoring rubrics for all assessment questions

2. Conduct group or team scoring (grading) practice sessions on a sample of student work and responses

3. Discuss and resolve differences of opinion regarding discrepant scores by multiple scoring of student samples by different teachers, checking for agreement on the students' grades (inter-rater reliability), and reaching agreement on the score for the students' grades (calibration of teacher grading)

Reeves (2011) points out that collaborative scoring techniques not only improve accuracy of the initial grades students receive on the assessment but also save time for you as part of a teacher team. As you work with your team, your speed for grading and using the assessment scoring rubrics improves over time.

An important aspect of collaboratively agreeing on scoring for assessments is the level and quality of specific feedback you and your collaborative team are willing to provide. More importantly is what students do with that feedback.

Grading Feedback Must Be Specific

Scoring and grading a lab, project, quiz, or a test has traditionally been a deeply personal and private act. In this new paradigm of using assessment tools such as projects, quizzes, and tests for formative purposes, the type of specific feedback you and your team provide to students as you score the exams must be consistent.

As your collaborative team discusses the nature of specific feedback to students, what should *specific feedback* look like? Traditionally, in high school mathematics classes, feedback is limited to the test's total percent score followed by a letter grade. This feedback is too general and only serves a diagnostic purpose. However, feedback that is process or task oriented and requires the student to respond to the errors (and your feedback about the errors) will increase student achievement over time. This is especially true in vertically connected (students need last year's content knowledge to understand this year's) courses such as mathematics.

Thus, your collaborative team–designed scoring rubric used for each question on the lab, project, quiz, or test assessment instrument is a prime example of specific feedback. Deciding as a team how much each question should be worth and what type of errors will receive partial credit with specific feedback on the error creates consistent feedback across all teachers on the team. Your collaborative team's agreed-on rubrics provide a clear description to students of the criteria needed to achieve a certain level of mastery. When scoring rubrics for various assessment tasks are given to the students before they complete their work, they have a better understanding of how they will be assessed. Using collaboratively designed scoring rubrics decreases the subjectivity of a grade and impacts overall grading accuracy for the course. (Visit www.insidemathematics.org or http://map .mathshell.org/materials/index.php for specific feedback with rubrics.)

Once students know that the grade is more than just a one-shot learning experience, and they can actually learn from the specific feedback you provide to them on the assessment instrument or exam—both the scoring feedback and the written feedback to certain question errors—students are more motivated to learn. However, the positive impact of your feedback is lost when you fail to allow students to rework their errors for an improved grade or fail to allow them to improve a weak learning target area (Canady & Hotchkiss, 1989).

Grading Feedback Must Be Timely

As your collaborative team examines the impact of your grading practices on student learning, you will also need to improve a third characteristic of effective feedback—timeliness. Reeves (2011) indicates that timeliness refers to feedback provided to students with sufficient promptness to influence their future performance. Does that describe the work of every teacher on your team? Grading feedback that is accurate and specific has no benefit if it is provided to students too late to impact their future performance. How do you and your team attend to this critical area of feedback?

Your grading feedback needs to be *immediate.* In the old assessment paradigm, the timeliness of grading feedback was a discretionary task of each teacher on your team. This is not so in the new paradigm. Do not schedule an assessment if you know that the feedback (scoring, grading, and opportunity for students to use the instrument formatively) will not be provided to the students within one or two days. Students are more motivated to prepare for an assessment if they know they will receive feedback either the same or next day (Hattie, 2009). They know to take the assessment seriously because the teacher places a high value on the assessment as a learning instrument as well.

Grading Feedback Must Be Fair

How do you know if your grading practices are fair for every student in the course? First, fair evaluation of a student must be based primarily on academic performance.

Wormelli (2006) states, "Differentiation is doing what is fair for students" (p. 3). By using differentiation strategies to prepare students for the quiz and test assessments, teams are not making the content easier; they are making the content accessible. For your grading feedback to be fair, it would be disingenuous to lower your expectations for standards proficiency because of the gender, ethnicity, or socioeconomic status of students.

As indicated under timely feedback, your team must also be willing to allow student demonstration of performance over time before the summative grade is assigned. To ensure equitable grading of students' understanding and skill level, you need to allow multiple attempts of mastery on the unit learning targets. This is one of the great benefits of the assessment cycle. Wormelli (2006) notes, "It is more reasonable to allow students every opportunity to show their best side, not just one opportunity. . . . We are teaching adults in the making, not adults" (p. 31).

Fairness often surfaces as an issue with student homework (independent practice). Meaningful homework should be purposeful, efficient (for you and the student), personalized for student ownership, connected to the lesson, doable, and inviting (Vatterott, 2010). Most importantly, in the old paradigm of assessment, individual teachers on your team decided the homework assigned to students for a unit of study. In the new paradigm, one of the more important high-leverage activities of the high school collaborative team is to ensure an equitable and fair formative practice (such as homework) experience for all students in the algebra, geometry, mathematics 1 course, and so on as described in chapter 2.

Finally, your team must ask, "Are we using fair components to determine semester grades? How do missing assignments affect a student's overall grade in the course? Are students allowed to turn in homework late, or do they receive a zero? If students are allowed multiple attempts at mastering the learning targets, how do we address the grading of retake assessment instruments? Is it a fair and motivating process for all students?" This leads to the questions your team must ask regarding your overall grading practices. Visit http://allthingsplc.info for help in how to negotiate the difficult team conversations that are part of reaching these critical agreements for all students in the course, not just the ones you teach.

Effective Summative Grading Practices

To clearly establish a relationship between a student's grade and his or her demonstration of mathematical understanding, your collaborative teams should engage in honest conversations about your beliefs related to grading. Figure 4.11 (page 122) provides an activity for you and your team to investigate your potential areas for grading inequity and bias. You can use this activity to search for your own biases and to better understand whether or not your collaborative grading practices motivate or destroy student effort and learning.

By answering the questions in figure 4.11, you and your team will discover a lot about your own built-in biases and issues as they relate to the accuracy, timeliness, specificity,

In your collaborative team, complete the following, and describe your practices during a grading period.

1. List all components used to determine a student's grade in your course, such as tests, quizzes, homework, projects, and so on. Are the components and the percentages assigned to each component the same for every teacher on your team? Do the percentages align with the actual percentage of total points?

2. What is the grading scale your team uses? Is it the same for every member? How does your team address the issue of the "really bad" F, such as a 39 percent that distorts a student's overall grade performance?

3. What position does your team follow for assigning zeros to students? If teachers assign zeros, how does your team address the elimination of those zeros before the summative grade is assigned (the goal is not to assign students a zero—in a PLC, the goal is to motivate every student to do his or her mathematics homework, prepare for tests, complete assignments, and so on)? Do you:

   • Drop one homework grade from the grading period?

   • Drop one quiz or test score per grading period?

   • Allow for student makeup or retesting on weak learning targets?

4. What is your collaborative team's position on makeup work for class? Is your makeup policy fair for students, and do all members apply it equitably? Does your makeup policy encourage and motivate all students to keep trying?

5. How does your collaborative team prepare students for a major unit exam or quiz? Do all team members provide students with the same formative opportunities for preparing for the learning targets?

6. How does your team provide for the immediate and corrective feedback on major quiz and test instruments? Do all students receive results, identify areas of weakness, and then act on those results within two to three days?

7. Does your collaborative team average letter grades or use total points throughout the grading period? Explain your current grading system. How does your team address the inequity caused by total points as part of a summative grade cause (in which it is impossible to offset zeros and one really bad F with enough good grades to accurately represent overall performance)?

8. How does your team provide for the strategic use of technology tools as an aspect of evaluating student performance during the unit?

Source: Adapted from Kanold, 2011b.

Figure 4.11: A collaborative team analysis of grading practices.

Visit **go.solution-tree.com/commoncore** for a reproducible version of this figure.

and fairness of your grades. Furthermore, as question eight indicates, using technology to teach and assess student work accelerates learning. To not use technology in this CCSS era of high school mathematics is a disservice to the technologically motivated and ready students walking into your classroom and to the deep-level learning potential the technology provides.

Technology as an Assessment Tool

NCTM (2008) states, "All necessary resources for optimal learning and personal growth of students and teachers are allocated to students" (p. 1). Technology is one of these tools and has two purposes to ensure equity: (1) technology assists with creating rich instructional experiences for students beyond traditional mathematical tasks, and (2) technology can manage alignment of curriculum, instruction, and assessments for the data analysis necessary for identifying student needs.

Technology provides a powerful instructional tool. The CCSS Mathematical Practices expect students to develop mathematical models and use appropriate tools. Your collaborative team needs to embrace the use of technology as a way to build these Mathematical Practices in students. The question is not whether to use technology. The question is how well you and your team will integrate technology in a way that supports learning for each student. With today's 21st century digital tools, you will need to teach discernment in regard to which tool a student should access. For example, students can view multiple answers for a mathematical problem at many websites (such as www.wolframalpha.com) or through interactive algebra, geometry, or statistics apps. However, students also need to demonstrate how they interpret answers, understand the reasonableness of solutions, and make sense of those solutions and arguments regardless of the technology used to support their thinking.

Stacey and Wiliam (in press) point out that the increasing sophistication and power of technology will support the work of your collaborative team to engage students in tasks in different ways and "ensure that students adhere to constraints imposed on solutions." NCSM (2011) identifies four ways to integrate research-affirmed technology practices with teaching and learning practices:

1. Increase interactivity with content.

2. Make connections between multiple representations of the content standards.

3. Increase student-to-student collaboration.

4. Collect and organize feedback for students and teachers on formative assessments.

To build conceptual knowledge, students need opportunities to interact with mathematics and digital tools that can deliver this type of instruction and feedback to students. Your collaborative team needs to account for the influence of technology in the unit-by-unit teaching and learning of mathematics—including the development of proficiency in Mathematical Practice 6, Using tools strategically. Your collaborative team will need to purposefully plan how to *integrate* specific technologies to reach all students.

When planning a unit of instruction or task, you should identify which technological tool (graphing calculator, web 2.0 tools, interactive games, blogs, adaptive test generators, or so on) will assist in making the mathematics more *meaningful*. Once you identify the tool, teams should articulate the tool's formative purpose and how it will complement the expected student learning. Once agreed, all team members must allow students to benefit from using technology as *part* of the student assessment experience.

Your Focus on Large-Scale Assessment Data

You may feel like many high school mathematics teachers do—far removed from the decision-making realities of large-scale assessments and state assessment data, yet under pressure to respond. Under the curriculum guidelines of the K–12 CCSS expectations, a state assessment system must now provide a coherent and consistent formative system anchored in college- and career-ready expectations. Two state consortia are designing state-level common assessments for the high school standards. These common state assessments will reflect the high school expectations for the Mathematical Practices' content with large-scale assessments that measure beyond the traditional multiple-choice, bubble-in answer sheets. As Achieve (2010) notes, it is the hope and the expectation that these new exams will:

> Improve the quality and types of items included in on-demand tests to create more cognitively-challenging tasks that measure higher-order thinking and analytic skills, such as reasoning and problem solving; [and] move beyond a single, end-of-year test to open the door for performance measures and extended tasks that do a better job of measuring important college- and career-ready skills and model exemplary forms of classroom instruction. (p. 1)

Implementing Common Core mathematics is not likely to alter the scrutiny and pressure you will face as a high school mathematics teacher from large-scale assessments. Both consortia intend to implement their new state-level common assessments for high school during the 2014–2015 school year.

PARCC and SBAC also intend to provide adaptive online tests that will include a mix of constructed-response items, performance-based tasks, and computer-enhanced items that require the application of knowledge and skills. (You should check your state website or visit www.parcconline.org/about-parcc or www.smarterbalanced.org for the latest information about the assessment consortia progress.) It will be imperative that you and your team monitor the PARCC and SBAC assessment progress for interpretation of assessment items that will be used to establish the operational definitions of the standards.

Regardless of the opportunity for the PARCC and SBAC assessments to provide school districts formative assessment information on the state assessment instruments, what will make the most difference in terms of student learning is the shorter cycle, unit-by-unit classroom-based formative assessment described in this chapter. As Wiliam (2007a) writes, "If students have left the classroom before teachers have made adjustments to their teaching on the basis of what they have learned about students' achievement, then they are already playing catch-up" (p. 191).

In many ways, the work of this chapter is very similar to the work of advanced placement (AP) calculus courses and AP teachers across the United States. The AP exam provides formative feedback to the teacher in the longer-term cycle of once per year. However, it is the quality of the weekly, shorter-term assessment processes the teacher or teacher team has in place that allows for student success on the final summative AP test in May. Ultimately, any assessment your team uses can be formative if it is used to make decisions and take future action for improvement on learning target success and improve a student's summative grade. Your collaborative team is empowered to carry out this vision of assessment as an ongoing *cycle of formative learning* throughout the year—for both the students and each team member.

As Tate and Rousseau (2007) indicate in *Engineering Changes in Mathematics Education*, "Students' opportunities to learn mathematics are influenced by the assessment policies of the local district. Assessment policies often influence the nature of pedagogy in the classroom" (p. 1222). The questions every high school teacher must then ask are, "What is the vision of our assessment policies and practices in this department?" and "How will we work together so that assessment can become a motivational student bridge in the assessment cycle for our high school?" Your response will have a major positive impact on student motivation and the level of improved student learning in your course and in your mathematics program.

Chapter 4 Extending My Understanding

1. Using the definition of formative assessment on page 98, describe how your current assessment practices either do or do not meet this standard.

2. High-quality high school assessment practices function to integrate formative assessment processes for adult and student learning by:

    a. Implementing formative assessment classroom strategies and advancing and assessing questions that check for student understanding during the classroom period

    b. Using assessment instruments such as quizzes and tests as tools to support a formative learning process for teachers and students to take action

    How can your high school mathematics department and collaborative team use common classroom assessment instruments, along with other formative assessment information sources collected each day, to advance student learning and support students' active involvement in taking ownership of their own learning?

3. Examine the assessment cycle in figure 4.1 (page 99). For the following five steps, rate your current level of implementation, and explain what your team can do to improve in this assessment practice during the school year. Note there are two different step-one paths.

    ○ **Step one (in-class formative assessment):** How well do we understand and develop *in advance of teaching* the unit of study the student learning targets; the content standard clusters and domains; the common student tasks that will align with those targets; the use of technology to develop understanding of those targets; and the homework that will be assigned?

> **Step one (test instrument formative assessment)**: How well do we identify the agreed-on common assessment instruments, scoring rubrics for those instruments, and grading procedures that will *accurately reflect student achievement* of the learning targets for the unit?

> **Step two**: How well do we use daily classroom assessments that are formative, *build student confidence*, and require student goal setting and reflection on the learning targets they know and don't know?

> **Step three**: How well do we use diagnostic and formative assessment feedback that provides *frequent, descriptive, timely,* and *accurate* feedback for students during the unit—allowing members of our teacher team as well as our students to take action on specific insights regarding our strengths as well as how to improve?

> **Step four**: How well do we, as a team, ask students to *adjust and take action* based on the results of the common assessment instruments (quizzes and tests) used during the unit of study? Do we allow that action to improve their grade?

> **Step five**: How well do we, as a team, *adjust and differentiate our instruction* based on the results of formative assessment evidence as well the common assessment instruments used during the unit of study?

4. As a team, review the four formative assessment strategies listed in figure 4.6, page 107. Discuss how you might implement each of these strategies or how you might adapt them for your students. Also, discuss and share additional in-class formative assessment strategies that work for you.

5. As a team, examine figure 4.11 (page 122). Discuss your current grading practices, and judge those practices on whether or not you believe current practices meet the standards for effective feedback and result in motivating student performance. Discuss how your current team grading practices could improve.

Online Resources

Visit **go.solution-tree.com/commoncore** for links to these online resources.

- **Mathematics Common Core Coalition (www.nctm.org/standards /mathcommoncore)**: This site includes materials and links to information and resources that the organizations of the coalition provide to the public and the education community about the CCSS for mathematics.

- **Mathematics Assessment Project (http://map.mathshell.org.uk/materials)**: The Mathematics Assessment Program (MAP) brings life to the Common Core State Standards in a way that will help teachers and their students turn their aspirations for achieving them into classroom realities. MAP contains exemplar formative lessons, summative assessments, and rich mathematical tasks.

- **Partnership for Assessment of Readiness for College and Careers (www .parcconline.org):** This site provides content frameworks, sample instructional units, sample assessment tasks, professional development assessment modules, and more.

- **SMARTER Balanced Assessment Consortium (www.smarterbalanced.org):** This site provides content frameworks, sample instructional units, sample assessment tasks, professional development modules, and more.

- **Numerical pattering (www.insidemathematics.org/index.php/classroom -video-visits/public-lessons-numerical-patterning):** This resource provides a re-engagement lesson for learners to revisit a problem-solving task.

CHAPTER 5

Implementing Required Response to Intervention

Ultimately there are two kinds of schools: learning enriched schools and learning impoverished schools. I have yet to see a school where the learning curves . . . of the adults were steep upward and those of the students were not. Teachers and students go hand and hand as learners . . . or they don't go at all.

—Roland Barth

As the curriculum is written, the unit learning targets are set, and your assessments are in place, your current instructional processes need to meet the needs of *each* student in the courses you teach. As you read the high school Common Core mathematics for the first time, what went through your mind? Were you thinking about the students in your class, your campus, or part of your district and wondering, "Will they be able to respond positively to the rigor?" Did you reflect on how you would be able to develop the CCSS Mathematical Practices in each student? How will *each* student be able to succeed with rich and rigorous mathematical tasks? Are there different learning opportunities for different groups of students, depending on their mathematics ability or diversity? How can you generate equitable learning experiences so that *each* student is prepared to meet the demands of the Common Core mathematics as described in this book? The key to answering these questions is part of the essential work of your collaborative team. To create an equitable mathematics program, you and your colleagues must ensure current structures for teaching and learning will generate greater access, equity, and opportunity to learn for each student.

What does equity mean? Merriam-Webster defines equity as "justice according to natural law or right; specifically: freedom from bias or favoritism" (Equity, 2011). No matter how hard you are trying, your current instructional practices can be improved so that students' opportunities to learn are fair and impartial. Creating and sustaining a culture of equity is developed through a common effort by all participants of learning, including teachers, administrators, students, and the community (NCTM, 2008). All members are crucial in developing equitable practices that foster appropriate instruction, including support and resources that sustain student learning at every level (NCTM, 2008). It is no coincidence that *equity* is the first principle of the *PRIME Leadership Framework*. The principle makes clear it is the expectation and duty that school leaders "ensure high expectations and access to meaningful mathematics learning for every student" (2008c,

p. 11). In its equity position paper, NCSM (2008a) describes research-informed practices that support the vision of equity. In mathematics education, inequities are created when students do not have the same access and opportunities to learn based on the independent decisions of those serving on your collaborative team.

NCTM (2000), in *Principles and Standards for High School,* define equity in terms of having high expectations and support. With the focus on equity and support, NCTM (2011b) encourages the "use of increasingly intensive and effective instructional interventions for students who struggle in mathematics" (p. 1). When implementing appropriate interventions for each mathematics learner, the position statement goes on to state that you and your colleagues must possess "strong mathematical content knowledge for teaching, pedagogical content knowledge, and a wide range of instructional strategies" (p. 1).

Vision of Equity

The focus of this chapter is to define equity for mathematics teaching and learning and describe your intentional effort and collaborative team response to students who are not meeting the expected standards. This chapter will describe the fundamental paradigm shift for mathematics intervention and the collective response (from you or your collaborative team, school, or district) necessary for student learning in your department and school. In a PLC, collaborative teams ensure students have equitable learning environments that include the instruction, content, assessment, and grading procedures as described in chapters 2 through 4. Collaborative teams will be required to identify student needs and establish support structures to provide equitable access to the rich mathematical tasks needed to develop the conceptual understanding aspects of the CCSS. Collaborative teams demonstrate a vision for equity when they use an articulated plan to monitor student achievement and to ensure the needs of *each* student are being met. Equitable learning opportunities are essential to narrow the current achievement gap.

To pursue equity, you, your team, and mathematics leaders need to break through the social issues and disparities to engage each student in rich mathematics. Collaborative teams should identify the current barriers to student success and find ways to overcome them. It is no longer acceptable to say, "Our kids can't" in your collaborative meeting. Through collaboration, you and your colleagues work toward a common vision holding shared values and beliefs about student learning, ultimately leading toward a school culture that will support academic achievement for all (Alford & Niño, 2011).

Sources That Inform Equity in Mathematics

In spite of years of research, inequities still exist in U.S. high school mathematics classes. Wilkins and the Education Trust Staff (2006) find that less than a third of African American high school students are exposed to college preparatory mathematics classes, and students of color—including African American, Latino, and Native Americans—are twice as likely to be taught by inexperienced teachers. Access to college preparatory mathematics curriculum has traditionally been restricted to a small group of students. The idea of tracking students into lower-level mathematics courses is a traditional response to poor performance. Studies show that students who are placed into remedial courses have instruction that is focused on procedural skills limiting students' ability to learn rigorous, engaging, and meaningful mathematics (Darling-Hammond, 2010). Students historically identified as underperformers should have access to and be exposed to mathematics courses that teach students to think critically and reason about the mathematics and make sense of what they are learning. If students are to have opportunities to be successful beyond high school, college preparatory mathematics can no longer be available to a select few. Whether students pursue postsecondary education or go directly into the workforce, a richer college preparatory mathematics is a necessity (Achieve, 2005).

Doug Reeves's (2003) report on high performance of high-poverty schools dispels the myth that poverty and ethnicity are the only variables related to student learning. Over 90 percent of students met or exceeded academic achievement, determined by local assessments, in spite of 90 percent of the students receiving free and reduced lunch, and 90 percent or more being minority students. These are 90-90-90 schools. The following common themes emerged from these schools.

- Every work aspect of the school was focused on academic achievement.

- There were clear curriculum choices that emphasized the essential ideas of a subject in lieu of teaching every skill standard.

- Students' progress was effectively monitored weekly, and students had multiple opportunities to demonstrate understanding.

- There was a strong emphasis on nonfiction writing.

- Teachers collaboratively graded student work.

Kati Haycock (1998) examines schools that show academic gains for traditionally underperforming students. One study from Boston finds that consistent and excellent teaching in high school mathematics produced academic "gains on average that exceeded the national median (14.6 to 11.0 nationally) whereas the bottom third showed virtually no growth" (p. 8). Haycock's (Peske & Haycock, 2006) review on teacher effectiveness finds that schools with high-poverty or high-minority students were twice as likely to have mathematics teachers who were not mathematics majors. Differences in teacher quality and experience continue to affect student achievement, especially among diverse populations. Student success is predicated on teachers who have content and pedagogical expertise to meet students' learning needs. Using the data, researchers identified qualities associated with high teacher effectiveness, including strong verbal and mathematics skills, a depth of conceptual knowledge of mathematics, and strong pedagogical skills. Not surprisingly then, the more pedagogical content knowledge you possess, the more mathematics your students will learn. Your collaborative team's collective knowledge and the activities in which you and your team engage produce this positive outcome.

How can your collaborative team provide equity for each student? As NCSM (2008c) describes, "A vision for equity begins with understanding your responsibility to seek out and erase biases and inequities that exist in student learning and assessment experiences" (p. 10). When you and your colleagues focus on erasing inequities, students who traditionally underperform can make significant academic gains. Your current planning and classroom practices should be focused on bridging the opportunity gaps for your groups of diverse students. You and your collaborative team need to develop resources and interventions to reach linguistically diverse students. Your collaborative team ensures that high expectations are held for every student, regardless of race, language, socioeconomic status, or current proficiency level.

To ensure students reach the high expectations of the Common Core mathematics, collaborative teams are required to orchestrate strong interventions and support for each student. Interventions cannot be optional. It is a moral imperative for your team to monitor each student's individual progress toward meeting the learning targets of the unit and to require students to actively participate in your team's interventions. This moral imperative prevents your colleagues from opting out of providing students with the interventions your collaborative team has identified. Every teacher of the collaborative team is held accountable to each student of the team.

Reflection is a necessary component of improvement. To move forward and commit to equity improvement, collaborative teams are reflective and purposeful when creating a plan for intervention and support. To meet the demands of CCSS, your team needs to be reflective and plan purposefully to find a balance between holding high standards and finding ways to support struggling students. Complete the equity reflection activity in table 5.1 both individually and as a team, and then use it as a focus for future improvement.

Table 5.1: Equity Reflection Activity

Focus Area	Reflection Questions	Comments
Access	What process is used for mathematics placement into the freshman-level mathematics course?	
	Do students have opportunities to advance through the mathematics matriculation, and how does this get demonstrated or decided?	
	What percentage of students is enrolled in college preparatory mathematics courses?	
Grading	Is every team member's definition of an A, B, C, D, or F the same?	
	Does the team grade the assessments together to ensure equitable grading?	
	What feedback is provided to students?	

Focus Area	Reflection Questions	Comments
Data-Driven Practices	Are data broken down by subpopulations to ensure the needs of each learner are met? Are data reviewed to inform instructional practices? Are data collected on specific interventions and support to track and monitor effectiveness?	
Task Selection	When planning a unit of instruction, do teacher teams develop common artifacts to meet the learning needs of every student? Does the team select or develop rich mathematical tasks for each student to use? Does the team identify essential skills needed for an upcoming unit of instruction?	
Assessments	Does the team use rubrics on formative assessments? Are assessments high quality and representative of the Common Core mathematics? How are students involved in the assessment cycle?	
Interventions and support	Do teachers have time within the school day to collaborate on issues specific to student learning, students with disabilities, or English learners? What interventions are currently being offered? Are students required to attend intervention if deemed not meeting the standards?	

Visit **go.solution-tree.com/commoncore** for a reproducible version of this table.

To ensure learning for each student, teachers and collaborative teams cannot work alone. The reflection tool in table 5.1 is a beneficial tool for creating a schoolwide or district-wide commitment to pursue equity and to create a systematic process that ensures every child receives the additional time and support needed to learn mathematics at high levels. A PLC is committed to high standards of learning for each student, and with this collective responsibility, collaborative teams within the school work together to meet the needs of each student.

Student Learning Needs for Success

Your collaborative team has the responsibility to find out the current level of students' mathematics understanding to ensure each student's learning needs are met. During step two of the teaching-assessing-learning cycle (figure 4.1, page 99), teacher teams will use formative assessments to identify areas in which students need support and then map students' progress on the standards.

The current reality of student knowledge and understanding should be used to inform teaching and learning. Assessment data should not categorize students. Rather, these data can be used to drive instructional practices and inform teaching and learning to create an intentional *response to learning* during steps four and five of the teaching-assessing-learning cycle. It should not be used to place a student into a lower-level mathematics class, thereby perpetuating limited access to higher-level mathematics. Closing the opportunity gap means that students identified with learning gaps must have access to rich mathematics. When teachers are cognizant of where students are mathematically and provide scaffolding and support so students have access to meaningful mathematics, they model responsive teaching. In a PLC, collaborative teams identify students' background knowledge, both mathematical and linguistic, to properly plan and support them (Fisher, Frey, & Rothenberg, 2011). Your team assesses each student's current knowledge in order to develop or select mathematical tasks that include the underlying skills and knowledge needed to access the new content with understanding. Not only can you and your collaborative team use these data for instructional purposes, students can be taught to use the information to engage in self-assessment of their own mathematical knowledge and conceptual understanding, leading to the ability of characterizing their level of progress toward each learning target as described in chapter 4.

As the assessment cycle progresses, you and your collaborative teams, teacher leaders, and administrators capture data that measure student growth on specific course standards. Step five of the cycle describes how assessments can be used to inform teachers and students about students' current mathematical levels of understanding. To truly engage teachers in meeting the needs of each student, collaborative teams should monitor which standards are being met and monitor the progress or growth on each standard for the course using high-quality assessments that reflect the prescribed standards. This scrutiny of monitoring is called *progress monitoring*, which is a repeated measurement of academic performance. Progress monitoring will track current learning, and it is also used to chart students' growth progress to inform instruction of individual students (National Center for Response to Intervention [NCTRI], n.d.). During step two of the assessment cycle, you and your collaborative team should collect multiple points of data to monitor and review students' progress throughout a unit of instruction (before, during, and after). To map individual student growth on each standard, high school collaborative teams can use both formative data as well as data collected from assessment instruments.

Your collaborative team is required to embrace and implement a culture of data-driven practices as a vehicle to effectively monitor students' progress. Most districts are rich with data; however, they are poor in data analysis. As your team collaborates to develop highly engaging assessments to measure students' growth, you need to collectively decide what data will be useful. The checklist in table 5.2 can help you identify specific data to be collected and analyzed to monitor students' progress and discuss *why* a student is struggling (Buffum, Mattos, & Weber, 2012). The closer your work is to the classroom, the more frequently you need to analyze the data. Your collaborative team should review specific data weekly or with each unit of instruction, while school- and district-level teams may review data less frequently, depending on the essential questions in the table.

Table 5.2: High-Quality Data Checklist

Data Type	Essential Questions	What Data Can Answer This Question?	How Are Data Monitored? How Often?
Collaborative Teacher Teams			
Formative Data	What assessment tools are used to determine student learning?		
	Can we identify students (by name and need) who are not proficient?		
	How is feedback provided to students?		
	How are students expected to take action on the feedback?		
	Are rubrics given to students to assist with self-assessment?		
Tasks	What are the common student misconceptions for this learning target?		
	Is this a trend for all or just a specific subpopulation?		
	What are the literacy demands of the student mathematical tasks?		
Intervention	What interventions are provided in the class as well as outside the class?		
	How many students are attending the required intervention?		
	How frequent is the intervention?		
	How is the intervention deemed to be successful for students?		

continued →

Data Type	Essential Questions	What Data Can Answer This Question?	How Are Data Monitored? How Often?
Schoolwide or Districtwide Teams			
Summative Data	What percent of our students are achieving As, Bs, and Cs? What percent of students are receiving Ds and Fs? What percent of students are not proficient on the assessment instruments we use? Are there defined benchmark assessments that are not being met by the students?		
Accessibility	What is the student participation rate in each course by subgroups? What percent of students at each grade level are enrolled in college-readiness courses?		
Attendance	Do varying levels of attendance affect grade-distribution rates? How do you know?		

Visit **go.solution-tree.com/commoncore** for a reproducible version of this table.

In a PLC, your collaborative team will decide what data to analyze to assess students' knowledge. The decisions about data use will be the clear, nondiscretionary, and collaborative teacher actions needed for student success. (Visit www.allthingsplc.info and search the Tools & Resources for more information about specific data and dialogue prompts to ask while reviewing data.)

High school collaborative teams will be required to come together and embrace an intentional plan to support learning for each student. The plan must include (Knight, 2011):

- Research-informed practices for instruction
- High-quality assessments that provide meaningful feedback for action to students and teachers
- Cognitively demanding instructional tasks
- A strong behavioral expectation for teachers and students

Recall that when collaborative teams reflect on the four critical questions of a PLC, the answers drive the work of collaborative teams in PLCs (DuFour et al., 2008). The four questions are:

1. What are the knowledge, skills, and dispositions we want all students to acquire as a result of their experience in our course?

2. How will we know each student has acquired the intended knowledge, skills, and dispositions? What is our process for gathering information on each student's proficiency?

3. How will our team and school respond to students who experience difficulty in acquiring the intended knowledge and skills? How will we provide them with additional time and support for learning in a way that is timely, directive, precise, and systematic?

4. How will our team and school provide additional enrichment for students who are already proficient?

To meet the demands of the CCSS, create equity, and access rich mathematics, collaborative teams must be especially attentive to address and answer these last two questions through their response to intervention response.

The PLC Required Response to Learning

You and your colleagues should be able to provide a clear picture of the teacher collaboration, instructional approach, and mathematical interventions necessary to meet the needs of each learner. High school collaborative teams make certain that increasing access to the rich mathematics of the CCSS will not lead to increased failure (Seeley, 2009). In the pursuit of equity, your goal is to provide access to rich mathematics. You cannot think about raising standards and expectations without identifying appropriate support for students not meeting these standards. The collaborative team's response to the needs of students who are not meeting the standards must be purposefully planned, universal, and communicated. The purpose of intentional responses is to provide clarity for all members—including students, teachers, parents, administrators, and community members—about what is valued, what is assessed, and the progress of each student toward learning the Common Core mathematics content. These intentional responses are nondiscretionary for establishing equity and access.

To create a successful response to learning, you and your collaborative team will embrace the need to pursue equity, be reflective about your current instructional practices, clearly identify students who are not being successful with mathematics, and be able to brainstorm all the potential resources you might use for students who are struggling. Only then are you ready to evaluate the effectiveness of your current interventions (Buffum, Mattos, & Weber, 2009).

RTI is a framework designed to address each learner's needs and support increased student achievement by integrating assessment and intervention strategies within a multi-level system that reduces behavioral problems. According to the National Center for Response to Intervention (n.d.), RTI is a system that "integrates research-based practices, progress monitoring, and required support and is a systematic approach for improved teaching and learning" (p. 4). Buffum, Mattos, and Weber (2010) further state that

RTI's "underlying premise is that schools should not wait until students fall far enough behind to qualify for special education" (p. 10). RTI was part of the reauthorization of the Individuals With Disabilities Education Improvement Act (IDEIA) in 2004, so some schools view RTI as a requirement or as a way to identify students with special needs. RTI is not just about identifying students with special needs. The RTI framework can assist with defining how you pursue equity in your mathematics program. You and your team can utilize this framework to ensure equity and access to the curriculum for each student.

To reach the desired outcomes of CCSS, your students may require additional support and intervention beyond what is typically provided to high school students. Although all public schools are required to have an RTI plan, Johnson, Smith, and Harris (2009) highlight the differences in the purpose of RTI at the elementary and secondary level. At the elementary level, RTI is used to:

- Screen to identify at-risk students
- Provide early interventions to supplement the general curriculum
- Use student interventions as part of disability determination

At the secondary level, the purpose of RTI is focused on:

- Building the capacity of all learners
- Meeting the demands of diverse student populations
- Increasing graduation rate
- Using researched best practices for increased learning

RTI is a model for comprehensive school reform aimed intentionally to increase student achievement. The RTI framework enables all students to be successful in high school, which in turn supports schools as they progress in their continuous improvement plans (Johnson et al., 2009). While there are many forms of RTI, for the purpose of this book, the RTI framework we reference has three tiers.

Tier 1: What Is Your Differentiated Response to Learning?

Tier 1 instruction, research-informed practices designed to meet the needs of each learner, is the core of the RTI model and addresses the expected student outcomes. During this first stage of RTI, supports are provided to every student. Fisher et al. (2011) suggest that "interventions are an element of good teaching" (p. 2), and these interventions begin in the classroom. Therefore, it is imperative you and your collaborative team focus your work on meaningful and rigorous mathematical tasks delivered with high-quality instruction. Tier 1 instruction is the first line of defense for struggling students and can include but is not limited to:

- High-quality, researched-based instructional practices
- Differentiated instruction

- Screening and use of multiple assessment measures to monitor students' progress (Bender & Crane, 2011)

- Guided instruction with scaffolding and modeling that integrates listening, speaking, writing, and reading for ELs

- Language-acquisition intervention that supports learning of both content and language (Fisher et al., 2011)

In Tier 1, your team starts by making sure every student has access to rigorous high school mathematics courses, high-quality instruction, support, and the intervention necessary. Your *differentiated* response to learning will be required to ensure that all students are learning.

Wormelli (2006) states, "Differentiation is doing what is fair for students" (p. 3). *Fair* does not mean having the same learning experience. Differentiation requires teacher teams to make adjustments and do things differently for individual students. Teachers do this regularly without being explicit about what they are differentiating. Some students receive preferential seating to see the board, some students get extended time for tests, and some are challenged to think of other ways to solve a problem because you know they can explore a concept deeper than their classmates or from a different point of view. These are all basic examples of differentiation. Within the RTI framework, differentiation is explicit and is purposefully planned using a compilation of research-informed practices used to maximize student achievement starting with Tier 1. You and your collaborative team use formative assessment data, knowledge of students' prior knowledge, language, and diverse culture to offer students in the same class different teaching and learning opportunities to address their learning needs. By using differentiation strategies, teams are not making the content easier; they are making the content *accessible*. Consider the following sample problem in figure 5.1 related to the algebra domain Reasoning With Equations and Inequalities (see A-REI, page 173, in appendix C).

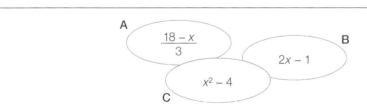

When x is zero, A is greater than both B and C.

- For what other values of x is A the greatest? (Your answer will include that zero value, of course.)

- For what x values is B the greatest? And C?

- Is there a value of x when neither A, B, or C is greater than the other two?

Source: The NRICH Project (http://nrich.math.org), n.d. Used with permission.

Figure 5.1: Sample problem for inequality.

Differentiated instruction is about providing students tools to problem solve and make meaning of mathematics, at whatever learning level they are. Not all students would want to set up inequalities for the task in figure 5.1; some students might set up tables to represent all of the possible solutions, and some might choose to graph the inequalities. Some students would be challenged to solve this with more complex methods. However, you might need to provide the tables up front as a scaffold to support the learning.

Buffum et al. (2012) state, "Prevention is the best intervention" (p. 61). As part of Tier 1 differentiated instruction, you need to assess students' prior knowledge necessary to master the new standard. Using a common formative assessment measuring requisite knowledge during the assessment cycle will help you plan preventative scaffolding and support for students. (Figure 2.8, page 58, provides a section on beginning-of-class routines and asks how the warm-up activity connects to student prior knowledge.)

Your collaborative team needs to find tasks that allow students multiple points of entry and to plan for differentiation. How you and your team address students' misconceptions or challenge students to think deeper about the content is one way to begin planning for differentiation. With your team, reflect on the prompts in table 5.3. Use this tool and the advancing and assessing questions you created in figure 2.8 (page 58) to analyze tasks to ensure your collaborative team is planning for differentiation.

Table 5.3: Tool for Your Differentiated Response to Learning

Questions to Consider	Reflection
What is the learning target for all, for some, or for few? What is the expected level of mastery of the standard?	
Does this task provide opportunities for different student readiness levels?	
Are there multiple ways to make sense of the mathematics for this standard?	
How can the task be adjusted to challenge students more deeply?	
Can the task be adjusted to increase access to students who are still struggling with background or prior knowledge?	

Visit **go.solution-tree.com/commoncore** for a reproducible version of this table.

No matter what scaffolds or supports you provide, students should be able to demonstrate their understanding. How you and your colleagues design and use differentiated practices to create access and equity and provide instruction in Tier 1 will maximize students' learning (Wormelli, 2006). A primary message of Tier 1 is that the responsibility falls on you and your collaborative team to determine various teaching strategies that support improved student proficiency in the learning target for the unit. The descriptions of formative assessment practices (chapters 2 and 3) and the PLC teaching-assessing-learning cycle (figure 4.1, page 99) will be helpful as you and your team explore what is required in Tier 1.

Tier 2: What Is Your Targeted Response to Learning?

Tier 2 interventions are directed more toward specific Common Core mathematics skills or understanding of learning targets and will include academic and behavioral interventions. These interventions are more intensive and intended for students who continue to struggle even after Tier 1 differentiated instruction is shown to be ineffective. Tier 2 interventions are supplemental and not intended for each student. Examples of Tier 2 interventions include (Fisher et al., 2011):

- Increased frequency and duration of interventions

- Small-group instruction

- Additional instructional time outside of the regular mathematics class

- Intensive development of language proficiency to develop content knowledge

To generate a *targeted* response to learning, Tier 2 requires intensive progress monitoring as a means to clearly identify students' learning gaps. Ongoing formative assessment of student progress toward identified learning targets aligned to the unit or chapter enables customized additional support. Step three of the assessment cycle also requires students to take action on feedback and is a tool for engaging students in Tier 2 strategies. Students can reflect on their learning using the formative assessment strategies in figure 4.8 (page 110) and use the self-reflection as a guide to inform teachers what targeted learning gaps need to be addressed.

Additional mathematics support and interventions in Tier 2 should look significantly different from the first learning experience. Think about students who fail a typical algebra or freshman-level course. When they take the course a second time, what is the passing rate of *repeater* courses in your school or district? Is the learning experience significantly different in order to increase the likelihood of improved student achievement? When you and your team reflect on instructional strategies, you will need to determine which instructional strategies are most effective. Students who are in need of Tier 2 interventions do not need more of the same thing (Buffum et al., 2009). The *targeted* intervention—whether it be in an after-school program, a special-assigned support period, or before-school session—needs to provide the student with an opportunity for action on the specific learning target gaps.

Tier 3: What Is Your Intensive Response to Learning?

Tier 3 interventions are intensive in nature as students who need these interventions usually have multiple needs. Tier 3 interventions are greater in intensity, with increasing frequency and duration (Buffum et al., 2009). Interventions at this stage can include, but are not limited to, placement into inclusion classrooms, one-on-one tutoring, or specific learning and behavioral interventions (Johnson et al., 2009). The intensive assistance is in addition to classroom instruction, not in lieu of classroom instruction. Your role in

Tier 3 interventions is to continually monitor each student's progress and increase the amount of time and frequency of interventions. Your *intensive* response to learning should be individualized and based on addressing multiple academic and behavioral needs.

A Major Paradigm Shift in High School Mathematics Intervention Practices

To guarantee equity for each student, interventions at any tier cannot be optional. Students should not be able to elect to participate in targeted or intensive Tier 2 or Tier 3 support. The CCSS require a shift in how you and your colleagues respond to learning, realizing that interventions are no longer optional. This is the fifth fundamental second-order paradigm shift required for each student to demonstrate learning and understanding of the Common Core mathematics, and your collaborative team is pivotal in the intervention plans. In a PLC culture, you and your collaborative teams must implement a *required response to intervention* (R^2TI). At the high school level, interventions cannot be optional. When high school students are struggling, their response to their academic challenges is to retreat from the challenge, become nonparticipants in their learning, passively engage in the classwork, or ultimately drop out of school. Buffum et al. (2009) say, "As adults, we understand the long-term consequences of educational failure far better than our students do. We should never allow them to embark upon that path" (p. 62). To effectively implement the RTI framework, collaborative teams, schools, and districtwide efforts should be focused on how to require interventions at every tier, hence R^2TI.

The lack of coordination of school improvement efforts will often lead to school failure because collaborative teams and schoolwide teams are not working together toward the same goals. When identifying interventions, your collaborative team needs to be intentional about the requirements of R^2TI. According to Johnson et al. (2009), "RTI as a systems framework has the potential to coordinate various programs so that they work in concert with one another to achieve the desired outcomes" (p. 17). For the R^2TI model to impact student achievement, you, your collaborative team, and school administrators should identify required interventions based on data and individual needs (refer to table 5.2, page 135). By requiring interventions at the high school level, school improvement efforts will not be destroyed by dwindling support or misunderstanding of the purpose. Individually or as a team, complete table 5.4 (page 143) to identify the current interventions or strategies implemented to support struggling students and to articulate how all stakeholders monitor the interventions.

As you consider your responses for table 5.4, what percent of students needing intervention are actually attending the support programs? To ensure academic achievement for each learner, support systems and interventions should be required. Students must be *required to participate in interventions.* Opening an extra algebra support class or offering after-school tutoring is good, but not sufficient. If students are to meet the challenges of the CCSS learning targets, you will need to establish systematic interventions as part of the R^2TI plan. Buffum et al. (2012) state, "It is disingenuous for a school to claim that its mission is to ensure that all students learn at high levels, yet allow its students to choose failure" (p. 133).

Table 5.4: School and District Intervention Reflection Questions

What Initiatives Are You Utilizing to Meet the Varying Needs of Students?	Who Is Responsible for the Intervention?	What Is the Current Level of Success of Each Subpopulation Participating in the Intervention?	What Data Are Being Reviewed to Monitor Students' Progress?	Which Students Are Participating in the Collaborative Team's Interventions?

Visit **go.solution-tree.com/commoncore** for a reproducible version of this table.

Not only do high school collaborative teams need to think about the nature of Tier 1 instruction for all students and more intensive interventions at Tier 2 and Tier 3 for selected students, teams need to be intentional and purposeful in student access to the R²TI strategies.

As you, your collaborative teams, and your schoolwide leadership teams determine the appropriate interventions, you should ensure that academic intervention is not a *happenstance* opportunity. Collaborative teams define the learning targets for a given unit or define a level of mastery of the content by a rubric or common evaluation instrument. Your collaborative team's response to each student's learning should address the following questions.

- Is the intervention needed on an individual basis, or does the gap exist in all students or particular subpopulations?
- Do students need differentiated instruction (Tier 1) or targeted interventions (Tier 2)?
- Is the intervention tailored to meet the needs of a specific subpopulation?
- For ELs, what research-based best practices for content literacy are being used?
- For inclusion students, what accommodations or modifications are being implemented to differentiate learning?
- What responsive teaching is needed for all students to be successful?

Tier 1 differentiated instruction for ELs requires creating a gradual release model of instruction (Fisher et al., 2011). Although specific for ELs, the intent of the interventions is about developing prerequisite language and literary skills to effectively support students learning the mathematics detailed in the CCSS. For students who have little or no literacy skills, either in English or their primary language, collaborative teams plan for building student responsibility into the learning experiences. Fisher et al. (2011) suggest several strategies to prepare students for a specific task:

- Tap into prior knowledge.
- Set clear learning targets.

- Explain and model the concept (I do, we do, you do).

- Create a visual representation of the expected learning.

- Focus on building academic language and vocabulary.

- Provide examples and nonexamples.

The skills needed to develop language proficiency—listening, speaking, reading, and writing—are all essential components to developing students' mathematical understanding.

Required Interventions at Work: A Model

Phoenix Union High School District, in Phoenix, Arizona, is an urban district that serves close to 25,000 students. The diverse student population includes 78 percent Hispanic, 10 percent African American, and 6 percent Anglo, Native American, Asian, or two or more races. Eighty-two percent of the student population qualifies for the free and reduced lunch program. While about 5 percent of the students are deemed EL, only 40 percent of students' primary language at home is English. To meet the needs of the diverse populations, a PLC requires that collaborative teams have a laser-like focus on student achievement. The collaborative teams in this school worked together to create student conversations around the reasoning and sense making of mathematics, using student-team cooperative learning structures and creating common artifacts and lesson plans that promoted equitable learning environments.

During the first years of implementation, structures were put in place to identify student needs and assist with academic support. Using seventh-grade Arizona's Instrument to Measure Standards (AIMS) scores, campuses began identifying students as being at-risk prior to entering high school. Rather than tracking students into lower-level mathematics courses, these students were placed in algebra lab classes in addition to their algebra 1 course. In 2004, before implementing these structures, 60 percent of all incoming freshmen were placed into a below-algebra, or prealgebra, course. In 2010, the percent of incoming freshmen placed into this introductory class fell to 13 percent.

Beginning in 2006, the Algebra Team for one high school, Metro Tech, met to discuss the challenges and reality of students' lack of success. In discussing the results, teachers consistently cited a lack of student motivation toward homework completion. The team had offered three different options for tutoring (before school, during lunch, and after school), and only a few students took advantage.

Refusing to give up on their students, the team members brainstormed other strategies. The team members devised a solution that was twofold. First, they examined current homework assignments to ensure they were meaningful and contained focused practice tasks (not just problems from the textbook). Second, they needed to embrace the PLC mantra, "Make it harder to fail than to pass." Students who were not passing the algebra class with a C or better started lunch five minutes earlier and received Tier 2 targeted assistance thirty minutes per day five days a week for the duration of the grading period. Each team member committed to assisting with the lunch tutoring and shared the responsibility. Instead of spending lunch with friends, students received the needed and *required* tutoring to be successful in algebra. Additionally, students from upper-level math classes assisted as peer tutors and worked as part of the teacher team.

Another layer of student support involved daily instructional Tier 1 differentiated instruction. Collaborative team members integrated student self-assessments with assessment *for* learning strategies to increase student engagement in formative assessments (Stiggins, 2007). Learning targets were written to include language objectives to assist with developing academic language proficiency. During the first pilot year, Metro Tech Academic Support Center (MASC) began with about one hundred students daily. By the end of the first month, students needing required tutoring dwindled to about 10 percent of the students in the course.

Through the dedication and commitment of the Algebra Team to use research-informed teaching practices, identify specific students' learning needs, and provide required interventions, the failure rate in the team's course decreased from 22 percent to 14 percent, and students' final-exam passing rate increased from 47 percent to 80 percent. In 2011, Metro Tech out-performed the state in the number of students meeting and exceeding the state standards on AIMS—66 percent compared to 60 percent. Because of the team's systematic approach to address failing students and administrative support of the tutoring intervention, students who once were permitted to fail are finding success in learning mathematics. Table 5.5 provides an excerpt from the algebra team's intervention and planning model.

Table 5.5: Metro Tech's Algebra Intervention and Planning Model Excerpt

Intervention	Tier	What Students Need Intervention?	How Often Do Students Get Support?	How Will Students Receive Intervention?
Academic Support Center	Tier 1	Students who are not passing with a C or better require intervention.	Every lunch Monday through Friday	Students will be walked from their classroom to the tutoring center.
Student Self-Assessment Strategies	Tier 1	All students will use this when completing reviews for unit exams.	For every unit assessment, each student will set goals and identify his or her strengths and weaknesses.	Teams will create student self-assessments during team time, and all teachers will bring samples of student work to discuss after each assessment cycle.

Source: Used with permission from Metro Tech High School.

Phoenix Union's story addresses the need to pursue required interventions with a systematic approach that will respond to the core challenges of learning high school mathematics. As you and your collaborative team make decisions regarding specific support and intervention programs, you will need to know when students have learned the content and what will be done for students who have not been successful. Collaborative teams should discuss what is working instructionally, what is not working, and how utilizing effective instructional strategies is impacting student achievement (see chapter 2 for strategies). To answer the critical questions of a PLC, you will need to focus your intervention efforts continuously through the assessment cycle. Use table 5.6 to begin planning your intentional *response to learning* within each tier. This tool provides reflection questions about your current interventions and identifies opportunities to improve your current R²TI framework. (Refer to table 5.4, page 143, for your current list of interventions.)

Table 5.6: Tier 1, Tier 2, or Tier 3 Diagnostic Tool

	Diagnostic Question	Comments
Student Needs	What Tier 1, Tier 2, or Tier 3 supports are needed for our course?	
	What data are we using to support this claim?	
	How does our team support students from special populations (such as students with special needs or ELs)?	
	What professional development is needed for the members of our team?	
Tier 1: Differentiated Response to Learning	Our team currently implements what type of differentiated instruction?	
	What are the accommodations or modifications currently implemented?	
	Are the teachers on our team identifying language barriers to student learning?	
	What language-proficiency issues need to be addressed?	
Tier 2: Targeted Response to Learning	How will our team increase the intensity of interventions?	
	What is the small-group instruction we need to provide?	
	What is the intensive development of language proficiency needed?	

Tier 3: Intensive Response to Learning	What is the current schedule of intensive support?	
	What is the current frequency of that support?	
	Are there academic and behavioral interventions needed for the students?	
Evidence	How are students placed and required to participate in the intervention?	
Implementation	Who will be responsible for implementing the support?	
	What evidence does the team need to monitor implementation success?	
	What support from administration or other personnel is needed to sustain the required intervention?	
Accountability	What data will be used to determine intervention effectiveness?	

Visit **go.solution-tree.com/commoncore** for a reproducible version of this table.

Once collaborative teams accept the responsibility to meet the needs of each learner, conversations are no longer centered on trivial items that have little or no impact on student achievement. Conversations are about learning experiences, equitable instructional practices, and cognitive-demand tasks that meet the vision of the CCSS for mathematics.

As your team focuses on the nondiscretionary actions of a professional learning community, you will build the capacity of your team members and increase shared knowledge of how best to meet the needs of all students. You and your collaborative team—focused on creating learning environments that develop mathematical capacity by integrating research-informed practices around a R^2TI framework with differentiated, targeted, and intensive response to learning—will meet the needs of your diverse learners.

Your Intentional R²TI for Learning

After your collaborative team plans for student intervention and support, you should communicate the plan for monitoring students within each R^2TI tier. High school mathematics programs struggle severely with managing interventions if they do not specify how students are engaged within each intervention (Johnson et al., 2009). How will students move in and out of specific interventions? You and your collaborative team need to communicate what data are going to be used, specify the interventions that will meet specific academic needs, and identify resources needed to support each intervention. In addition, collaborative teams measure the impact of academic interventions to determine their effectiveness. Table 5.7 is a template to assist with planning for your R²TI model.

Table 5.7: Intervention-Planning Tool

Intervention	Tier	What Students Need Intervention?	How Often Do Students Get Support?	How Will Students Receive Intervention?

Visit **go.solution-tree.com/commoncore** for a reproducible version of this table.

R²TI is the framework for academic support that will meet the demands of the increased rigor of the Common Core mathematics. Collaboratively communicating targeted support is a critical component of the framework. Reflecting on the Phoenix Union story, the collaborative team did not work in isolation from other stakeholders. The team needed campus personnel's assistance to accompany students to the lunch tutoring. Campus administration did its part by vigorously pursuing students who chose to decline or escape the required tutoring. Students who made the poor decision to skip lunch tutoring were escorted from their last class of the day to attend a longer tutoring session after school. The collaborative teacher team anticipated the nuances of the intervention plan and was able to communicate to every stakeholder the requirements needed to make this a successful intervention. Through letters and emails, parents and faculty were made aware of students in need of additional tutoring.

The Phoenix Union story models how multiple levels of teams work collaboratively to problem solve for increased student learning. Kanold (2011a) defines three varying levels of teams needed for continuous school improvement.

1. District-level team for continuous improvement of all districtwide programs

2. A school-level principal or school-site leader-led team for continuous improvement of school-based programs

3. Grade-level or course-based teacher-led teams for continuous improvement of student achievement

Figure 5.2 provides an example of the Phoenix Union High School District R²TI framework that was developed collaboratively through the district and school level. This R²TI framework is shared with administrators, social workers, counselors, mathematics teachers, and community members. Tier 1 *differentiated response to learning* includes instructional strategies for meeting the needs of all learners, support programs, and

Tier 3

- Individualized instruction
- Intervention team support
- Continued tutoring

- Counseling
- Outside sources
- More frequent support

Tier 2

Credit and Concept Recovery
- Summer and evening school
- Web-based concept or credit recovery
- Fluency and Automaticity Through Systematic Teaching With Technology Mathematics (FASTT Math)

Required Tutoring
- Before, after, and during school day
- Saturday

Assessments to Identify Specific Needs
- Arizona English Language Learner Assessment
- Course benchmarks assessments

Accelerated and Enriched Coursework
- AP coursework
- Honors classes
- Gifted

Focused AIMS Support
- Tutoring
- AIMS prep
- Web-based concept recovery
- Mentoring

Inclusion Teachers

Academic Contracts
- Test-taking strategies (small group)

Tier 1

Freshman Summer School

Teachers Plan for Success
- Guiding expectations

Education and Career Action Plans

Forty-five-day new student screening

Tutoring Opportunities
- Before and after school
- Lunch
- College tutors

Mastery Learning
- Multiple opportunities to reassess mastery

Assessment for Learning

Advancement Via Individual Determination Strategies (AVID)

Advisory Periods

Enrichment Seminar

Lab-Support Classes
- Algebra 1–2
- Geometry 1–2
- Algebra 3–4

E² Mathematics
- Cooperative learning
- Technology
- Differentiated instruction
- High student engagement

Progress Monitoring on D²SC

Completion Opportunities
- Saturday school
- Completion lab

Parent Conferences

Source: Used with permission from Phoenix Union High School District.

Figure 5.2: Phoenix Union R²TI support structure.

required progress monitoring. Tier 2 *targeted response to learning* includes support for high-stakes state assessments and English learner assessments, in addition to specific-to-face and web-based concept (learning target) recovery options.

To support R²TI, modeled on the Phoenix Union structure, high school leaders must develop an infrastructure that will effectively monitor and adjust student interventions. With shared leadership and a PLC culture, district high school leaders develop support teams that monitor one specific aspect of R²TI. Whether it is the intervention team, support team, data team, screening team, or assessment team, it is imperative that R²TI is a collaborative effort capitalizing on informative data, identifying tiered interventions necessary to enable each student to learn the CCSS for mathematics. (Visit www.allthingsplc.info for more RTI models.) Figure 5.3 is a template to plan collaborative team–specific tiered interventions.

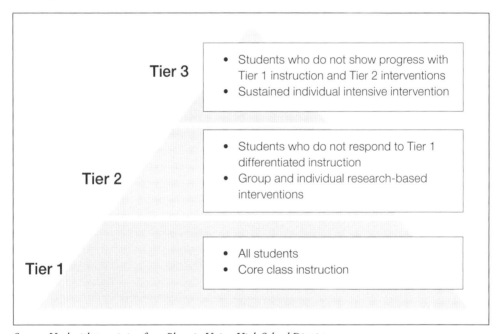

Source: Used with permission from Phoenix Union High School District.

Figure 5.3: Tool to plan for R²TI.

Visit **go.solution-tree.com/commoncore** for a reproducible version of this figure.

Looking Ahead

To create an equitable mathematics program, teachers, leaders, and administrators should ensure that the current processes and R²TI framework create access and equity for each student. The focus of this chapter was to define equity and to design a reflective path and intentional plan through the R²TI framework for establishing equitable access to mathematics learning for each student. Collaborative teams ensure students have equitable learning environments, which includes curriculum, instruction, and assessment, within a supportive R²TI framework. While implementing R²TI, teacher teams must identify student needs and establish support structures to provide student access to the rich mathematical tasks needed to develop the conceptual understanding aspect of the CCSS. Collaborative teams with a vision for equity and a fully developed R^2TI model in place to monitor student achievement will make certain the needs of each student are being met. Your collaborative pursuit of a positive, richly embedded, and *required* RTI system for each student will not be easy. However, it will be so worthwhile as you pursue the social justice and equitable opportunities to ensure high school mathematics learning for every child in your school.

Chapter 5 Extending My Understanding

1. Refer to your reflections in tables 5.1 (page 132) and 5.2 (page 135). What is your current reality of equitable learning experiences? What are your leadership responsibilities needed to pursue equity?

2. Refer to table 5.3 (page 140). What data do you have or what data do you need to effectively monitor students' CCSS learning?

3. Think about the Tier 1 differentiated instruction (page 138). What is your differentiated response to learning? How are you and your collaborative team making content accessible for each student?

4. Thinking back to the mathematical task in figure 5.1 (page 139), you and your collaborative team would need to identify students who did not meet or demonstrate mastery and plan for an appropriate intervention. What would an appropriate *targeted* Tier 2 intervention look like? How would the intervention be significantly different from the first time you used the task or taught the concept?

5. Refer to three varying levels of teams (page 148). What teams do you have at your high school and what level of support is provided for implementing the R^2TI framework? How does the work of each team support the shared vision for equity and access to rich mathematics?

6. As you develop your R^2TI framework, what are your next steps for ensuring it is implemented with fidelity? What are your current strengths? What will be your challenges? What additional support or professional development will be needed to solidify you and your collaborative team's response to learning?

Online Resources

Visit **go.solution-tree.com/commoncore** for links to these resources.

- **RTI Action Network for High School (www.rtinetwork.org/high-school):** The RTI Action Network is dedicated to the effective implementation of RTI in U.S. school districts. This website offers specific high school research, strategies for tiered interventions, and tools for implementation.

- **Classroom-Focused Improvement Process (School Improvement in Maryland, 2010; http://mdk12.org/process/cfip):** The Classroom-Focused Improvement Process is a six-step process for increasing student achievement that teachers plan and carry out during grade-level or cross-level team meetings as a part of their regular lesson-planning cycle.

- **National Center on Response to Intervention (www.rti4success.org):** This site provides a wealth of resources to plan, implement, and screen RTI, including professional development modules that teacher learning teams can use to initiate or improve an RTI program in schools, districts, or states.

- **Mathematics Leadership Resources (www.mathedleadership.org):** The National Council of Supervisors of Mathematics is an organization that assists mathematics educators in interpreting and understanding the CCSS to support the development and implementation of comprehensive, coherent instruction and assessment systems.

- **RTI books and reproducibles (go.solution-tree.com/rti):** This site offers free reproducibles and numerous resources on RTI, including *Simplifying Response to Intervention: Four Essential Guiding Principles* (Buffum et al., 2012).

EPILOGUE

Your Mathematics Professional Development Model

Implementing the Common Core Mathematics Standards for High School presents you with both new challenges and new opportunities. The unprecedented adoption of a common set of mathematics standards by nearly every state provides the opportunity for U.S. educators to press the reset button on mathematics education (Larson, 2011). Collectively, you and your colleagues have the opportunity to rededicate yourselves to ensuring all students are provided with exemplary teaching and learning experiences, and you have access to the supports necessary to guarantee all students the opportunity to develop mathematical proficiency.

The CCSS college and career aspirations and vision for teaching, learning, and assessing students usher in an opportunity for unprecedented implementation of research-informed practices in your school or district's mathematics program. In order to meet the expectations of the five fundamental paradigm shifts described in this book, you will want to assess your current practice and reality as a school against the roadmap to implementation described in figure E.1 (page 154).

Figure E.1 describes the essential paradigm shifts for your collaborative team (chapter 1) focus in the four critical areas of instruction (chapter 2), content (chapter 3), assessment (chapter 4), and intervention (chapter 5) in your mathematics program. As you professionally develop through your interaction and work as members of a collaborative team, your students will not only be better prepared for the Common Core mathematics assessment expectations but also for the college and career readiness that is an expectation for all students K–12—whether your state is part of the CCSS or not. Each sector in figure E.1 describes three vital collaborative team behaviors for that area of change. If you hope to break through any current areas of student stagnation in your mathematics program and achieve greater student success than ever before, then these paradigms provide part of your mindset for never-ending change, growth, and improvement within the reasoning and sense-making focus of the mathematics instruction your students receive in your school.

Working collaboratively in a grade-level team will make the CCSS attainable not only for you but ultimately for your students. Working within a PLC culture is the best vehicle available to support you and your colleagues as you work together to interpret the Common Core State Standards, develop new pedagogical approaches through intensive collaborative planning, engage students in their progress toward meeting the standards, and provide the targeted supports necessary to ensure that all students meet

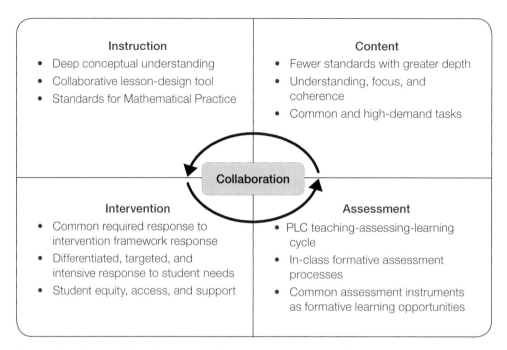

Figure E.1: PLCs at Work implementing Common Core mathematics.

Visit **go.solution-tree.com/commoncore** for a reproducible version of this figure.

mathematical opportunities of the Common Core mathematics. But perhaps most significantly, collaborative learning teams in a PLC can foster an environment in which you work to support one another and develop a culture that is fun for you, your colleagues, and the students in each course you teach. High school mathematics, as described in the Common Core, is intended to be rigorous, engaging, and focused on improved student learning as well as your continuous instructional improvement as an outcome of working together.

APPENDIX A

Changes in Mathematics Standards, 1989–2012

Helping students use their prior knowledge to enable them to recognize what is new and different in their learning is a key element of scaffolded instruction. Similarly, as you explore the CCSS for mathematics, it will be helpful to compare aspects of mathematics standards that have framed your previous instruction so that you can identify what is familiar, what is new and challenging, and what changes are required in the content delivered to your students. As you examine the CCSS for mathematics, you may find it helpful to refer to the standards that have formed the basis of your instruction recently. The release of the CCSS for mathematics comes on the heels of a long history of mathematics research and reform efforts. Consider the following dates.

- **1957**: Launch of *Sputnik* resulted in the "new math" movement, with an emphasis on the abstract nature of mathematical structure, set theory, and number bases

- **1970s**: Back-to-basics movement in which rote memorization was emphasized— the teacher was the dominant figure in instruction with good management skills and a focus on basic skills.

- **1983**: *A Nation at Risk* brought education into the spotlight and included recommendations for three years of high school mathematics. This document was critical of the back-to-basics movement and supported NCTM's 1980 policy statement *An Agenda for Action*.

- **1989**: NCTM publishes *Curriculum and Evaluation Standards for School Mathematics*, emphasizing more problem solving and reasoning of mathematics.

- **1991**: NCTM publishes *Professional Standards for Teaching Mathematics*.

- **1995**: NCTM publishes *Assessment Standards for School Mathematics*.

- **2000**: NCTM publishes *Principles and Standards for School Mathematics* (PSSM) providing a vision for teaching and learning mathematics, including the Process Standards (problem solving, reasoning and proof, communication, representation, and connections).

- **2001**: In *Adding It Up: Helping Children Learn Mathematics*, the National Research Council identifies five strands that comprise mathematical proficiency (adaptive reasoning, strategic competence, conceptual understanding, procedural fluency, and productive disposition).

- **2006, 2009:** NCTM releases *Curriculum Focal Points for Prekindergarten Through Grade 8: A Quest for Coherence* and *Focus on High School Mathematics: Reasoning and Sense Making,* two documents that further develop the conceptual ideas captured in PSSM.

- **2010:** The CCSS for mathematics are released, and forty-five state governments adopt them.

What becomes readily apparent in this brief history is that content standards are not new for you. Research confirms the notion that learning mathematics goes beyond a demonstration of knowledge of the content and must also include the ways in which students reason and make sense of the mathematics they are learning.

The placement of content standards and mathematical processes is an important consideration in any set of standards. The content and process standards within the *Principles and Standards for School Mathematics* (NCTM, 2000) were the same across all the grade-level bands (preK–2, 3–5, 6–8, and 9–12) and are most likely familiar to you.

The Common Core State Standards (NGA & CCSSO, 2010) differ significantly from the *Principles and Standards for School Mathematics* (NCTM, 2000) and *Focus in High School Mathematics: Reasoning and Sense Making* (NCTM, 2009) in the descriptive language used to define the content standards. The CCSS reference their content areas for the high school grades in *conceptual categories* rather than broad *standards.* Within the conceptual categories are *domains* instead of *strands.* Similarly, the conceptual categories in CCSS are unique to the high school level and do not span preK–12. These differences are illustrated in table A.1, which shows content topics defined in the *Principles and Standards for School Mathematics* and the content domains defined in the Common Core State Standards. You can use this table with your collaborative learning team to focus discussion on these questions:

1. How familiar are the terms describing conceptual categories and content domains?

2. How does the depth and coverage of content compare to what you have followed in the past?

3. What are your teacher professional development needs and differences between the *Principles and Standards for School Mathematics* and the Common Core State Standards content?

Table A.1: Mathematics Content—*Principles and Standards for School Mathematics* and the Common Core State Standards

PSSM—Content Topics Grades PreK–12	CCSS—Content Domains Grades K–5	CCSS—Content Domains Grades 6–8	CCSS— Conceptual Categories High School
Number and Operations	Counting and Cardinality (K only)	Ratios and Proportional Relationships (Grades 6–7)	Number and Quantity

PSSM—Content Topics Grades PreK–12	CCSS—Content Domains Grades K–5	CCSS—Content Domains Grades 6–8	CCSS—Conceptual Categories High School
	Number and Operations in Base Ten	The Number System	
	Number and Operations—Fractions (Grades 3–5 only)		
Algebra	Operations and Algebraic Thinking	Expressions and Equations	Algebra
Geometry	Geometry	Geometry	Geometry
Measurement		Functions (Grade 8 only)	Functions
Data Analysis and Probability	Measurement and Data	Statistics and Probability	Statistics and Probability
			Modeling

Visit **go.solution-tree.com/commoncore** for a reproducible version of this table.

In its publication *Making It Happen*, NCTM (2010) makes a similar comparison to the Standards for Mathematical Practices with NCTM's process standards as articulated in *Principles and Standards for School Mathematics* (2000) and the reasoning habits in *Focus in High School Mathematics* (FHSM; 2009). You can use table A.2 with your collaborative team to focus discussion on these questions:

1. To what extent has your team previously addressed student development of these processes or Mathematical Practices?

2. What do you see as the challenges to incorporating student development of the Mathematical Practices?

3. What are your teacher professional development needs and differences between the *Principles and Standards for School Mathematics* process standards and the CCSS Mathematical Practices?

Table A.2: Mathematics Process—*Principles and Standards for School Mathematics* and the Common Core State Standards Mathematical Practices

PSSM—Process Standards	FHSM—Reasoning Habits	CCSS—Mathematical Practices
Problem solving Communication Representation	Analyzing a problem Seeking and using connections Implementing a strategy Reflecting on a solution	**Mathematical Practice 1:** Make sense of problems and persevere in solving them.

continued →

PSSM—Process Standards	FHSM—Reasoning Habits	CCSS—Mathematical Practices
Problem solving Reasoning and proof	Analyzing a problem	**Mathematical Practice 2:** Reason abstractly and quantitatively.
Reasoning and proof Communication Representation	Analyzing a problem Implementing a strategy Reflecting on a solution	**Mathematical Practice 3:** Construct viable arguments and critique the reasoning of others.
Problem solving Reasoning and proof Connections Representations	Analyzing a problem Seeking and using connections Reflecting on a solution	**Mathematical Practice 4:** Model with mathematics.
Problem solving Representation	Analyzing a problem Reflecting on a solution	**Mathematical Practice 5:** Use appropriate tools strategically.
Problem solving Communication	Analyzing a problem Reflecting on a solution	**Mathematical Practice 6:** Attend to precision.
Problem solving Reasoning and proof Connections	Analyzing a problem Implementing a strategy	**Mathematical Practice 7:** Look for and make use of structure.
Problem solving Connections	Analyzing a problem Implementing a strategy	**Mathematical Practice 8:** Look for and express regularity in repeated reasoning.

Visit **go.solution-tree.com/commoncore** for a reproducible version of this table.

In 2010, the U.S. Department of Education awarded $330 million in Race to the Top funds to two consortia, representing the majority of states, to develop assessments aligned with the CCSS. The SMARTER Balanced Assessment Consortium (SBAC), representing more than thirty states, received $160 million, and the Partnership for Assessment of Readiness for College and Careers (PARCC), representing more than twenty-five states, received $176 million. As of this publication, eleven states are members of both consortia (Porter et al., 2011). Both consortia intend to implement their new state-level common assessments for grades 3–8 and high school during the 2014–2015 school year.

Both assessment consortia aim to design *common* state assessments that are consistent with the vision of the CCSS to include items that assess higher-order thinking, reasoning and conceptual understanding, and problem-solving abilities. If the assessments take the form their designers intend, then these new common state assessments will go beyond assessment of low-level procedural skills that typify many current state-administered assessments. Because "students' opportunities to learn mathematics are influenced by the assessment policies of the local district . . . [and influenced by] . . . the nature of pedagogy in the classroom" (Tate & Rousseau, 2007, p. 1222), these new common assessments can serve as a lever to promote desired instructional changes in favor of an emphasis on deep understanding and reasoning.

When discussing the standards over the next few years, collaborative teams will frequently ask, "What does that really mean?" in regard to a standard or content standard cluster. The assessment instruments or tasks you choose to validate a standard will become the operational definition of that standard—it's what you expect students to do based on your understanding of the standard. Monitoring the progress of the two assessment consortia will be an important way for you to anticipate the next steps in providing the necessary focus for and connections to the CCSS content as well as the student behaviors described in the Standards for Mathematical Practice.

APPENDIX B
Standards for Mathematical Practice

Source: NGA & CCSSO, 2010, pp. 6–8. © Copyright 2010. National Governors Association Center for Best Practices and Council of Chief State School Officers. All rights reserved. Used with permission.

The Standards for Mathematical Practice describe varieties of expertise that mathematics educators at all levels should seek to develop in their students. These practices rest on important "processes and proficiencies" with longstanding importance in mathematics education. The first of these are the NCTM process standards of problem solving, reasoning and proof, communication, representation, and connections. The second are the strands of mathematical proficiency specified in the National Research Council's report *Adding It Up:* adaptive reasoning, strategic competence, conceptual understanding (comprehension of mathematical concepts, operations and relations), procedural fluency (skill in carrying out procedures flexibly, accurately, efficiently and appropriately), and productive disposition (habitual inclination to see mathematics as sensible, useful, and worthwhile, coupled with a belief in diligence and one's own efficacy).

1. **Make sense of problems and persevere in solving them.** Mathematically proficient students start by explaining to themselves the meaning of a problem and looking for entry points to its solution. They analyze givens, constraints, relationships, and goals. They make conjectures about the form and meaning of the solution and plan a solution pathway rather than simply jumping into a solution attempt. They consider analogous problems, and try special cases and simpler forms of the original problem in order to gain insight into its solution. They monitor and evaluate their progress and change course if necessary. Older students might, depending on the context of the problem, transform algebraic expressions or change the viewing window on their graphing calculator to get the information they need. Mathematically proficient students can explain correspondences between equations, verbal descriptions, tables, and graphs or draw diagrams of important features and relationships, graph data, and search for regularity or trends. Younger students might rely on using concrete objects or pictures to help conceptualize and solve a problem. Mathematically proficient students check their answers to problems using a different method, and they continually ask themselves, "Does this make sense?" They can understand the approaches of others to solving complex problems and identify correspondences between different approaches.

2. **Reason abstractly and quantitatively.** Mathematically proficient students make sense of quantities and their relationships in problem situations. They bring two complementary abilities to bear on problems involving quantitative relationships: the ability to *decontextualize*—to abstract a given situation and represent it symbolically and manipulate the representing symbols as if they have a life of their own, without necessarily attending to their referents—and the ability to *contextualize*, to pause as needed during

the manipulation process in order to probe into the referents for the symbols involved. Quantitative reasoning entails habits of creating a coherent representation of the problem at hand; considering the units involved; attending to the meaning of quantities, not just how to compute them; and knowing and flexibly using different properties of operations and objects.

3. Construct viable arguments and critique the reasoning of others. Mathematically proficient students understand and use stated assumptions, definitions, and previously established results in constructing arguments. They make conjectures and build a logical progression of statements to explore the truth of their conjectures. They are able to analyze situations by breaking them into cases, and can recognize and use counterexamples. They justify their conclusions, communicate them to others, and respond to the arguments of others. They reason inductively about data, making plausible arguments that take into account the context from which the data arose. Mathematically proficient students are also able to compare the effectiveness of two plausible arguments, distinguish correct logic or reasoning from that which is flawed, and—if there is a flaw in an argument—explain what it is. Elementary students can construct arguments using concrete referents such as objects, drawings, diagrams, and actions. Such arguments can make sense and be correct, even though they are not generalized or made formal until later grades. Later, students learn to determine domains to which an argument applies. Students at all grades can listen or read the arguments of others, decide whether they make sense, and ask useful questions to clarify or improve the arguments.

4. Model with mathematics. Mathematically proficient students can apply the mathematics they know to solve problems arising in everyday life, society, and the workplace. In early grades, this might be as simple as writing an addition equation to describe a situation. In middle grades, a student might apply proportional reasoning to plan a school event or analyze a problem in the community. By high school, a student might use geometry to solve a design problem or use a function to describe how one quantity of interest depends on another. Mathematically proficient students who can apply what they know are comfortable making assumptions and approximations to simplify a complicated situation, realizing that these may need revision later. They are able to identify important quantities in a practical situation and map their relationships using such tools as diagrams, two-way tables, graphs, flowcharts and formulas. They can analyze those relationships mathematically to draw conclusions. They routinely interpret their mathematical results in the context of the situation and reflect on whether the results make sense, possibly improving the model if it has not served its purpose.

5. Use appropriate tools strategically. Mathematically proficient students consider the available tools when solving a mathematical problem. These tools might include pencil and paper, concrete models, a ruler, a protractor, a calculator, a spreadsheet, a computer algebra system, a statistical package, or dynamic geometry software. Proficient students are sufficiently familiar with tools appropriate for their grade or course to make sound decisions about when each of these tools might be helpful, recognizing both the insight to be gained and their limitations. For example, mathematically proficient high school students analyze graphs of functions and solutions generated using a graphing calculator. They detect possible errors by strategically using estimation and other mathematical knowledge. When making mathematical models, they know that technology can enable them to visualize the results of varying assumptions, explore consequences, and compare predictions with data. Mathematically proficient students at various grade levels are able to identify relevant external mathematical resources, such as digital content located on a website, and use them to pose or solve problems. They are able to use technological tools to explore and deepen their understanding of concepts.

6. **Attend to precision.** Mathematically proficient students try to communicate precisely to others. They try to use clear definitions in discussion with others and in their own reasoning. They state the meaning of the symbols they choose, including using the equal sign consistently and appropriately. They are careful about specifying units of measure, and labeling axes to clarify the correspondence with quantities in a problem. They calculate accurately and efficiently, express numerical answers with a degree of precision appropriate for the problem context. In the elementary grades, students give carefully formulated explanations to each other. By the time they reach high school they have learned to examine claims and make explicit use of definitions.

7. **Look for and make use of structure.** Mathematically proficient students look closely to discern a pattern or structure. Young students, for example, might notice that three and seven more is the same amount as seven and three more, or they may sort a collection of shapes according to how many sides the shapes have. Later, students will see 7×8 equals the well remembered $7 \times 5 + 7 \times 3$, in preparation for learning about the distributive property. In the expression $x^2 + 9x + 14$, older students can see the 14 as 2×7 and the 9 as $2 + 7$. They recognize the significance of an existing line in a geometric figure and can use the strategy of drawing an auxiliary line for solving problems. They also can step back for an overview and shift perspective. They can see complicated things, such as some algebraic expressions, as single objects or as being composed of several objects. For example, they can see $5 - 3(x - y)^2$ as 5 minus a positive number times a square and use that to realize that its value cannot be more than 5 for any real numbers x and y.

8. **Look for and express regularity in repeated reasoning.** Mathematically proficient students notice if calculations are repeated, and look both for general methods and for shortcuts. Upper elementary students might notice when dividing 25 by 11 that they are repeating the same calculations over and over again, and conclude they have a repeating decimal. By paying attention to the calculation of slope as they repeatedly check whether points are on the line through (1, 2) with slope 3, middle school students might abstract the equation $(y - 2)/(x - 1) = 3$. Noticing the regularity in the way terms cancel when expanding $(x - 1)(x + 1)$, $(x - 1)(x^2 + x + 1)$, and $(x - 1)(x^3 + x^2 + x + 1)$ might lead them to the general formula for the sum of a geometric series. As they work to solve a problem, mathematically proficient students maintain oversight of the process, while attending to the details. They continually evaluate the reasonableness of their intermediate results.

Connecting the Standards for Mathematical Practice to the Standards for Mathematical Content

The Standards for Mathematical Practice describe ways in which developing student practitioners of the discipline of mathematics increasingly ought to engage with the subject matter as they grow in mathematical maturity and expertise throughout the elementary, middle and high school years. Designers of curricula, assessments, and professional development should all attend to the need to connect the mathematical practices to mathematical content in mathematics instruction.

The Standards for Mathematical Content are a balanced combination of procedure and understanding. Expectations that begin with the word "understand" are often especially good opportunities to connect the practices to the content. Students who lack understanding of a topic may rely on procedures too heavily. Without a flexible base from which to work, they may be less likely to consider analogous problems, represent problems coherently, justify conclusions, apply the mathematics to practical situations, use technology mindfully to work with the mathematics, explain the mathematics accurately to other students, step back for an overview, or deviate from a known procedure to find a shortcut. In short, a lack of understanding effectively prevents a student from engaging in the mathematical practices.

In this respect, those content standards which set an expectation of understanding are potential "points of intersection" between the Standards for Mathematical Content and the Standards for Mathematical Practice. These points of intersection are intended to be weighted toward central and generative concepts in the school mathematics curriculum that most merit the time, resources, innovative energies, and focus necessary to qualitatively improve the curriculum, instruction, assessment, professional development, and student achievement in mathematics.

APPENDIX C

Standards for Mathematical Content, High School

Source: NGA & CCSSO, 2010, pp. 57–83. © Copyright 2010. National Governors Association Center for Best Practices and Council of Chief State School Officers. All rights reserved. Used with permission.

The high school standards specify the mathematics that all students should study in order to be college and career ready. Additional mathematics that students should learn in order to take advanced courses such as calculus, advanced statistics, or discrete mathematics is indicated by (+), as in this example:

> (+) Represent complex numbers on the complex plane in rectangular and polar form (including real and imaginary numbers).

All standards without a (+) symbol should be in the common mathematics curriculum for all college and career ready students. Standards with a (+) symbol may also appear in courses intended for all students. The high school standards are listed in conceptual categories:

- Number and Quantity
- Algebra
- Functions
- Modeling
- Geometry
- Statistics and Probability

Conceptual categories portray a coherent view of high school mathematics; a student's work with functions, for example, crosses a number of traditional course boundaries, potentially up through and including calculus.

Modeling is best interpreted not as a collection of isolated topics but in relation to other standards. Making mathematical models is a Standard for Mathematical Practice, and specific modeling standards appear throughout the high school standards indicated by a star symbol (★). The star symbol sometimes appears on the heading for a group of standards; in that case, it should be understood to apply to all standards in that group.

Mathematics | High School—Number and Quantity

Numbers and Number Systems. During the years from kindergarten to eighth grade, students must repeatedly extend their conception of number. At first, "number" means "counting number": 1, 2, 3 . . . Soon after that, 0 is used to represent "none" and the whole numbers are formed by the counting numbers together with zero. The next extension is fractions. At first, fractions are barely numbers and tied strongly to pictorial representations. Yet by the time students understand division of fractions, they have a strong concept of fractions as numbers and have connected them, via their decimal representations, with the base-ten system used to represent the whole numbers. During middle school, fractions are augmented by negative fractions to form the rational numbers. In Grade 8, students extend this system once more, augmenting the rational numbers with the irrational numbers to form the real numbers. In high school, students will be exposed to yet another extension of number, when the real numbers are augmented by the imaginary numbers to form the complex numbers.

With each extension of number, the meanings of addition, subtraction, multiplication, and division are extended. In each new number system—integers, rational numbers, real numbers, and complex numbers—the four operations stay the same in two important ways: They have the commutative, associative, and distributive properties and their new meanings are consistent with their previous meanings.

Extending the properties of whole-number exponents leads to new and productive notation. For example, properties of whole-number exponents suggest that $(5^{1/3})^3$ should be $5^{(1/3)^3} = 5^1 = 5$ and that $5^{1/3}$ should be the cube root of 5.

Calculators, spreadsheets, and computer algebra systems can provide ways for students to become better acquainted with these new number systems and their notation. They can be used to generate data for numerical experiments, to help understand the workings of matrix, vector, and complex number algebra, and to experiment with non-integer exponents.

Quantities. In real world problems, the answers are usually not numbers but quantities: numbers with units, which involves measurement. In their work in measurement up through Grade 8, students primarily measure commonly used attributes such as length, area, and volume. In high school, students encounter a wider variety of units in modeling, e.g., acceleration, currency conversions, derived quantities such as person-hours and heating degree days, social science rates such as per-capita income, and rates in everyday life such as points scored per game or batting averages. They also encounter novel situations in which they themselves must conceive the attributes of interest. For example, to find a good measure of overall highway safety, they might propose measures such as fatalities per year, fatalities per year per driver, or fatalities per vehicle-mile traveled. Such a conceptual process is sometimes called quantification. Quantification is important for science, as when surface area suddenly "stands out" as an important variable in evaporation. Quantification is also important for companies, which must conceptualize relevant attributes and create or choose suitable measures for them.

Number and Quantity Overview

The Real Number System

- Extend the properties of exponents to rational exponents
- Use properties of rational and irrational numbers.

Quantities

- Reason quantitatively and use units to solve problems

The Complex Number System

- Perform arithmetic operations with complex numbers
- Represent complex numbers and their operations on the complex plane
- Use complex numbers in polynomial identities and equations

Vector and Matrix Quantities

- Represent and model with vector quantities.
- Perform operations on vectors.
- Perform operations on matrices and use matrices in applications.

The Real Number System N-RN

Extend the properties of exponents to rational exponents.

1. Explain how the definition of the meaning of rational exponents follows from extending the properties of integer exponents to those values, allowing for a notation for radicals in terms of rational exponents. *For example, we define $5^{1/3}$ to be the cube root of 5 because we want $(5^{1/3})^3 = 5^{(1/3)3}$ to hold, so $(5^{1/3})^3$ must equal 5.*

2. Rewrite expressions involving radicals and rational exponents using the properties of exponents.

Use properties of rational and irrational numbers.

3. Explain why the sum or product of two rational numbers is rational; that the sum of a rational number and an irrational number is irrational; and that the product of a nonzero rational number and an irrational number is irrational.

Quantities* N-Q

Reason quantitatively and use units to solve problems.

1. Use units as a way to understand problems and to guide the solution of multi-step problems; choose and interpret units consistently in formulas; choose and interpret the scale and the origin in graphs and data displays.

2. Define appropriate quantities for the purpose of descriptive modeling.

3. Choose a level of accuracy appropriate to limitations on measurement when reporting quantities.

The Complex Number System N-CN

Perform arithmetic operations with complex numbers.

1. Know there is a complex number i such that $i^2 = -1$, and every complex number has the form $a + bi$ with a and b real.

2. Use the relation $i^2 = -1$ and the commutative, associative, and distributive properties to add, subtract, and multiply complex numbers.

3. (+) Find the conjugate of a complex number; use conjugates to find moduli and quotients of complex numbers.

Represent complex numbers and their operations on the complex plane.

4. (+) Represent complex numbers on the complex plane in rectangular and polar form (including real and imaginary numbers), and explain why the rectangular and polar forms of a given complex number represent the same number.

5. (+) Represent addition, subtraction, multiplication, and conjugation of complex numbers geometrically on the complex plane; use properties of this representation for computation. *For example, $(-1 + \sqrt{3}\,i)^3 = 8$ because $(-1 +\sqrt{3}\,i)$ has modulus 2 and argument 120°.*

6. (+) Calculate the distance between numbers in the complex plane as the modulus of the difference, and the midpoint of a segment as the average of the numbers at its endpoints.

Use complex numbers in polynomial identities and equations.

7. Solve quadratic equations with real coefficients that have complex solutions.

8. (+) Extend polynomial identities to the complex numbers. *For example, rewrite $x^2 + 4$ as $(x + 2i)(x - 2i)$.*

9. (+) Know the Fundamental Theorem of Algebra; show that it is true for quadratic polynomials.

Vector and Matrix Quantities N-VM

Represent and model with vector quantities.

1. (+) Recognize vector quantities as having both magnitude and direction. Represent vector quantities by directed line segments, and use appropriate symbols for vectors and their magnitudes (e.g., v, $|v|$, $\|v\|$, v).

2. (+) Find the components of a vector by subtracting the coordinates of an initial point from the coordinates of a terminal point.

3. (+) Solve problems involving velocity and other quantities that can be represented by vectors.

Perform operations on vectors.

4. (+) Add and subtract vectors.

    a. Add vectors end-to-end, component-wise, and by the parallelogram rule. Understand that the magnitude of a sum of two vectors is typically not the sum of the magnitudes.

b. Given two vectors in magnitude and direction form, determine the magnitude and direction of their sum.

c. Understand vector subtraction $v - w$ as $v + (-w)$, where $-w$ is the additive inverse of w, with the same magnitude as w and pointing in the opposite direction. Represent vector subtraction graphically by connecting the tips in the appropriate order, and perform vector subtraction component-wise.

5. (+) Multiply a vector by a scalar.

a. Represent scalar multiplication graphically by scaling vectors and possibly reversing their direction; perform scalar multiplication component-wise, e.g., as $c(V_x, V_y) = c(V_x, V_y)$.

b. Compute the magnitude of a scalar multiple cv using $\|cv\| = |c|v$. Compute the direction of cv knowing that when $|c|v \neq 0$, the direction of cv is either along $\mathbf{v}$ (for $c > 0$) or against v (for $c < 0$).

Perform operations on matrices and use matrices in applications.

6. (+) Use matrices to represent and manipulate data, e.g., to represent payoffs or incidence relationships in a network.

7. (+) Multiply matrices by scalars to produce new matrices, e.g., as when all of the payoffs in a game are doubled.

8. (+) Add, subtract, and multiply matrices of appropriate dimensions.

9. (+) Understand that, unlike multiplication of numbers, matrix multiplication for square matrices is not a commutative operation, but still satisfies the associative and distributive properties.

10. (+) Understand that the zero and identity matrices play a role in matrix addition and multiplication similar to the role of 0 and 1 in the real numbers. The determinant of a square matrix is nonzero if and only if the matrix has a multiplicative inverse.

11. (+) Multiply a vector (regarded as a matrix with one column) by a matrix of suitable dimensions to produce another vector. Work with matrices as transformations of vectors.

12. (+) Work with 2×2 matrices as transformations of the plane, and interpret the absolute value of the determinant in terms of area.

Mathematics | High School—Algebra

Expressions. An expression is a record of a computation with numbers, symbols that represent numbers, arithmetic operations, exponentiation, and, at more advanced levels, the operation of evaluating a function. Conventions about the use of parentheses and the order of operations assure that each expression is unambiguous. Creating an expression that describes a computation involving a general quantity requires the ability to express the computation in general terms, abstracting from specific instances.

Reading an expression with comprehension involves analysis of its underlying structure. This may suggest a different but equivalent way of writing the expression that exhibits some different aspect of its meaning. For example, $p + 0.05p$ can be interpreted as the addition of a 5% tax to a price p. Rewriting $p + 0.05p$ as $1.05p$ shows that adding a tax is the same as multiplying the price by a constant factor.

Algebraic manipulations are governed by the properties of operations and exponents, and the conventions of algebraic notation. At times, an expression is the result of applying operations to simpler expressions. For example, $p + 0.05p$ is the sum of the simpler expressions p and $0.05p$. Viewing an expression as the result of operation on simpler expressions can sometimes clarify its underlying structure.

A spreadsheet or a computer algebra system (CAS) can be used to experiment with algebraic expressions, perform complicated algebraic manipulations, and understand how algebraic manipulations behave.

Equations and inequalities. An equation is a statement of equality between two expressions, often viewed as a question asking for which values of the variables the expressions on either side are in fact equal. These values are the solutions to the equation. An identity, in contrast, is true for all values of the variables; identities are often developed by rewriting an expression in an equivalent form.

The solutions of an equation in one variable form a set of numbers; the solutions of an equation in two variables form a set of ordered pairs of numbers, which can be plotted in the coordinate plane. Two or more equations and/or inequalities form a system. A solution for such a system must satisfy every equation and inequality in the system.

An equation can often be solved by successively deducing from it one or more simpler equations. For example, one can add the same constant to both sides without changing the solutions, but squaring both sides might lead to extraneous solutions. Strategic competence in solving includes looking ahead for productive manipulations and anticipating the nature and number of solutions.

Some equations have no solutions in a given number system, but have a solution in a larger system. For example, the solution of $x + 1 = 0$ is an integer, not a whole number; the solution of $2x + 1 = 0$ is a rational number, not an integer; the solutions of $x^2 - 2 = 0$ are real numbers, not rational numbers; and the solutions of $x^2 + 2 = 0$ are complex numbers, not real numbers.

The same solution techniques used to solve equations can be used to rearrange formulas. For example, the formula for the area of a trapezoid, $A = ((b_1 + b_2)/2)h$, can be solved for h using the same deductive process.

Inequalities can be solved by reasoning about the properties of inequality. Many, but not all, of the properties of equality continue to hold for inequalities and can be useful in solving them.

Connections to Functions and Modeling. Expressions can define functions, and equivalent expressions define the same function. Asking when two functions have the same value for the same input leads to an equation; graphing the two functions allows for finding approximate solutions of the equation. Converting a verbal description to an equation, inequality, or system of these is an essential skill in modeling.

Algebra Overview

Seeing Structure in Expressions

- Interpret the structure of expressions
- Write expressions in equivalent forms to solve problems

Arithmetic with Polynomials and Rational Expressions

- Perform arithmetic operations on polynomials
- Understand the relationship between zeros and factors of polynomials
- Use polynomial identities to solve problems
- Rewrite rational expressions

Creating Equations

- Create equations that describe numbers or relationships

Reasoning with Equations and Inequalities

- Understand solving equations as a process of reasoning and explain the reasoning
- Solve equations and inequalities in one variable
- Solve systems of equations
- Represent and solve equations and inequalities graphically

Seeing Structure in Expressions A-SSE

Interpret the structure of expressions

1. Interpret expressions that represent a quantity in terms of its context.★

   a. Interpret parts of an expression, such as terms, factors, and coefficients.

   b. Interpret complicated expressions by viewing one or more of their parts as a single entity. *For example, interpret $P(1+r)^n$ as the product of P and a factor not depending on P.*

2. Use the structure of an expression to identify ways to rewrite it. *For example, see $x^4 - y^4$ as $(x^2)^2 - (y^2)^2$, thus recognizing it as a difference of squares that can be factored as $(x^2 - y^2)(x^2 + y^2)$.*

Write expressions in equivalent forms to solve problems

3. Choose and produce an equivalent form of an expression to reveal and explain properties of the quantity represented by the expression.★

   a. Factor a quadratic expression to reveal the zeros of the function it defines.

   b. Complete the square in a quadratic expression to reveal the maximum or minimum value of the function it defines.

   c. Use the properties of exponents to transform expressions for exponential functions. *For example the expression* 1.15^t *can be rewritten as* $(1.15^{1/12})^{12t}$ $\approx 1.012^{12t}$ *to reveal the approximate equivalent monthly interest rate if the annual rate is 15%.*

4. Derive the formula for the sum of a finite geometric series (when the common ratio is not 1), and use the formula to solve problems. *For example, calculate mortgage payments.*★

Arithmetic with Polynomials and Rational Expressions A-APR

Perform arithmetic operations on polynomials

1. Understand that polynomials form a system analogous to the integers, namely, they are closed under the operations of addition, subtraction, and multiplication; add, subtract, and multiply polynomials.

Understand the relationship between zeros and factors of polynomials

2. Know and apply the Remainder Theorem: For a polynomial $p(x)$ and a number a, the remainder on division by $x - a$ is $p(a)$, so $p(a) = 0$ if and only if $(x - a)$ is a factor of $p(x)$.

3. Identify zeros of polynomials when suitable factorizations are available, and use the zeros to construct a rough graph of the function defined by the polynomial.

Use polynomial identities to solve problems

4. Prove polynomial identities and use them to describe numerical relationships. *For example, the polynomial identity* $(x^2 + y^2)^2 = (x^2 - y^2)^2 + (2xy)^2$ *can be used to generate Pythagorean triples.*

5. (+) Know and apply the Binomial Theorem for the expansion of $(x + y)_n$ in powers of x and y for a positive integer n, where x and y are any numbers, with coefficients determined for example by Pascal's Triangle.

Rewrite rational expressions

6. Rewrite simple rational expressions in different forms; write $a(x)/b(x)$ in the form $q(x) + r(x)/b(x)$, where $a(x)$, $b(x)$, $q(x)$, and $r(x)$ are polynomials with the degree of $r(x)$ less than the degree of $b(x)$, using inspection, long division, or, for the more complicated examples, a computer algebra system.

7. (+) Understand that rational expressions form a system analogous to the rational numbers, closed under addition, subtraction, multiplication, and division by a nonzero rational expression; add, subtract, multiply, and divide rational expressions.

Creating Equations★ A-CED

Create equations that describe numbers or relationships

1. Create equations and inequalities in one variable and use them to solve problems. *Include equations arising from linear and quadratic functions, and simple rational and exponential functions.*

2. Create equations in two or more variables to represent relationships between quantities; graph equations on coordinate axes with labels and scales.

3. Represent constraints by equations or inequalities, and by systems of equations and/or inequalities, and interpret solutions as viable or nonviable options in a modeling context. *For example, represent inequalities describing nutritional and cost constraints on combinations of different foods.*

4. Rearrange formulas to highlight a quantity of interest, using the same reasoning as in solving equations. *For example, rearrange Ohm's law V = IR to highlight resistance R.*

Reasoning with Equations and Inequalities A-REI

Understand solving equations as a process of reasoning and explain the reasoning

1. Explain each step in solving a simple equation as following from the equality of numbers asserted at the previous step, starting from the assumption that the original equation has a solution. Construct a viable argument to justify a solution method.

2. Solve simple rational and radical equations in one variable, and give examples showing how extraneous solutions may arise.

Solve equations and inequalities in one variable

3. Solve linear equations and inequalities in one variable, including equations with coefficients represented by letters.

4. Solve quadratic equations in one variable.

    a. Use the method of completing the square to transform any quadratic equation in x into an equation of the form $(x - p)^2 = q$ that has the same solutions. Derive the quadratic formula from this form.

    b. Solve quadratic equations by inspection (e.g., for $x^2 = 49$), taking square roots, completing the square, the quadratic formula and factoring, as appropriate to the initial form of the equation. Recognize when the quadratic formula gives complex solutions and write them as a ± *bi* for real numbers *a* and *b*.

Solve systems of equations

5. Prove that, given a system of two equations in two variables, replacing one equation by the sum of that equation and a multiple of the other produces a system with the same solutions.

6. Solve systems of linear equations exactly and approximately (e.g., with graphs), focusing on pairs of linear equations in two variables.

7. Solve a simple system consisting of a linear equation and a quadratic equation in two variables algebraically and graphically. *For example, find the points of intersection between the line $y = -3x$ and the circle $x^2 + y^2 = 3$.*

8. (+) Represent a system of linear equations as a single matrix equation in a vector variable.

9. (+) Find the inverse of a matrix if it exists and use it to solve systems of linear equations (using technology for matrices of dimension 3×3 or greater).

Represent and solve equations and inequalities graphically

10. Understand that the graph of an equation in two variables is the set of all its solutions plotted in the coordinate plane, often forming a curve (which could be a line).

11. Explain why the *x*-coordinates of the points where the graphs of the equations $y = f(x)$ and $y = g(x)$ intersect are the solutions of the equation $f(x) = g(x)$; find the solutions approximately, e.g., using technology to graph the functions, make tables of values, or find successive approximations. Include cases where $f(x)$ and/or $g(x)$ are linear, polynomial, rational, absolute value, exponential, and logarithmic functions.★

12. Graph the solutions to a linear inequality in two variables as a half-plane (excluding the boundary in the case of a strict inequality), and graph the solution set to a system of linear inequalities in two variables as the intersection of the corresponding half-planes.

Mathematics | High School—Functions

Functions describe situations where one quantity determines another. For example, the return on $10,000 invested at an annualized percentage rate of 4.25% is a function of the length of time the money is invested. Because we continually make theories about dependencies between quantities in nature and society, functions are important tools in the construction of mathematical models.

In school mathematics, functions usually have numerical inputs and outputs and are often defined by an algebraic expression. For example, the time in hours it takes for a car to drive 100 miles is a function of the car's speed in miles per hour, v; the rule $T(v)$ = 100/v expresses this relationship algebraically and defines a function whose name is T.

The set of inputs to a function is called its domain. We often infer the domain to be all inputs for which the expression defining a function has a value, or for which the function makes sense in a given context.

A function can be described in various ways, such as by a graph (e.g., the trace of a seismograph); by a verbal rule, as in, "I'll give you a state, you give me the capital city;" by an algebraic expression like $f(x) = a + bx$; or by a recursive rule. The graph of a function is often a useful way of visualizing the relationship of the function models, and manipulating a mathematical expression for a function can throw light on the function's properties.

Functions presented as expressions can model many important phenomena. Two important families of functions characterized by laws of growth are linear functions, which grow at a constant rate, and exponential functions, which grow at a constant percent rate. Linear functions with a constant term of zero describe proportional relationships.

A graphing utility or a computer algebra system can be used to experiment with properties of these functions and their graphs and to build computational models of functions, including recursively defined functions.

Connections to Expressions, Equations, Modeling, and Coordinates.

Determining an output value for a particular input involves evaluating an expression; finding inputs that yield a given output involves solving an equation. Questions about when two functions have the same value for the same input lead to equations, whose solutions can be visualized from the intersection of their graphs. Because functions describe relationships between quantities, they are frequently used in modeling. Sometimes functions are defined by a recursive process, which can be displayed effectively using a spreadsheet or other technology.

Functions Overview

Interpreting Functions

- Understand the concept of a function and use function notation
- Interpret functions that arise in applications in terms of the context
- Analyze functions using different representations

Building Functions

- Build a function that models a relationship between two quantities
- Build new functions from existing functions

Linear, Quadratic, and Exponential Models

- Construct and compare linear, quadratic, and exponential models and solve problems

- Interpret expressions for functions in terms of the situation they model

Trigonometric Functions

- Extend the domain of trigonometric functions using the unit circle

- Model periodic phenomena with trigonometric functions

- Prove and apply trigonometric identities

Interpreting Functions F-IF

Understand the concept of a function and use function notation

1. Understand that a function from one set (called the domain) to another set (called the range) assigns to each element of the domain exactly one element of the range. If f is a function and x is an element of its domain, then $f(x)$ denotes the output of f corresponding to the input x. The graph of i is the graph of the equation $y = f(x)$.

2. Use function notation, evaluate functions for inputs in their domains, and interpret statements that use function notation in terms of a context.

3. Recognize that sequences are functions, sometimes defined recursively, whose domain is a subset of the integers. *For example, the Fibonacci sequence is defined recursively by f(0) = f(1) = 1, f(n + 1) = f(n) + f(n – 1) for n ≥ 1.*

Interpret functions that arise in applications in terms of the context

4. For a function that models a relationship between two quantities, interpret key features of graphs and tables in terms of the quantities, and sketch graphs showing key features given a verbal description of the relationship. *Key features include: intercepts; intervals where the function is increasing, decreasing, positive, or negative; relative maximums and minimums; symmetries; end behavior; and periodicity.*★

5. Relate the domain of a function to its graph and, where applicable, to the quantitative relationship it describes. *For example, if the function h(n) gives the number of person-hours it takes to assemble n engines in a factory, then the positive integers would be an appropriate domain for the function.*★

6. Calculate and interpret the average rate of change of a function (presented symbolically or as a table) over a specified interval. Estimate the rate of change from a graph.★

Analyze functions using different representations

7. Graph functions expressed symbolically and show key features of the graph, by hand in simple cases and using technology for more complicated cases.★

    a. Graph linear and quadratic functions and show intercepts, maxima, and minima.

   b. Graph square root, cube root, and piecewise-defined functions, including step functions and absolute value functions.

   c. Graph polynomial functions, identifying zeros when suitable factorizations are available, and showing end behavior.

   d. (+) Graph rational functions, identifying zeros and asymptotes when suitable factorizations are available, and showing end behavior.

   e. Graph exponential and logarithmic functions, showing intercepts and end behavior, and trigonometric functions, showing period, midline, and amplitude.

8. Write a function defined by an expression in different but equivalent forms to reveal and explain different properties of the function.

   a. Use the process of factoring and completing the square in a quadratic function to show zeros, extreme values, and symmetry of the graph, and interpret these in terms of a context.

   b. Use the properties of exponents to interpret expressions for exponential functions. *For example, identify percent rate of change in functions such as $y = (1.02)^t$, $y = (0.97)^t$, $y = (1.01)^{12t}$, $y = (1.2)^{t/10}$, and classify them as representing exponential growth or decay.*

9. Compare properties of two functions each represented in a different way (algebraically, graphically, numerically in tables, or by verbal descriptions). *For example, given a graph of one quadratic function and an algebraic expression for another, say which has the larger maximum.*

Building Functions F-BF

Build a function that models a relationship between two quantities

1. Write a function that describes a relationship between two quantities.★

   a. Determine an explicit expression, a recursive process, or steps for calculation from a context.

   b. Combine standard function types using arithmetic operations. *For example, build a function that models the temperature of a cooling body by adding a constant function to a decaying exponential, and relate these functions to the model.*

   c. (+) Compose functions. *For example, if T(y) is the temperature in the atmosphere as a function of height, and h(t) is the height of a weather balloon as a function of time, then T(h(t)) is the temperature at the location of the weather balloon as a function of time.*

2. Write arithmetic and geometric sequences both recursively and with an explicit formula, use them to model situations, and translate between the two forms.★

Build new functions from existing functions

3. Identify the effect on the graph of replacing $f(x)$ by $f(x) + k$, $k\,f(x)$, $f(kx)$, and $f(x + k)$ for specific values of k (both positive and negative); find the value of k given the graphs. Experiment with cases and illustrate an explanation of the effects on the graph using technology. *Include recognizing even and odd functions from their graphs and algebraic expressions for them.*

4. Find inverse functions.

    a. Solve an equation of the form f(x) = c for a simple function f that has an inverse and write an expression for the inverse. *For example, f(x) = 2 x³ or f(x) = (x + 1)/(x – 1) for x ≠ 1.*

    b. (+) Verify by composition that one function is the inverse of another.

    c. (+) Read values of an inverse function from a graph or a table, given that the function has an inverse.

    d. (+) Produce an invertible function from a non-invertible function by restricting the domain.

5. (+) Understand the inverse relationship between exponents and logarithms and use this relationship to solve problems involving logarithms and exponents.

Linear, Quadratic, and Exponential Models∗ F-LE

Construct and compare linear, quadratic, and exponential models and solve problems

1. Distinguish between situations that can be modeled with linear functions and with exponential functions.

    a. Prove that linear functions grow by equal differences over equal intervals, and that exponential functions grow by equal factors over equal intervals.

    b. Recognize situations in which one quantity changes at a constant rate per unit interval relative to another.

    c. Recognize situations in which a quantity grows or decays by a constant percent rate per unit interval relative to another.

2. Construct linear and exponential functions, including arithmetic and geometric sequences, given a graph, a description of a relationship, or two input-output pairs (include reading these from a table).

3. Observe using graphs and tables that a quantity increasing exponentially eventually exceeds a quantity increasing linearly, quadratically, or (more generally) as a polynomial function.

4. For exponential models, express as a logarithm the solution to $ab^{ct} = d$ where a, c, and d are numbers and the base b is 2, 10, or e; evaluate the logarithm using technology.

Interpret expressions for functions in terms of the situation they model

5. Interpret the parameters in a linear or exponential function in terms of a context.

Trigonometric Functions F-TF

Extend the domain of trigonometric functions using the unit circle

1. Understand radian measure of an angle as the length of the arc on the unit circle subtended by the angle.

2. Explain how the unit circle in the coordinate plane enables the extension of trigonometric functions to all real numbers, interpreted as radian measures of angles traversed counterclockwise around the unit circle.

3. (+) Use special triangles to determine geometrically the values of sine, cosine, tangent for $\pi/3$, $\pi/4$ and $\pi/6$, and use the unit circle to express the values of sine, cosine, and tangent for $\pi - x$, $\pi + x$, and $2\pi - x$ in terms of their values for x, where x is any real number.

4. (+) Use the unit circle to explain symmetry (odd and even) and periodicity of trigonometric functions.

Model periodic phenomena with trigonometric functions

5. Choose trigonometric functions to model periodic phenomena with specified amplitude, frequency, and midline.★

6. (+) Understand that restricting a trigonometric function to a domain on which it is always increasing or always decreasing allows its inverse to be constructed.

7. (+) Use inverse functions to solve trigonometric equations that arise in modeling contexts; evaluate the solutions using technology, and interpret them in terms of the context.★

Prove and apply trigonometric identities

8. Prove the Pythagorean identity $\sin^2(\theta) + \cos^2(\theta) = 1$ and use it to find $\sin(\theta)$, $\cos(\theta)$, or $\tan(\theta)$ given $\sin(\theta)$, $\cos(\theta)$, or $\tan(\theta)$ and the quadrant of the angle.

9. (+) Prove the addition and subtraction formulas for sine, cosine, and tangent and use them to solve problems.

Mathematics | High School—Modeling

Modeling links classroom mathematics and statistics to everyday life, work, and decision-making. Modeling is the process of choosing and using appropriate mathematics and statistics to analyze empirical situations, to understand them better, and to improve decisions. Quantities and their relationships in physical, economic, public policy, social, and everyday situations can be modeled using mathematical and statistical methods.

When making mathematical models, technology is valuable for varying assumptions, exploring consequences, and comparing predictions with data.

A model can be very simple, such as writing total cost as a product of unit price and number bought, or using a geometric shape to describe a physical object like a coin. Even such simple models involve making choices. It is up to us whether to model a coin as a three-dimensional cylinder, or whether a two-dimensional disk works well enough for our purposes. Other situations—modeling a delivery route, a production schedule, or a comparison of loan amortizations—need more elaborate models that use other tools from the mathematical sciences. Real-world situations are not organized and labeled for analysis; formulating tractable models, representing such models, and analyzing them is appropriately a creative process. Like every such process, this depends on acquired expertise as well as creativity.

Some examples of such situations might include:

- Estimating how much water and food is needed for emergency relief in a devastated city of 3 million people, and how it might be distributed.

- Planning a table tennis tournament for 7 players at a club with 4 tables, where each player plays against each other player.

- Designing the layout of the stalls in a school fair so as to raise as much money as possible.

- Analyzing stopping distance for a car.

- Modeling savings account balance, bacterial colony growth, or investment growth.

- Engaging in critical path analysis, e.g., applied to turnaround of an aircraft at an airport.

- Analyzing risk in situations such as extreme sports, pandemics, and terrorism.

- Relating population statistics to individual predictions.

In situations like these, the models devised depend on a number of factors: How precise an answer do we want or need? What aspects of the situation do we most need to understand, control, or optimize? What resources of time and tools do we have? The range of models that we can create and analyze is also constrained by the limitations of our mathematical, statistical, and technical skills, and our ability to recognize significant variables and relationships among them. Diagrams of various kinds, spreadsheets and other technology, and algebra are powerful tools for understanding and solving problems drawn from different types of real-world situations.

One of the insights provided by mathematical modeling is that essentially the same mathematical or statistical structure can sometimes model seemingly different situations. Models can also shed light on the mathematical structures themselves, for example, as when a model of bacterial growth makes more vivid the explosive growth of the exponential function.

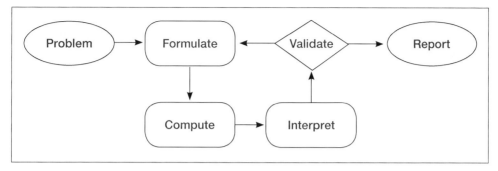

The basic modeling cycle is summarized in the diagram. It involves (1) identifying variables in the situation and selecting those that represent essential features, (2) formulating a model by creating and selecting geometric, graphical, tabular, algebraic, or statistical representations that describe relationships between the variables, (3) analyzing and performing operations on these relationships to draw conclusions, (4) interpreting the results of the mathematics in terms of the original situation, (5) validating the conclusions by comparing them with the situation, and then either improving the model or, if it is acceptable, (6) reporting on the conclusions and the reasoning behind them. Choices, assumptions, and approximations are present throughout this cycle.

In descriptive modeling, a model simply describes the phenomena or summarizes them in a compact form. Graphs of observations are a familiar descriptive model— for example, graphs of global temperature and atmospheric CO_2 over time.

Analytic modeling seeks to explain data on the basis of deeper theoretical ideas, albeit with parameters that are empirically based; for example, exponential growth of bacterial colonies (until cut-off mechanisms such as pollution or starvation intervene) follows from a constant reproduction rate. Functions are an important tool for analyzing such problems.

Graphing utilities, spreadsheets, computer algebra systems, and dynamic geometry software are powerful tools that can be used to model purely mathematical phenomena (e.g., the behavior of polynomials) as well as physical phenomena.

Modeling Standards *Modeling is best interpreted not as a collection of isolated topics but rather in relation to other standards. Making mathematical models is a Standard for Mathematical Practice, and specific modeling standards appear throughout the high school standards indicated by a star symbol (★).*

Mathematics | High School—Geometry

An understanding of the attributes and relationships of geometric objects can be applied in diverse contexts—interpreting a schematic drawing, estimating the amount of wood needed to frame a sloping roof, rendering computer graphics, or designing a sewing pattern for the most efficient use of material.

Although there are many types of geometry, school mathematics is devoted primarily to plane Euclidean geometry, studied both synthetically (without coordinates) and analytically (with coordinates). Euclidean geometry is characterized most importantly by the Parallel Postulate, that through a point not on a given line there is exactly one parallel line. (Spherical geometry, in contrast, has no parallel lines.)

During high school, students begin to formalize their geometry experiences from elementary and middle school, using more precise definitions and developing careful proofs. Later in college some students develop Euclidean and other geometries carefully from a small set of axioms.

The concepts of congruence, similarity, and symmetry can be understood from the perspective of geometric transformation. Fundamental are the rigid motions: translations, rotations, reflections, and combinations of these, all of which are here assumed to preserve distance and angles (and therefore shapes generally). Reflections and rotations each explain a particular type of symmetry, and the symmetries of an object offer insight into its attributes—as when the reflective symmetry of an isosceles triangle assures that its base angles are congruent.

In the approach taken here, two geometric figures are defined to be congruent if there is a sequence of rigid motions that carries one onto the other. This is the principle of superposition. For triangles, congruence means the equality of all corresponding pairs of sides and all corresponding pairs of angles. During the middle grades, through experiences drawing triangles from given conditions, students notice ways to specify enough measures in a triangle to ensure that all triangles drawn with those measures are congruent. Once these triangle congruence criteria (ASA, SAS, and SSS) are established using rigid motions, they can be used to prove theorems about triangles, quadrilaterals, and other geometric figures.

Similarity transformations (rigid motions followed by dilations) define similarity in the same way that rigid motions define congruence, thereby formalizing the similarity ideas of "same shape" and "scale factor" developed in the middle grades. These transformations lead to the criterion for triangle similarity that two pairs of corresponding angles are congruent.

The definitions of sine, cosine, and tangent for acute angles are founded on right triangles and similarity, and, with the Pythagorean Theorem, are fundamental in many real-world and theoretical situations. The Pythagorean Theorem is generalized to non-right triangles by the Law of Cosines. Together, the Laws of Sines and Cosines embody the triangle congruence criteria for the cases where three pieces of information suffice to completely solve a triangle. Furthermore, these laws yield two possible solutions in the ambiguous case, illustrating that Side-Side-Angle is not a congruence criterion.

Analytic geometry connects algebra and geometry, resulting in powerful methods of analysis and problem solving. Just as the number line associates numbers with locations in one dimension, a pair of perpendicular axes associates pairs of numbers with locations in two dimensions. This correspondence between numerical coordinates and geometric points allows methods from algebra to be applied to geometry and vice versa.

The solution set of an equation becomes a geometric curve, making visualization a tool for doing and understanding algebra. Geometric shapes can be described by equations, making algebraic manipulation into a tool for geometric understanding, modeling, and proof. Geometric transformations of the graphs of equations correspond to algebraic changes in their equations.

Dynamic geometry environments provide students with experimental and modeling tools that allow them to investigate geometric phenomena in much the same way as computer algebra systems allow them to experiment with algebraic phenomena.

Connections to Equations. The correspondence between numerical coordinates and geometric points allows methods from algebra to be applied to geometry and vice versa. The solution set of an equation becomes a geometric curve, making visualization a tool for doing and understanding algebra. Geometric shapes can be described by equations, making algebraic manipulation into a tool for geometric understanding, modeling, and proof.

Geometry Overview

Congruence

- Experiment with transformations in the plane
- Understand congruence in terms of rigid motions
- Prove geometric theorems
- Make geometric constructions

Similarity, Right Triangles, and Trigonometry

- Understand similarity in terms of similarity transformations
- Prove theorems involving similarity
- Define trigonometric ratios and solve problems involving right triangles
- Apply trigonometry to general triangles

Circles

- Understand and apply theorems about circles
- Find arc lengths and areas of sectors of circles

Expressing Geometric Properties with Equations

- Translate between the geometric description and the equation for a conic section
- Use coordinates to prove simple geometric theorems algebraically

Geometric Measurement and Dimension

- Explain volume formulas and use them to solve problems
- Visualize relationships between two-dimensional and three-dimensional objects

Modeling with Geometry

- Apply geometric concepts in modeling situations

Congruence G-CO

Experiment with transformations in the plane

1. Know precise definitions of angle, circle, perpendicular line, parallel line, and line segment, based on the undefined notions of point, line, distance along a line, and distance around a circular arc.

2. Represent transformations in the plane using, e.g., transparencies and geometry software; describe transformations as functions that take points in the plane as inputs and give other points as outputs. Compare transformations that preserve distance and angle to those that do not (e.g., translation versus horizontal stretch).

3. Given a rectangle, parallelogram, trapezoid, or regular polygon, describe the rotations and reflections that carry it onto itself.

4. Develop definitions of rotations, reflections, and translations in terms of angles, circles, perpendicular lines, parallel lines, and line segments.

5. Given a geometric figure and a rotation, reflection, or translation, draw the transformed figure using, e.g., graph paper, tracing paper, or geometry software. Specify a sequence of transformations that will carry a given figure onto another.

Understand congruence in terms of rigid motions

6. Use geometric descriptions of rigid motions to transform figures and to predict the effect of a given rigid motion on a given figure; given two figures, use the definition of congruence in terms of rigid motions to decide if they are congruent.

7. Use the definition of congruence in terms of rigid motions to show that two triangles are congruent if and only if corresponding pairs of sides and corresponding pairs of angles are congruent.

8. Explain how the criteria for triangle congruence (ASA, SAS, and SSS) follow from the definition of congruence in terms of rigid motions.

Prove geometric theorems

9. Prove theorems about lines and angles. *Theorems include: vertical angles are congruent; when a transversal crosses parallel lines, alternate interior angles are congruent and corresponding angles are congruent; points on a perpendicular bisector of a line segment are exactly those equidistant from the segment's endpoints.*

10. Prove theorems about triangles. *Theorems include: measures of interior angles of a triangle sum to 180°; base angles of isosceles triangles are congruent; the segment joining midpoints of two sides of a triangle is parallel to the third side and half the length; the medians of a triangle meet at a point.*

11. Prove theorems about parallelograms. *Theorems include: opposite sides are congruent, opposite angles are congruent, the diagonals of a parallelogram bisect each other, and conversely, rectangles are parallelograms with congruent diagonals.*

Make geometric constructions

12. Make formal geometric constructions with a variety of tools and methods (compass and straightedge, string, reflective devices, paper folding, dynamic geometric software, etc.). *Copying a segment; copying an angle; bisecting a segment; bisecting an angle; constructing perpendicular lines, including the perpendicular bisector of a line segment; and constructing a line parallel to a given line through a point not on the line.*

13. Construct an equilateral triangle, a square, and a regular hexagon inscribed in a circle.

Similarity, Right Triangles, and Trigonometry G-SRT

Understand similarity in terms of similarity transformations

1. Verify experimentally the properties of dilations given by a center and a scale factor:

   a. A dilation takes a line not passing through the center of the dilation to a parallel line, and leaves a line passing through the center unchanged.

   b. The dilation of a line segment is longer or shorter in the ratio given by the scale factor.

2. Given two figures, use the definition of similarity in terms of similarity transformations to decide if they are similar; explain using similarity transformations the meaning of similarity for triangles as the equality of all corresponding pairs of angles and the proportionality of all corresponding pairs of sides.

3. Use the properties of similarity transformations to establish the AA criterion for two triangles to be similar.

Prove theorems involving similarity

4. Prove theorems about triangles. *Theorems include: a line parallel to one side of a triangle divides the other two proportionally, and conversely; the Pythagorean Theorem proved using triangle similarity.*

5. Use congruence and similarity criteria for triangles to solve problems and to prove relationships in geometric figures.

Define trigonometric ratios and solve problems involving right triangles

6. Understand that by similarity, side ratios in right triangles are properties of the angles in the triangle, leading to definitions of trigonometric ratios for acute angles.

7. Explain and use the relationship between the sine and cosine of complementary angles.

8. Use trigonometric ratios and the Pythagorean Theorem to solve right triangles in applied problems.★

Apply trigonometry to general triangles

9. (+) Derive the formula $A = 1/2\ ab\ \sin(C)$ for the area of a triangle by drawing an auxiliary line from a vertex perpendicular to the opposite side.

10. (+) Prove the Laws of Sines and Cosines and use them to solve problems.

11. (+) Understand and apply the Law of Sines and the Law of Cosines to find unknown measurements in right and non-right triangles (e.g., surveying problems, resultant forces).

Circles G-C

Understand and apply theorems about circles

1. Prove that all circles are similar.

2. Identify and describe relationships among inscribed angles, radii, and chords. *Include the relationship between central, inscribed, and circumscribed angles; inscribed angles on a diameter are right angles; the radius of a circle is perpendicular to the tangent where the radius intersects the circle.*

3. Construct the inscribed and circumscribed circles of a triangle, and prove properties of angles for a quadrilateral inscribed in a circle.

4. (+) Construct a tangent line from a point outside a given circle to the circle.

Find arc lengths and areas of sectors of circles

5. Derive using similarity the fact that the length of the arc intercepted by an angle is proportional to the radius, and define the radian measure of the angle as the constant of proportionality; derive the formula for the area of a sector.

Expressing Geometric Properties with Equations G-GPE

Translate between the geometric description and the equation for a conic section

1. Derive the equation of a circle of given center and radius using the Pythagorean Theorem; complete the square to find the center and radius of a circle given by an equation.

2. Derive the equation of a parabola given a focus and directrix.

3. (+) Derive the equations of ellipses and hyperbolas given the foci, using the fact that the sum or difference of distances from the foci is constant.

Use coordinates to prove simple geometric theorems algebraically

4. Use coordinates to prove simple geometric theorems algebraically. *For example, prove or disprove that a figure defined by four given points in the coordinate plane is a rectangle; prove or disprove that the point $(1,\ \sqrt{3})$ lies on the circle centered at the origin and containing the point $(0, 2)$.*

5. Prove the slope criteria for parallel and perpendicular lines and use them to solve geometric problems (e.g., find the equation of a line parallel or perpendicular to a given line that passes through a given point).

6. Find the point on a directed line segment between two given points that partitions the segment in a given ratio.

7. Use coordinates to compute perimeters of polygons and areas of triangles and rectangles, e.g., using the distance formula.★

Geometric Measurement and Dimension G-GMD

Explain volume formulas and use them to solve problems

1. Give an informal argument for the formulas for the circumference of a circle, area of a circle, volume of a cylinder, pyramid, and cone. *Use dissection arguments, Cavalieri's principle, and informal limit arguments.*

2. (+) Give an informal argument using Cavalieri's principle for the formulas for the volume of a sphere and other solid figures.

3. Use volume formulas for cylinders, pyramids, cones, and spheres to solve problems.★

Visualize relationships between two-dimensional and three-dimensional objects

4. Identify the shapes of two-dimensional cross-sections of three-dimensional objects, and identify three-dimensional objects generated by rotations of two-dimensional objects.

Modeling with Geometry G-MG

Apply geometric concepts in modeling situations

1. Use geometric shapes, their measures, and their properties to describe objects (e.g., modeling a tree trunk or a human torso as a cylinder).★

2. Apply concepts of density based on area and volume in modeling situations (e.g., persons per square mile, BTUs per cubic foot).★

3. Apply geometric methods to solve design problems (e.g., designing an object or structure to satisfy physical constraints or minimize cost; working with typographic grid systems based on ratios).★

Mathematics | High School—Statistics and Probability★

Decisions or predictions are often based on data—numbers in context. These decisions or predictions would be easy if the data always sent a clear message, but the message is often obscured by variability. Statistics provides tools for describing variability in data and for making informed decisions that take it into account.

Data are gathered, displayed, summarized, examined, and interpreted to discover patterns and deviations from patterns. Quantitative data can be described in terms of key characteristics: measures of shape, center, and spread. The shape of a data distribution might be described as symmetric, skewed, flat, or bell shaped, and it might be summarized by a statistic measuring center (such as mean or median) and a statistic measuring spread (such as standard deviation or interquartile range). Different distributions can be compared numerically using these statistics or compared visually using plots. Knowledge of center and spread are not enough to describe a distribution. Which statistics to compare, which plots to use, and what the results of a comparison might mean, depend on the question to be investigated and the real-life actions to be taken.

Randomization has two important uses in drawing statistical conclusions. First, collecting data from a random sample of a population makes it possible to draw valid conclusions about the whole population, taking variability into account. Second, randomly assigning individuals to different treatments allows a fair comparison of the effectiveness of those treatments. A statistically significant outcome is one that is unlikely to be due to chance alone, and this can be evaluated only under the condition of randomness. The conditions under which data are collected are important in drawing conclusions from the data; in critically reviewing uses of statistics in public media and other reports, it is important to consider the study design, how the data were gathered, and the analyses employed as well as the data summaries and the conclusions drawn.

Random processes can be described mathematically by using a probability model: a list or description of the possible outcomes (the sample space), each of which is assigned a probability. In situations such as flipping a coin, rolling a number cube, or drawing a card, it might be reasonable to assume various outcomes are equally likely. In a probability model, sample points represent outcomes and combine to make up events; probabilities of events can be computed by applying the Addition and Multiplication Rules. Interpreting these probabilities relies on an understanding of independence and conditional probability, which can be approached through the analysis of two-way tables.

Technology plays an important role in statistics and probability by making it possible to generate plots, regression functions, and correlation coefficients, and to simulate many possible outcomes in a short amount of time.

Connections to Functions and Modeling. Functions may be used to describe data; if the data suggest a linear relationship, the relationship can be modeled with a regression line, and its strength and direction can be expressed through a correlation coefficient.

Statistics and Probability Overview

Interpreting Categorical and Quantitative Data

- Summarize, represent, and interpret data on a single count or measurement variable

- Summarize, represent, and interpret data on two categorical and quantitative variables

- Interpret linear models

Making Inferences and Justifying Conclusions

- Understand and evaluate random processes underlying statistical experiments

- Make inferences and justify conclusions from sample surveys, experiments and observational studies

Conditional Probability and the Rules of Probability

- Understand independence and conditional probability and use them to interpret data

- Use the rules of probability to compute probabilities of compound events in a uniform probability model

Using Probability to Make Decisions

- Calculate expected values and use them to solve problems

- Use probability to evaluate outcomes of decisions

Interpreting Categorical and Quantitative Data S-ID

Summarize, represent, and interpret data on a single count or measurement variable

1. Represent data with plots on the real number line (dot plots, histograms, and box plots).

2. Use statistics appropriate to the shape of the data distribution to compare center (median, mean) and spread (interquartile range, standard deviation) of two or more different data sets.

3. Interpret differences in shape, center, and spread in the context of the data sets, accounting for possible effects of extreme data points (outliers).

4. Use the mean and standard deviation of a data set to fit it to a normal distribution and to estimate population percentages. Recognize that there are data sets for which such a procedure is not appropriate. Use calculators, spreadsheets, and tables to estimate areas under the normal curve.

Summarize, represent, and interpret data on two categorical and quantitative variables

5. Summarize categorical data for two categories in two-way frequency tables. Interpret relative frequencies in the context of the data (including joint, marginal, and conditional relative frequencies). Recognize possible associations and trends in the data.

6. Represent data on two quantitative variables on a scatter plot, and describe how the variables are related.

   a. Fit a function to the data; use functions fitted to data to solve problems in the context of the data. *Use given functions or choose a function suggested by the context. Emphasize linear, quadratic, and exponential models.*

   b. Informally assess the fit of a function by plotting and analyzing residuals.

   c. Fit a linear function for a scatter plot that suggests a linear association.

Interpret linear models

7. Interpret the slope (rate of change) and the intercept (constant term) of a linear model in the context of the data.

8. Compute (using technology) and interpret the correlation coefficient of a linear fit.

9. Distinguish between correlation and causation.

Making Inferences and Justifying Conclusions S-IC

Understand and evaluate random processes underlying statistical experiments

1. Understand statistics as a process for making inferences about population parameters based on a random sample from that population.

2. Decide if a specified model is consistent with results from a given data-generating process, e.g., using simulation. *For example, a model says a spinning coin falls heads up with probability 0.5. Would a result of 5 tails in a row cause you to question the model?*

Make inferences and justify conclusions from sample surveys, experiments, and observational studies

3. Recognize the purposes of and differences among sample surveys, experiments, and observational studies; explain how randomization relates to each.

4. Use data from a sample survey to estimate a population mean or proportion; develop a margin of error through the use of simulation models for random sampling.

5. Use data from a randomized experiment to compare two treatments; use simulations to decide if differences between parameters are significant.

6. Evaluate reports based on data.

Conditional Probability and the Rules of Probability S-CP

Understand independence and conditional probability and use them to interpret data

1. Describe events as subsets of a sample space (the set of outcomes) using characteristics (or categories) of the outcomes, or as unions, intersections, or complements of other events ("or," "and," "not").

2. Understand that two events *A* and *B* are independent if the probability of *A* and *B* occurring together is the product of their probabilities, and use this characterization to determine if they are independent.

3. Understand the conditional probability of *A* given *B* as *P(A and B)/P(B)*, and interpret independence of *A* and *B* as saying that the conditional probability of *A* given *B* is the same as the probability of *A*, and the conditional probability of *B* given *A* is the same as the probability of *B*.

4. Construct and interpret two-way frequency tables of data when two categories are associated with each object being classified. Use the two-way table as a sample space to decide if events are independent and to approximate conditional probabilities. *For example, collect data from a random sample of students in your school on their favorite subject among math, science, and English. Estimate the probability that a randomly selected student from your school will favor science given that the student is in tenth grade. Do the same for other subjects and compare the results.*

5. Recognize and explain the concepts of conditional probability and independence in everyday language and everyday situations. *For example, compare the chance of having lung cancer if you are a smoker with the chance of being a smoker if you have lung cancer.*

Use the rules of probability to compute probabilities of compound events in a uniform probability model

6. Find the conditional probability of *A* given *B* as the fraction of *B*'s outcomes that also belong to *A*, and interpret the answer in terms of the model.

7. Apply the Addition Rule, P(A or B) = P(A) + P(B) – P(A and B), and interpret the answer in terms of the model.

8. (+) Apply the general Multiplication Rule in a uniform probability model, P(A and B) = P(A)P(B|A) = P(B)P(A|B), and interpret the answer in terms of the model.

9. (+) Use permutations and combinations to compute probabilities of compound events and solve problems.

Using Probability to Make Decisions S-MD

Calculate expected values and use them to solve problems

1. (+) Define a random variable for a quantity of interest by assigning a numerical value to each event in a sample space; graph the corresponding probability distribution using the same graphical displays as for data distributions.

2. (+) Calculate the expected value of a random variable; interpret it as the mean of the probability distribution.

3. (+) Develop a probability distribution for a random variable defined for a sample space in which theoretical probabilities can be calculated; find the expected value. *For example, find the theoretical probability distribution for the number of correct answers obtained by guessing on all five questions of a multiple-choice test where each question has four choices, and find the expected grade under various grading schemes.*

4. (+) Develop a probability distribution for a random variable defined for a sample space in which probabilities are assigned empirically; find the expected value. *For example, find a current data distribution on the number of TV sets per household in the United States, and calculate the expected number of sets per household. How many TV sets would you expect to find in 100 randomly selected households?*

Use probability to evaluate outcomes of decisions

5. (+) Weigh the possible outcomes of a decision by assigning probabilities to payoff values and finding expected values.

   a. Find the expected payoff for a game of chance. *For example, find the expected winnings from a state lottery ticket or a game at a fast-food restaurant.*

   b. Evaluate and compare strategies on the basis of expected values. *For example, compare a high-deductible versus a low-deductible automobile insurance policy using various, but reasonable, chances of having a minor or a major accident.*

6. (+) Use probabilities to make fair decisions (e.g., drawing by lots, using a random number generator).

7. (+) Analyze decisions and strategies using probability concepts (e.g., product testing, medical testing, pulling a hockey goalie at the end of a game).

References and Resources

Achieve. (2005). *Rising to the challenge: Are high school graduates prepared for college and work?* Washington, DC: Author.

Achieve. (2010). *On the road to implementation.* Accessed at www.achieve.org/files/CCSS &Assessments.pdf on November 14, 2011.

Ainsworth, L. (2007). Common formative assessments: The centerpiece of an integrated standards-based assessment system. In D. Reeves (Ed.), *Ahead of the curve: The power of assessment to transform teaching and learning* (pp. 79–101). Bloomington, IN: Solution Tree Press.

Alford, B. J., & Niño, M. C. (2011). *Leading academic achievement for English language learners: A guide for principals.* Thousand Oaks, CA: Corwin Press.

Baccellieri, P. (2010). *Professional learning communities: Using data in decision making to improve student learning.* Huntington Beach, CA: Shell Education.

Ball, D. L., & Bass, H. (2003). Making mathematics reasonable in school. In J. Kilpatrick, W. G. Martin, & D. Schifter (Eds.), *A research companion to principles and standards for school mathematics* (pp. 27–44). Reston, VA: National Council of Teachers of Mathematics.

Barber, M., & Mourshed, M. (2007). *How the world's best performing school systems come out on top.* Accessed at http://mckinseyonsociety.com/downloads/reports/Education/Worlds _School_Systems_Final.pdf on January 23, 2012.

Barth, R. S. (2001). *Learning by heart.* San Francisco: Jossey-Bass.

Barth, R. S. (2006). Improving relationships within the schoolhouse. *Educational Leadership, 63*(6), 8–13.

Bender, W. N., & Crane, D. (2011). *RTI in math: Practical guidelines for elementary teachers.* Bloomington, IN: Solution Tree Press.

Bowgren, L., & Sever, K. (2010). *Differentiated professional development in a professional learning community.* Bloomington, IN: Solution Tree Press.

Brown, S., Seidelmann, A., & Zimmermann, G. (2006). *In the trenches: Three teacher's perspectives on moving beyond the math wars.* Accessed at http://mathematicallysane.com/in -the-trenches on April 11, 2012.

Buffum, A., Mattos, M., & Weber, C. (2009). *Pyramid response to intervention: RTI, professional learning communities, and how to respond when kids don't learn.* Bloomington, IN: Solution Tree Press.

Buffum, A., Mattos, M., & Weber, C. (2010). The why behind RTI. *Educational Leadership, 68*(2), 10–16.

Buffum, A., Mattos, M., & Weber, C. (2012). *Simplifying response to intervention: Four essential guiding principles.* Bloomington, IN: Solution Tree Press.

Burke, K. (2010). *Balanced assessment: From formative to summative.* Bloomington, IN: Solution Tree Press.

Bush, W. S., Briars, D. J., Confrey, J., Cramer, K., Lee, C., Martin, W. G., et al. (2011). *Common core state standards (CCSS) mathematics curriculum materials analysis project.* Accessed at

www.mathedleadership.org/docs/ccss/CCSSO%20Mathematics%20Curriculum%20
Analysis%20Project.Whole%20Document.6.1.11.Final.docx on November 15, 2011.

Canady, R. L., & Hotchkiss, P. R. (1989). It's a good score, just a bad grade! *Phi Delta Kappan, 71*(1), 68–71.

Cazden, C. B. (2001). *Classroom discourse: The language of teaching and learning* (2nd ed.). Portsmouth, NH: Heinemann.

Center for Comprehensive School Reform and Improvement. (2009). *Professional learning communities: Web sites.* Accessed at www.centerforcsri.org/plc/websites.html on November 15, 2011.

Cobb, P., Yackel, E., & Wood, T. (1992). Interaction and learning in mathematics classroom situations. *Educational Studies in Mathematics, 23*(1), 99–122.

Collins, J., & Hansen, M. (2011). *Great by choice.* Harper-Collins: New York.

Common Core State Standards Initiative. (2011). *Mathematics: Introduction: Standards for mathematical practice.* Accessed at www.corestandards.org/the-standards/mathematics/introduction /standards-for-mathematical-practice on November 15, 2011.

Conley, D. T., Drummond, K. V., de Gonzalez, A., Rooseboom, J., & Stout, O. (2011). *Reaching the goal: The applicability and importance of the common core state standards to college and career readiness.* Eugene, OR: Educational Policy Improvement Center. Accessed at www.epiconline .org/files/pdf/ReachingtheGoal-FullReport.pdf on January 20, 2012.

Danielson, C. (2009). *Talk about teaching!: Leading professional conversations.* Thousand Oaks, CA: Corwin Press.

Darling-Hammond, L. (2010). *The flat world and education: How America's commitment to equity will determine our future.* New York: Teachers College Press.

Daro, P., McCallum, W., & Zimba, J. (2012, February 16). *The structure is the standards* [Web log post]. Accessed at http://commoncoretools.me/2012/02/16/the-structure-is-the-standards /on March 11, 2012.

DuFour, R., DuFour, R., & Eaker, R. (2008). *Revisiting professional learning communities at work: New insights for improving schools.* Bloomington, IN: Solution Tree Press.

DuFour, R., DuFour, R., Eaker, R., & Many, T. (2006). *Learning by doing: A handbook for professional learning communities at work.* Bloomington, IN: Solution Tree Press.

Dweck, C. (2006). *Mindset: The new psychology of success.* New York: Random House.

Easton, L. B. (Ed). (2008). *Powerful designs for professional learning* (2nd ed.). Oxford, OH: National Staff Developers Council.

Equity. (2011). In *Merriam-Webster's online dictionary* (11th ed.). Accessed at www.merriam-webster .com/dictionary/equity on June 4, 2011.

Fennema, E., Sowder, J., & Carpenter, T. P. (1999). Creating classrooms that promote understanding. In E. Fennema & T. A. Romberg (Eds.), *Mathematics classrooms that promote understanding* (pp. 185–199). Mahwah, NJ: Erlbaum.

Ferrini-Mundy, J., Graham, K., Johnson, L., & Mills, G. (1998). *Making change in mathematics education: Learning from the field.* Reston, VA: National Council of Teachers of Mathematics.

Fisher, D., Frey, N., & Rothenberg, C. (2011). *Implementing RTI with English learners.* Bloomington, IN: Solution Tree Press.

Flinders, D. J., Noddings, N., & Thornton, S. J. (1986). The null curriculum: Its theoretical basis and practical implications. *Curriculum Inquiry, 16*(1), 33–42.

Forman, E. (2003). A sociocultural approach to mathematics reform: Speaking, inscribing, and doing mathematics within communities of practice. In J. J. Kilpatrick, W. G. Martin, & D. Schifter (Eds.), *A research companion to principles and standards for school mathematics* (pp. 289–303). Reston, VA: National Council of Teachers of Mathematics.

Fullan, M. (2008). *The six secrets of change: What the best leaders do to help their organizations survive and thrive.* San Francisco, CA: Jossey-Bass.

Garmston, R. J., & Wellman, B. M. (2009). *The adaptive school: A sourcebook for developing collaborative groups.* Norwood, MA: Christopher-Gordon.

Ginsburg, H. P., & Dolan, A. O. (2011). Assessment. In F. Fennell (Ed.), *Achieving fluency: Special education and mathematics* (pp. 85–103). Reston, VA: National Council of Teachers of Mathematics.

Graham, K., Cuoco, A., & Zimmermann, G. (2010). *Focus in high school mathematics: Reasoning and sense making in algebra.* Reston, VA: National Council of Teachers of Mathematics.

Graham, P., & Ferriter, B. (2008). One step at a time. *Journal of Staff Development, 29*(3), 38–42.

Grover, R. (1996). *Collaboration: Lessons learned series.* Chicago: American Association of School Librarians.

Hattie, J. A. C. (2009). *Visible learning: A synthesis of over 800 meta-analyses relating to achievement.* New York: Routledge.

Hattie, J. A. C. (2012). *Visible learning for teachers* New York: Routledge.

Haycock, K. (1998). *Good teaching matters . . . a lot.* Santa Cruz, CA: The Center for the Future of Teaching and Learning. Accessed at www.cftl.org/documents/K16.pdf on June 5, 2011.

Hiebert, J., Carpenter, T. P., Fennema, E., Fuson, K. C., Kearne, D., Murray, H., et al. (1997). *Making sense: Teaching and learning mathematics with understanding.* Portsmouth, NH: Heinemann.

Hiebert, J., Gallimore, R., Garnier, H., Bogard Givvin, K., Hollingsworth, H., Jacobs, J., et al. (2003). *Highlights from the 1999 TIMSS video study of eighth-grade mathematics teaching* (NCES 2003–011). Washington, DC: National Center for Education Statistics.

Hiebert, J., & Stigler, J. (1999). *The teaching gap: Best ideas from the world's teachers for improving education in the classroom.* New York: The Free Press.

Horn, I. S. (2010). Teaching replays, teaching rehearsals, and re-visions of practice: Learning from colleagues in a mathematics teacher community. *Teachers College Record, 112*(1), 225-259.

Inside Mathematics. (2010a). *Common core standards for mathematical practice.* Accessed at http://insidemathematics.org/index.php/common-core-standards on November 15, 2011.

Inside Mathematics. (2010b). *Tools for principals and administrators.* Accessed at www.insidemathematics.org/index.php/tools-for-teachers/tools-for-principals-and-administrators on November 15, 2011.

Institute for Mathematics and Education. (2007). *Progressions documents for the common core math standards.* Accessed at http://ime.math.arizona.edu/progressions on November 15, 2011.

Johnson, D. (1990). *Every minute counts: Making your math class work.* Palo Alto, CA: Seymour.

Johnson, E. S., Smith, L., & Harris, M. L. (2009). *How RTI works in secondary schools.* Thousand Oaks, CA: Corwin Press.

Kanold, T. D. (2011a). *The five disciplines of PLC leaders.* Bloomington, IN: Solution Tree Press.

Kanold, T. (2011b, April 18). Formative assessment in a summative assessment world! [Web log post]. Accessed at http://tkanold.blogspot.com/2011/04/formative-assessment-in -summative.html on November 14, 2011.

Kanold, T. D., Briars, D. J., & Fennell, F. (2012). *What principals need to know about teaching and learning mathematics.* Bloomington, IN: Solution Tree Press.

Kantowski, M. G. (1980). Some thoughts on teaching for problem solving. In S. Krulik & R. Reys (Eds.), *Problem solving in school mathematics: 1980 yearbook* (pp. 195–203). Reston, VA: National Council of Teachers of Mathematics.

Knight, J. (2011). *Unmistakable impact: A partnership approach for dramatically improving instruction.* Thousand Oaks, CA: Corwin Press.

Kohn, A. (2011). Corridor wit: Talking back to our teachers. *Education Week, 31*(5), 28.

Learning Forward. (2011). *Standards for professional learning.* Oxford, OH: Author. Accessed at www .learningforward.org/standards/standards.cfm on November 15, 2011.

Lewis, C. C. (2002). *Lesson study: A handbook of teacher-led instructional change.* Philadelphia: Research for Better Schools.

Loucks-Horsley, S., Stiles, K., Mundry, S., Love, N., & Hewson, P. (2009). *Designing professional development for teachers of science and mathematics* (3rd ed.). Thousand Oaks, CA: Corwin Press.

Loveless, T. (2012). How well are American students learning? *The 2012 Brown Center Report on American Education*, *3*(1), 1–36. Accessed at www.brookings.edu/~/media/Files/rc /reports/2012/0216_brown_education_loveless/0216_brown_education_loveless.pdf on April 11, 2012.

Maine West Mathematics Department. (n.d.). *Common core math initiative.* Accessed at https://sites .google.com/a/maine207.org/mw-math-department/home/common-core on November 15, 2011.

Martin, T. S. (Ed.). (2007). *Mathematics teaching today: Improving practice, improving student learning.* Reston, VA: National Council of Teachers of Mathematics.

Marzano, R. J. (2003). *What works in schools: Translating research into action.* Alexandria, VA: Association for Supervision and Curriculum Development.

Marzano, R. J. (2007). *The art and science of teaching: A comprehensive framework for effective instruction.* Alexandria, VA: Association for Supervision and Curriculum Development.

McCallum, B., Black, A., Umland, K., & Whitesides, E. (n.d.). [Common Core Mathematical Practices model]. *Tools for the Common Core standards.* Accessed at http://commoncoretools .files.wordpress.com/2011/03/practices.pdf on March 7, 2012.

McCallum, W. G. (2005). *Assessing the strands of student proficiency in elementary algebra.* Accessed at http://math.arizona.edu/~wmc/Research/AssessingAlgebra.pdf on November 14, 2011.

Middleton, J., & Spanias, P. (2002). Findings from research on motivation in mathematics education: What matters in coming to value mathematics. In J. T. Sowder & B. P. Schappelle (Eds.), *Lessons learned from research* (pp. 9–16). Reston, VA: National Council of Teachers of Mathematics.

Morris, A. K., & Hiebert, J. (2011). Creating shared instructional products: An alternative approach to improving teaching. *Educational Researcher, 40*(1), 5–14.

Morris, A. K., Hiebert, J., & Spitzer, S. M. (2009). Mathematical knowledge for teaching in planning and evaluating instruction: What can preservice teachers learn? *Journal for Research in Mathematics Education, 40*(5), 491–529.

Mourshed, M., Chijioke, C., & Barber, M. (2010). *How the world's most improved school systems keep getting better.* Accessed at www.mckinsey.com/Client_Service/Social_Section /Latest-thinking/Worlds_most_improved_schools.aspx on January 10, 2012.

National Board for Professional Teaching Standards. (2010). *Mathematics standards for teachers of students ages 11–18+.* Arlington, VA: Author.

National Center for Response to Intervention. (n.d.). *Monitoring progress.* Accessed at www .rti4success.org on June 15, 2011.

National Commission on Teaching and America's Future. (2006). *STEM teachers in professional learning communities: From good teachers to great teaching.* Accessed at www.nctaf.org /NCTAFReportNSFKnowledgeSynthesis.htm on November 15, 2011.

National Council of Supervisors of Mathematics. (2007). Improving student achievement by leading effective and collaborative teams of mathematics teachers. *The NCSM Improving Student Achievement Series, Fall*(1), 1–4.

National Council of Supervisors of Mathematics. (2008a). Improving student achievement by leading the pursuit of a vision for equity. *The NCSM Improving Student Achievement Series, Spring*(3), 1–4.

National Council of Supervisors of Mathematics. (2008b). The PRIME leadership framework: Principles and indicators for mathematics education leaders. *The NCSM Improving Student Achievement Series, Fall*(1), 1–4.

National Council of Supervisors of Mathematics. (2008c). *The PRIME leadership framework: Principles and indicators for mathematics education leaders.* Bloomington, IN: Solution Tree Press.

National Council of Supervisors of Mathematics. (2011a). Improving student achievement in mathematics by systematically integrating effective technology. *The NCSM Improving Student Achievement Series, Spring*(8), 1–6.

National Council of Supervisors of Mathematics. (2011b). Improving student achievement in mathematics by promoting positive self-beliefs. *The NCSM Improving Student Achievement Series, Spring*(9), 1–5.

National Council of Teachers of Mathematics. (1980). *Agenda for action: Problem solving.* Accessed at www.nctm.org/standards/content.aspx?id=17279 on June 25, 2011.

National Council of Teachers of Mathematics. (1989). *Curriculum and evaluation standards for school mathematics.* Reston, VA: Author.

National Council of Teachers of Mathematics. (1991). *Professional standards for teaching mathematics.* Reston, VA: Author.

National Council of Teachers of Mathematics. (1995). *Assessment standards for school mathematics.* Reston, VA: Author.

National Council of Teachers of Mathematics. (2000). *Principles and standards for school mathematics.* Reston, VA: Author.

National Council of Teachers of Mathematics. (2006). *Curriculum focal points for prekindergarten through grade 8: A quest for coherence.* Reston, VA: Author.

National Council of Teachers of Mathematics. (2008). *Equity in mathematics education: A position of the National Council of Teachers of Mathematics.* Accessed at www.nctm.org/about/content .aspx?id=13490 on October 15, 2011.

National Council of Teachers of Mathematics. (2009). *Focus in high school mathematics: Reasoning and sense making.* Reston, VA: Author.

National Council of Teachers of Mathematics. (2010). *Making it happen: A guide to interpreting and implementing common core state standards for mathematics.* Reston, VA: Author.

National Council of Teachers of Mathematics. (2011a). *Discourse: Questioning.* Accessed at www.nctm.org/resources/content.aspx?id=6730&itemid=6730&linkidentifier=id&menu_id=598 on November 15, 2011.

National Council of Teachers of Mathematics. (2011b). *Intervention: A position of the National Council of Teachers of Mathematics.* Accessed at www.nctm.org/about/content.aspx?id=30506 on October 15, 2011.

National Governors Association Center for Best Practices and Council of Chief State School Officers. (2010). *Common core state standards for mathematics.* Washington, DC: Authors. Accessed at www.corestandards.org/assets/CCSSI_Math%20Standards.pdf on January 20, 2012.

National Governors Association Center for Best Practices and Council of Chief State School Officers. (2011). *Resources: Common core implementation video series.* Accessed at www.ccsso.org/Resources/Digital_Resources/Common_Core_Implementation_Video_Series.html on November 15, 2011.

National Research Council. (2001). *Adding it up: Helping children learn mathematics.* Washington, DC: National Academies Press.

NRICH Project. (n.d.). *Almost total inequality: Enriching mathematics.* Accessed at http://nrich.maths.org/5966 on June 5, 2011.

PBS Teachers. (n.d.). *Resource roundups.* Accessed at www.pbs.org/teachers/resourceroundups on November 15, 2011.

Peske, H. G., & Haycock, K. (2006). *Teaching inequality: How poor and minority students are short-changed on teacher quality.* Washington, DC: The Education Trust. Accessed at www.edtrust.org/sites/edtrust.org/files/publications/files/TQReportJune2006.pdf on July 21, 2011.

Pink, D. (2009). *Drive: The surprising truth about what motivates us.* New York: Riverhead.

Pölya, G. (1957). *How to solve it* (2nd ed.). Princeton, NJ: Princeton University Press.

Popham, W. J. (2007). *Classroom assessment: What teachers need to know* (5th ed.). Boston: Allyn & Bacon.

Popham, W. J. (2008). *Transformative assessment.* Alexandria, VA: Association for Supervision and Curriculum Development.

Popham, W. J. (2011a). *Transformative assessment in action: An inside look at applying the process.* Alexandria, VA: Association for Supervision and Curriculum Development.

Popham, W. J. (2011b). Formative assessment—A process, not a test. *Education Week, 30*(21), 35–37.

Porter, A., McMaken, J., Hwang, J., & Yang, R. (2011). Common core standards: The new U.S. intended curriculum. *Educational Researcher, 40*(3), 103–116.

Rasmussen, C., Yackel, E., & King, K. (2003). Social and sociomathematical norms in mathematics classrooms. In H. L. Schoen & R. I. Charles (Eds.), *Teaching mathematics through problem solving: Grades 6–12* (pp. 143–154). Reston, VA: National Council of Teachers of Mathematics.

Raymond, A. M. (1997). Inconsistency between a beginning elementary school teacher's mathematics beliefs and teaching practice. *Journal for Research in Mathematics Education, 28*(5), 550–576.

Reeves, D. B. (2003). *High performance in high poverty schools: 90/90/90 and beyond.* Denver, CO: Center for Performance Assessment. Accessed at www.sjboces.org/nisl/high%20performance%2090%2090%2090%20and%20beyond.pdf on June 5, 2011.

Reeves, D. B. (2006). *The learning leader: How to focus school improvement for better results*. Alexandria, VA: Association for Supervision and Curriculum Development.

Reeves, D. B. (2009). *Leading change in your school: How to conquer myths, build commitment, and get results*. Alexandria, VA: Association for Supervision and Curriculum Development.

Reeves, D. B. (2010). *Transforming professional development into student results*. Alexandria, VA: Association for Supervision and Curriculum Development.

Reeves, D. (2011). *Elements of grading: A guide to effective practices*. Bloomington, IN: Solution Tree Press.

Reys, R., Lindquist, M. M., Lambdin, D. V., & Smith, N. L. (2009). *Helping children learn mathematics* (9th ed.). Hoboken, NJ: Wiley.

School Improvement in Maryland. (2010). *Introduction to the classroom-focused improvement process (CFIP)*. Accessed at http://mdk12.org/process/cfip on November 15, 2011.

Seeley, C. (2009). *Faster isn't smarter: Messages about math, teaching, and learning in the 21st century*. Sausalito, CA: Math Solutions.

Siegler, R. (2003). Implications of cognitive science research for mathematics education. In J. J. Kilpatrick, W. G. Martin, & D. Schifter (Eds.), *A research companion to principles and standards for school mathematics* (pp. 289–303). Reston, VA: National Council of Teachers of Mathematics.

Smith, M. S., & Stein, M. K. (2011). *Five practices for orchestrating productive mathematics discussions*. Reston, VA: National Council of Teachers of Mathematics.

Snyder, B. R. (1973). *The hidden curriculum*. Cambridge, MA: MIT Press.

Stacey, K. C., & Wiliam, D. (in press). *Technology and assessment in mathematics*. In M. A. Clements, A. Bishop, C. Keitel, J. Kilpatrick, & F. Leung (Eds.), *Third international handbook of mathematics education*. Dordrecht, Netherlands: Springer.

Standards Management System. (n.d.). *Math questioning strategies: The art of questioning in mathematics*. Accessed at http://sms.sdcoe.net/SMS/mas/mathQuestionStrategy.asp on November 15, 2011.

Stein, M. K., Remillard, J., & Smith, M. S. (2007). How curriculum influences student learning. In F. K. Lester (Ed.), *Second handbook of research on mathematics teaching and learning* (pp. 319–370). Charlotte, NC: Information Age.

Stein, M., Smith, M., Henningsen, M., & Silver, E. (2009). *Implementing standards-based mathematics instruction: A casebook for professional development* (2nd ed.). New York: Teachers College Press.

Stepanek, J., Appel, G., Leong, M., Managan, M. T., & Mitchell, M. (2007). *Leading lesson study: A practical guide for teachers and facilitators*. Thousand Oaks, CA: Corwin Press.

Stiggins, R. (2007). Assessment for learning: An essential foundation of productive instruction. In D. B. Reeves (Ed.), *Ahead of the curve: The power of assessment to transform teaching and learning* (pp. 59–76). Bloomington, IN: Solution Tree Press.

Stiggins, R. J., Arter, J. A., Chappuis, J., & Chappuis, S. (2007). *Classroom assessment for student learning: Doing it right—Using it well*. Upper Saddle River, NJ: Pearson Education.

Stigler, J. W., Gonzales, P., Kawanaka, T., Knoll, S., & Serrano, A. (1999). *The TIMSS videotape classroom study: Methods and findings from an exploratory research project on eighth-grade mathematics instruction in Germany, Japan, and the United States (1995)*. Washington, DC: U.S. Department of Education, National Center for Education Statistics.

Stronge, J. H. (2007). *Qualities of effective teachers* (2nd ed.). Alexandria, VA: Association for Supervision and Curriculum Development.

Tate, W. F., & Rousseau, C. (2007). Engineering change in mathematics education: Research, policy, and practice. In F. K. Lester (Ed.), *Second handbook of research on mathematics teaching and learning* (pp. 1209–1246). Charlotte, NC: Information Age.

U.S. Census Bureau. (2011). *World population 1950–2050*. Accessed at www.census.gov/population /international/data/idb/worldpopgraph.php on October 23, 2011.

U.S. Department of Education. (1983). *A nation at risk: The imperative for educational reform*. Accessed at www2.ed.gov/pubs/NatAtRisk/index.html on December 10, 2011.

Ushomirsky, N., & Hall, D. (2010). *Stuck schools: A framework for identifying schools where students need change—now*. Accessed at www.edtrust.org/sites/edtrust.org/files/publications/files /StuckSchools.pdf on February 26, 2012.

Vatterott, C. (2010). Five hallmarks of good homework. *Educational Leadership, 68*(1), 10–15.

Waters, T., Marzano, R., & McNulty B. (2003). *Balanced leadership: What 30 years of research tells us about the effect of leadership on student achievement*. Denver, CO: McREL.

Webb, N. L. (1997). *Criteria for alignment of expectations and assessments in mathematics and science and education*. Washington, DC: Council of Chief State School Officers. Accessed at http:// facstaff.wcer.wisc.edu/normw/WEBBMonograph6criteria.pdf on April 5, 2012.

Wellman, B., & Lipton, L. (2004). *Data-driven dialogue: A facilitator's guide to collaborative inquiry*. Arlington, MA: MiraVia.

Wiliam, D. (2007a). Content then process: Teacher learning communities in the service of formative assessment. In D. B. Reeves (Ed.), *Ahead of the curve: The power of assessment to transform teaching and learning* (pp. 183–205). Bloomington, IN: Solution Tree Press.

Wiliam, D. (2007b). Keeping learning on track: Classroom assessment and the regulation of learning. In F. K. Lester (Ed.), *Second handbook of research on mathematics teaching and learning* (pp. 1053–1098). Reston, VA: National Council of Teachers of Mathematics.

Wiliam, D. (2011). *Embedded formative assessment*. Bloomington, IN: Solution Tree Press.

Wiliam, D., Lee, C., Harrison, C., & Black, P. (2004). Teachers developing assessment for learning: Impact on student achievement. *Assessment in Education: Principles, Policy & Practice, 11*(1), 49–65.

Wiliam, D., & Thompson, M. (2008). Integrating assessment with instruction: What will it take to make it work? In C. A. Dwyer (Ed.), *The future of assessment: Shaping teaching and learning*. Mahwah, NJ: Erlbaum.

Wilkins, A., & Education Trust Staff. (2006). *Yes we can: Telling truths and dispelling myths about race and education in America*. Washington, DC: The Education Trust. Accessed at http:// diversity.ucf.edu/documents/resources/YesWeCan.pdf on June 5, 2011.

Wise, L. L., & Alt, M. (2005). *Assessing vertical alignment*. Alexandria, VA: Human Resources Research Organization.

Wormelli, R. (2006). *Fair is not always equal*. Portland, ME: Stenhouse.

Yackel, E., & Cobb, P. (1996). Sociomathematical norms, argumentation, and autonomy in mathematics. *Journal for Research in Mathematics Education, 27*(4), 458–477.

Index

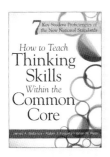

How to Teach Thinking Skills Within the Common Core
7 Key Student Proficiencies of the New National Standards
James A. Bellanca, Robin J. Fogarty, and Brian M. Pete
Empower your students to thrive across the curriculum. Packed with examples and tools, this practical guide prepares teachers across all grade levels and content areas to teach the most critical cognitive skills from the Common Core State Standards.
BKF576

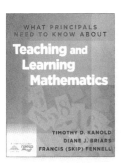

What Principals Need to Know About Teaching and Learning Mathematics
Timothy D. Kanold, Diane J. Briars, and Francis (Skip) Fennell
This must-have resource offers support and encouragement for improved mathematics achievement across every grade level. With an emphasis on Principles and Standards for School Mathematics and Common Core State Standards, this book covers the importance of mathematics content, learning and instruction, and mathematics assessment.
BKF501

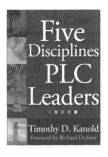

The Five Disciplines of PLC Leaders
Timothy D. Kanold
Foreword by Richard DuFour
Effective leadership in a professional learning community requires practice, patience, and skill. Through engaging examples and accessible language, this book offers a focused framework that will help educators maintain balance and consistent vision as they strengthen the skills of PLC leadership.
BKF495

Learning by Doing
A Handbook for Professional Learning Communities at Work™
Richard DuFour, Rebecca DuFour, Robert Eaker, and Thomas Many
Learning by Doing is an action guide for closing the knowing-doing gap and transforming schools into PLCs. It also includes seven major additions that equip educators with essential tools for confronting challenges.
BKF416

Solution Tree's mission is to advance the work of our authors. By working with the best researchers and educators worldwide, we strive to be the premier provider of innovative publishing, in-demand events, and inspired professional development designed to transform education to ensure that all students learn.

The National Council of Teachers of Mathematics is a public voice of mathematics education, supporting teachers to ensure equitable mathematics learning of the highest quality for all students through vision, leadership, professional development, and research.